AN
INNOCENT
IN
IRELAND

AN
INNOCENT
IN
IRELAND

Curious Rambles and Singular Encounters

DAVID W. McFADDEN

M&S

Canadian Cataloguing in Publication Data
McFadden, David, date.
An innocent in Ireland : curious rambles and
singular encounters

Includes index.
ISBN 0-7710-5527-7

1. McFadden, David, date. – Journeys – Ireland.
2. Ireland – Description and travel. I. Title.

DA978.2.M34 1995   914.15'04824   C95-930821-0

Design: Andrew Skuja
Map by Visutronx
Typesetting: M&S, Toronto

The publishers acknowledge the support of the Canada Council
and the Ontario Arts Council for their publishing program.

Printed and bound in Canada on acid-free paper.

McClelland & Stewart Inc.
The Canadian Publishers
481 University Avenue
Toronto, Ontario
M5G 2E9

1 2 3 4 5   99 98 97 96 95

for my daughters

"In Ireland it happens sometimes that the insane are taken to be saints of a kind. Legends in Ireland are born almost every day."

— William Trevor

CONTENTS

Preface/ ix

Map of Ireland/ x

1   In Search of Morton / 1

2   The Flowing Tide / 7

3   Phoenix Park / 16

4   Lourdes Brasil / 26

5   The Bridges on the Liffey / 35

6   Glendalough / 45

7   The Longest Arms of Any Man / 51

8   The Browne's Hill Dolmen / 60

9   Dunbrody Abbey / 71

10   Stained Glass, Swans, and Greyhounds / 79

11   The Verger of Saint Canice / 85

12   Cormac's Chapel / 90

13   The Monks of Mount Melleray / 99

14   Mr. Looney / 105

15   The Well of Jesus / 117

16   Corktown Interlude / 125

17   Everyday Life in Rath Luirc / 136

18   Drooping Rhododendrons / 146

19   Trouble in Tinkertown / 153

20 The Poet's Corner / *168*

21 The Darker Side of Dingle / *176*

22 The Man Who Believed in Fairies / *191*

23 Diarmuid O'Duibhne and Gráinne / *206*

24 The Hag of Béara / *212*

25 Uragh / *219*

26 Famous Players of Ballydehob / *229*

27 Visions of Ancient Ireland / *234*

28 The Old Reprobate / *245*

29 The Way People Talk in Ireland / *259*

30 Under Ben Bulben / *266*

31 Farmer Trollope / *274*

32 Many a Song Was Sung at Tara / *285*

33 Motte Knockgraffon / *296*

Index/ 309

PREFACE

This book is intended to be a work of non-fiction, yet a certain amount of fictionalization was unavoidable. For instance, in order to prevent the slightest possibility of embarrassment, some characters have had their names changed. In other cases, circumstances and locales have been altered. In some cases, one real-life character has been divided into two literary characters, and in other cases two real-life characters have been combined into one. In a few instances characters had to be invented.

Essentially, however, this book remains a work of non-fiction and is faithful to the spirit of Ireland as it presented itself. Indeed, the author immodestly recommends this book for anyone planning – or dreaming of – a trip to this enchanted, complex, and poorly understood island.

Thanks are extended to the many people who engaged me in so many strange, poetical, comical, tragical, delightful, and illuminating conversations, little suspecting, and, I trust, little caring, that these conversations would wind up in a book. As is my custom, I told no one on this trip that I was a writer, nor that I was planning a book on Ireland. In fact, although I couldn't resist taking copious notes each night, I still hadn't formed any real intent to write a book. Such an intent didn't form until after my return to Canada.

Thanks are also due to friends who read the manuscript, and to the Ontario Arts Council's Works-in-Progress program for financial support for the task of transforming my notes into a book that, I hope, could, without blushing, sit on the same shelf alongside H. V. Morton's trail-blazing *In Search of Ireland*.

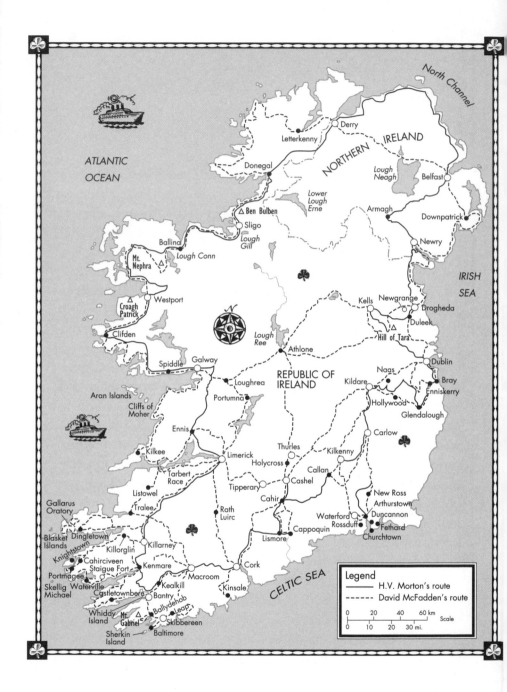

ATLANTIC
OCEAN

North Channel

Derry
Letterkenny
NORTHERN IRELAND
Donegal
Lough Neagh
Belfast
△ Ben Bulben
Lower Lough Erne
Armagh
Downpatrick
Sligo
Lough Gill
Newry
Ballina
Lough Conn
IRISH SEA
Mt. Nephra △
△ Croagh Patrick
Westport
Kells
Newgrange
Drogheda
Duleek
Clifden
Lough Ree
Hill of Tara △
Spiddle
Galway
Athlone
REPUBLIC OF IRELAND
Dublin
Loughrea
Naas
Bray
Aran Islands
Portumna
Kildare
Enniskerry
Cliffs of Moher
Hollywood
Glendalough
Ennis
Carlow
Thurles
Kilkee
Limerick
Holycross
Kilkenny
Tarbert Race
Callan
New Ross
Listowel
Tipperary
Cashel
Arthurstown
Tralee
Cahir
Waterford
Duncannon
Rath Luirc
Cappoquin
Rossduff
Fethard
Gallarus Oratory
Lismore
Churchtown
Blasket Islands
Dingletown
Killarney
Knightstown
Killorglin
Cork
Cahirciveen
Staigue Fort
Kenmare
Macroom
Kinsale
CELTIC SEA
Portmagee
Waterville
Kealkill
Skellig Michael
Castletownbere
Bantry
Whiddy Island
Ballydehob
Leap
Mt. Gabriel △
Skibbereen
Sherkin Island
Baltimore

Legend
—— H.V. Morton's route
- - - David McFadden's route

0   20   40   60 km
0   10   20   30 mi.   Scale

IN SEARCH OF MORTON

The commuter train continued south over the Liffey and past Tara Street, Pearse Station, Lansdowne Road (location of the rugby stadium), Sandymount, Dalkey (near the Martello tower featured in the first chapter of *Ulysses* and now a James Joyce museum), and offered melancholy views out over "the murderous innocence of the sea" (Yeats) and "the great sweet mother of the snotgreen sea, empty save for the smokeplume of the mailboat vague on the bright skyline" (Joyce). It continued out over the formerly prosperous and still-handsome Anglo-Irish suburbs, spreading along the coastal plain and up to the feet of the lavender Dublin Mountains.

But I was tired after an overnight flight from Canada, and kept jetlagging off. Eventually I was awakened by a polite and serious eight-year-old in a grammar-school uniform. Strapped to his back was an oversize leather book-bag.

"Excuse me, sir," he said, softly, "but this is the last stop."

The child stood before me at solemn attention. When he was certain I was awake, he turned and scurried off.

In Toronto, where I usually hang out, this would never have happened. I'd have been left to sleep it off, I'd have had my bag stolen, or I'd have been punched on the shoulder by a transit employee.

But this was Dublin, another world.

Cultural homogeneity was still not universal, though it had certainly progressed since J. B. Priestley wrote his novel *The Good Companions*, in which Messrs. Oakroyd and Oglethorpe come to the conclusion, after a lengthy debate, that people and places are as "different as chalk is from cheese."

Coincidentally, *The Good Companions* was published in 1929, one year before H. V. Morton's *In Search of Ireland*, which I was intending to use as a guide of sorts on this trip.

We had *In Search of Ireland* in our house when I was a kid and I read it several times. Morton was a nice man, people responded well to him, and, if they hadn't, he wouldn't have noticed. He was a well-wisher, an optimist, a Pollyanna, a rank sentimentalist, a gladhander, a promoter of peace and goodwill, a schmoozer, and he always seemed to be on the lookout for a free meal. He was funnier than he realized. He was a certifiable Everyman.

I imagined him with a gap between his two front teeth, and wearing a tweed three-piece suit and a bowler hat splotched with bird droppings. If I were to run away to Ireland, I'd be surrounded by happy Irish people holding hands and dancing and singing. Morton's Irish were eminently lovable, but a somewhat dark and devilish people who were not to be taken seriously and not to be given undue responsibility. They had a tendency to be bibulous, lazy, tribal, superstitious, irrational, a bit primitive, and fierce if unduly annoyed.

"The Irish are, of course, sometimes unfair," Morton wrote, "which, I think, proceeds from the fact that they possess no sense of historical perspective."

You got your money's worth with a book by H. V. Morton.

He was entertaining, and very popular in his day. He wrote a whole string of "In Search of . . ." books, but *In Search of Ireland* was the only one I've read to this day, and I've never seen a picture of him. Someone told me he eventually settled in South Africa and died at a very advanced age.

When Morton made his trip to Ireland, almost seventy summers ago, he found himself noticing all the differences between Irish and English temperaments, between the Catholics and the Protestants, between the Irish Irish, the Irish English, the English Irish, and so on.

He left no stereotype unconfirmed.

He had an eye for "typical" Irish pugnacity, tipsiness, sentimentality, wit, superstition. "Typical" was his favourite word, though he seemed to be putting a different spin on it than we do today. He celebrated the "typical" the way we might celebrate the "atypical."

Yet he was an attractive man with a sunny soul. He was no tormented poet. He thought that men of goodwill such as himself, armed with nothing but a festoon of racial stereotypes, could turn the world around. The British Empire was still intact, the Irish Free State being part of it, sort of, and Hitler was an obscure watercolourist.

My plan was to follow Morton's route through Ireland, to match my perceptions with his, and to try to determine how things had changed since his visit, and how things had remained the same. In retrospect I'm amazed at how many of the traditional values noted by Morton (not necessarily with his approval) were intact – the tradition of tremendous hospitality, the tradition of great seriousness and great levity, the tradition of great conversation, the tradition of the Irish as a race of poets, an oasis of benign lunacy in an ugly world.

Besides rereading Morton's book, I attended the Irish Film Festival at the Metropolitan Theatre in Toronto. Fortuitously, it happened to coincide with the two weeks prior to my departure.

There was a Super-8 film about a priest who got his housekeeper in the family way, was kicked out of the church, then took revenge by writing a book about it. The film started out in colour, switched to black and white for the flashback, then back to colour for the ending.

There was a feature about some crooks selling fire extinguishers door to door in the County Mayo town of Knock, north of Galway. They would drop hints to the townspeople that, if they didn't buy a fire extinguisher, their houses would burn down for dead certain. The gang leader, a respectable-looking gentleman who dressed like a senator, was found shot dead behind the wheel of his white Mercedes on a lonely country road. His beautiful daughter was the chief suspect. This was a political allegory, though it went over my head at the time.

The final film finished two hours before my flight.

Also I read Edna O'Brien's *Mother Ireland*, Hugh Kenner's *A Colder Eye: The Irish Modern Writers*, some poetry, mostly from the standard anthologies, and, among other things, some political histories that radically contradicted each other and only left me more unsure of my footing, while at the same time doing great damage to whatever "historical perspective" I might have had on the subject of Ireland.

A well-travelled friend startled me by predicting, erroneously as it turned out, that everywhere I went people would be saying, "What are ye, Catholic or Protestant?"

On the way over I felt secure in my ignorance. I had no preconceived opinions about Ireland, except for a general feeling that people shouldn't kill each other, Irish or not, and so I figured I'd be able to stay out of trouble. I had no plans to write a book, but I did pack a thick new notebook, just in case something happened that seemed worth recording. When I returned home five weeks later, the notebook, which had a bright green cover, was full, both sides of each page.

Upon arrival at Dublin Airport I cashed a fifty-dollar traveller's cheque. The teller gave me twenty-six pounds, eight pence.

"I'd better cash another," I said, innocently. "This looks as if it won't go very far."

"Well," she said, sternly, "fifty dollars wouldn't go very far in Canada either now, would it?"

I felt chastised, told myself this was a serious country, and vowed to watch the sarcasm and irony. Let the Irish tell the jokes, if they had a mind to. I also vowed to let "I am a camera" be my motto.

From the airport one turns left for Belfast, right for Dublin.

The sky was blue, the grass was green, and the flowers were yellow. There were daffodils and forsythias everywhere, even along the highway median. And it was cold and windy.

Two billboards dominated the Dublin skyline: "Welcome to Dublin – Heineken," with a small pink hand holding a large green bottle, and "Welcome to Dublin – Guinness," with a large pink hand holding a big black pint with a fringe of thick white foam on top. Another large billboard advertised "Great Values in Deep Base and Six-Leg Beds" and featured numerous beds, some with six legs and some with no legs at all.

In the Beshoff Fresh Fish Restaurant on O'Connell Street I ordered a fresh prawn sandwich, and the first of a series of supernatural coincidences occurred.

While waiting for the sandwich I sat listening to a phone-in show on my little breast-pocket radio. A call came in from a cheery and loquacious professor named Paul McNulty. He said he taught in the food-engineering department at University College, Dublin, and a former student had phoned him yesterday with a report so strange he couldn't resist calling in.

The student had been abroad and, when he returned, he happened to buy a prawn sandwich at Dublin Airport. He had it wrapped, brought it home with him, unwrapped it, then left it sitting on the kitchen counter when he went to bed.

In the middle of the night he woke up, famished, went into the kitchen without bothering to turn on the light, and found the sandwich glowing in the dark.

The program host, Gay Byrne, neglected to ask the professor what his student had done with the sandwich. Gay got the caller off the phone real fast, perhaps on the off-chance he might have been an urban-legend prankster.

When my sandwich arrived, the fresh prawns had been ominously deep-fried in thick batter. Maybe it was the batter that was radioactive. I decided against taking the sandwich into the toilet and turning out the lights to see if it glowed. I just ate it.

If the highly respected Gay Byrne didn't take the report all that seriously, why should I? Eh?

THE FLOWING TIDE

At the bar of the Flowing Tide, across the street from the Abbey Theatre, the fellow on my right claimed to be a blocklayer, but as we chatted it became apparent he probably hadn't laid a block in a decade. His big passion was Irish literature, but it appeared, as our discussion continued, that he almost certainly hadn't read a book in his life – even though he was amazingly well-informed.

"My name is Robert O'Shea and I'm fifty-eight years old," he said.

"An Irishman, I presume?"

He snorted and laughed, forgiving me for my bad manners.

"And what, *sor*, is your name and how old would you be?" he said. "And what part of America would you be from? Ohio? California?" He didn't betray a jot of disappointment when I told him I was from Canada. In fact he cocked a cold eye at me. "I know all about the Canadians. They always cringe when they hear an Irishman refer to the U.S.A. as America. I know all about that."

7

"The Mexicans, too," I said, "and all those countries down there. The Americans have stolen our name, the scoundrels."

It wasn't only the Irish who were lumbered with nationalistic sensitivities, but nobody could blame Mr. O'Shea for taking a somewhat condescending attitude toward the New World and its agonies.

"Let the Yanks have it, I say," he said. "They stole the name of the continent, so let's have a new name for it. Let's call it, um, er —"

"Vespucci?"

"Good as any other, *sor*. But couldn't it be a bit more Irish?"

"O'Shea?"

"That's better."

"As good as it gets."

"But then they'd start calling themselves North and South O'Shea and the Yanks would start calling themselves the United States of O'Shea. So we'd be back where we started."

"This is true."

"But maybe I'd be getting better service in the pub."

"You and all the members of your clan."

Mr. O'Shea didn't care what the Yanks called themselves. "The Americans steal everything," he said. "Just ask the Russians. And the French. And the English. And the Canadians."

"The Canadians? Just what did they steal from the Canadians? I know but I'm just testing you."

"The telephone. Basketball. And baseball. They haven't stolen hockey so far. They're not quite good enough at it yet."

"I have only been in Ireland a couple of hours, and I don't know. Are the Irish generally so well-versed in Canadian affairs?"

"I would say not. I'm special."

"You seem that way to me."

Mr. O'Shea kept mentioning Listowel – in County Kerry, in the west, south of the mouth of the Shannon, an area which suddenly seemed remote and exotic to me. I was dying to get out of Dublin, which already was beginning to feel like just another city – although one blessedly free of skyscrapers – and to immerse myself in the mystical Irish countryside. But first, according to my plan, I had to spend a few days in Dublin, as had H. V. Morton almost seventy years before. I was hoping to meet a poet in Dublin, as Morton had, but I was determined not to go looking for one. I had already made the decision not to look up any poets or painters, though I knew and admired the work of a few. Nor would I try to track down ancestors and distant cousins. I was aiming at a sort of purity, random and anonymous. It's my style.

My friend kept pronouncing Listowel a syllable short. It sounded like a cleaning powder, or an ancient kingdom where no one had to work very hard. When I told him I'd never heard of *Lestoil*, he seemed hurt and disappointed. When I asked him how it was spelled, he hesitated so long I almost repeated myself, but he finally said, "I'm not sure of the spelling just now."

The bartender rattled off the spelling matter-of-factly, and rolled his eyes to show that he couldn't imagine someone unable to spell the town in which he was born.

I told Mr. O'Shea we had a Listowel in Ontario, but we always pronounced it with three syllables so as not to confuse it with the more-celebrated Irish town. He looked pleased once again.

Mr. O'Shea had me down for at least a semi-educated soul, so he told me about one of the world's greatest playwrights – perhaps the greatest playwright of all time – who just happened to run a pub in Listowel. He wanted me to go there straightaway and ask for John B. King. At least that's what it sounded like.

"Now this John B. King, I tell you, he would be the greatest playwright of the twentieth century, for certain, with the possible exception of Sean O'Casey."

"Better than Synge?"

"Oh Lord." A little sneer formed on his lip and he bent closer to my ear. "Synge, you know, he never really lived the life of the people he wrote about."

This seemed a fair comment, since Synge is famous for having stayed for a while above a pub in the Aran Islands, at Yeats's suggestion, and boring a hole in the floor so he could eavesdrop and take notes on what was being said below, notes that were later used in his writing of *The Playboy of the Western World*. That, I suppose, would be a perfect example of a writer not living the life of the people he wrote about. It seemed a legitimate complaint on the part of Mr. O'Shea.

Yet the charge at the same time seemed unfair, because Synge was a shy man, and, as Yeats pointed out, Synge wasn't all that comfortable in any society. "Well-to-do Ireland never saw his plays nor spoke his name," Yeats lamented after Synge's death in 1909 at the age of thirty-seven. "Was he ever asked to any country house? Was he ever asked to a dinner party?"

In Yeats's *Autobiography*, he portrays Synge as a literary saint, one of those rare writers who never admits to the existence of other writers. Yeats declares that Synge ultimately did for Ireland what Robert Burns did for Scotland. And two years before Synge's death, when *Playboy* opened at the Abbey Theatre, the poor fellow had to endure what Hugh Kenner called "the skelping, squelching, scuttling of the critics."

With Synge, it was the Irish people that he was supposedly slandering, the true Irish, unspoiled by the outside world. In my heart I knew Mr. O'Shea was (relatively) right, but I didn't want to admit it. I blurted out that I thought *The Playboy of the Western World* was the greatest play since *Pericles*. And the Irish audiences that gave Synge such a hard time were the sort of simpletons who would prefer the sentimental lyrics of Percy French to the sumptuous poetry of W. B. Yeats.

"Well, if you feel that way," said Mr. O'Shea. Had I gone too far? He paused to take the last slug of his lager. I wasn't sure whether he was trying to remember who had written *Pericles* or whether he was becoming angry. His face was red. I thought I was in for it. But no, he was just getting tipsy and losing the thread of the conversation. He'd read my heart instead of my words and was convinced I was in agreement with him. "If you feel that way," he said, "you'll for sure love the plays of John B. King. Now there's a man who actually lives the life of the people he writes about. He's a man who has lived in the mountains, and he's lived in the country, and yet he's, um, er . . ."

"Sophisticated?"

"That's it, sophisticated. He lives in both worlds, he does, and his plays are full of real people."

The subject of Joyce arose, and he wanted to know if I had understood *Ulysses*. I told him Yeats had declared it unreadable, but I thought it easily as readable as Yeats. I regrettably said something about *Ulysses* being a work of genius – not a word to use in connection with Joyce, unless you happened to be lamenting his lack of it.

"Genius, *phht*," he said. "I didn't understand a word of it."

It seemed that Mr. O'Shea might have been involved in a bit of extravagant bluffing. He could claim to have read, say, *Ulysses*, thereby proving that he was no illiterate bumpkin, and no one could prove he hadn't read it because he had the grace, modesty, and most of all the honesty to admit he hadn't understood a word of it.

"And why didn't you understand a word of it?"

"Why, it's the author's fault, of course, for not having written simply enough, for the ordinary people, like me."

It turned out Mr. O'Shea had been referring not to John B. King but to John B. Keane, the author of such plays as *The Field*, which had recently been made into a feature film seen around the world. Keane is mentioned in surveys of Irish theatre, but the focus is usually on the man rather than the plays, descriptions of which are suspiciously hard to come across. Keane is described, however, as a short, stout, lovable character, a great talker, full of anecdote and gossip, and an excellent imitator of whales and mongooses. Also he has the distinction of having been expelled from college for writing plays. In his autobiography, *Self-Portrait*, he says the saddest day of his life was when as a young man he sailed for England. He and his wife settled down and bought a pub in Ireland in 1955 – in Listowel, in fact.

Mr. O'Shea seemed to feel it was self-evident that Joyce and Yeats would be poor writers, because they were of the Ascendancy – that is, of Anglo stock, no matter how far back the stock was stuck in Ireland and no matter if they were Protestant or Catholic. Along with Keane, Sean O'Casey was another denizen of O'Shea's literary pantheon. It would appear that the reason was not because Mr. O'Shea admired these plays in any real way. In fact, he was inadvertently giving the distinct impression he hadn't sat through a real play in his life.

The reason was rather because Keane and O'Casey had the proper demographics, artistic philosophy, and moral attitude. They were politically correct, no two ways about it. As tribal icons, they couldn't be more suitable, for they wrote for the Irish, pure and simple.

Dublin, says Hugh Kenner, remains obsessed with the writers it doesn't read. Mr. O'Shea was like that; he worshipped O'Casey as a great Irishman, yet was indifferent to his work. For instance, at first my friend didn't believe me when I told him that an O'Casey play was being performed directly across the street at the Abbey Theatre. I was forced to drag him to the door and point his nose at the marquee. Yet he didn't seem to be focusing on the actual words.

The play, *The Silver Tassie*, had just been panned in *What's On*, Dublin's weekly entertainment guide: "Shaun Davey's score," wrote the reviewer, Tom Mathews, "prevents the drooping of the eyelid as cliché rings on cliché." Mr. Mathews seemed to be involved in a campaign against long-windedness. He felt that former pop star Boy George, when he sings the line "War is stupid," conveys "much the same sort of message as the current Abbey production – only about sixty times less tediously." It would appear that Mr. Mathews wished to be transferred to the music beat. But, to his credit, his review was remarkably brief and not tedious at all.

Mr. O'Shea was spared the pain of being asked if he had read any of John B. Keane's plays or seen them performed. It was obvious he hadn't. He was interested in literary matters, and it was important for him to have the correct opinions on various literary issues of national interest. Who could condemn him for that? But that's as far as it went. It cost money to go to the theatre, money that would be better spent with real-life people in a pub. And as for books, well, the less said about that the better.

He was illiterate for sure – but he was tough and persuasive. It was obvious he'd been a loner from away back. It turned out that Mr. O'Shea was the youngest of thirteen. He had never married, he said, because being the youngest he had to take care of his old widowed mother. He had been in Dublin twenty years, and every drink he had drunk in that time showed in his potted and pitted nose and the rosacea that was gradually devouring his face. He kept poking me and shaking my hand vigorously. He must have shaken my hand twenty times in the course of our chat. He took each and every excuse to shake my hand. He had a beautiful manner of speaking, a pure Irish country accent, but he kept talking unnaturally low, as if he didn't want his manner of speaking to betray that he was, in spite of his twenty years in the capital, still a country lad. He would be mumbling along indistinctly then all of a sudden yell out: "Be yourself!"

One wouldn't dream of calling Mr. O'Shea a simple person. Indeed, he had his complexities, his passions, his inconsistencies, and his own brand of sophistication and wisdom. For instance, he called Brendan Behan an "overgrown idiot," and when we reached a certain point in that discussion, his eyes indicated he didn't think we should proceed any further.

His dislike of Behan didn't seem to fit the pattern set by his previously established likes and dislikes. But the attitude that Behan lacked authenticity, especially as reflected in his relationship with and attitude towards the media, turned out to be standard in Ireland.

"*Borstal Boy* was just a school essay. And he just got drunk to make himself famous, you know."

"But Brendan Behan was a very courageous fellow, wouldn't you say? After all, at the age of sixteen he was caught trying to plant a huge bomb on a British battleship."

"That's not courageous, that's just ignorant."

I still hadn't rested, but that was all right, because one soon discovers Ireland is a great country to be tired in. You're more likely to get a taste of mythic Ireland when you're ready to collapse. The myths still exist, if only in the minds of besotted insomniacs. In fact, as Mr. O'Shea rumbled on, I could see dozens of fairies in my peripheral vision. They were dancing merrily, but focusing on them made them disappear. This was definitely not a common every-day experience.

Mr. O'Shea had the most agonizing manner of making the simplest things complex. He spent ten minutes groping for the words to tell me that in my travels around Ireland I should be sure to leave the beaten track and stay away from tourist attractions. "The Blarney Stone is fake," he said. Meanwhile, the television set over the bar was showing a set of stained-glass windows, a bell started ringing, and Mr. O'Shea crossed himself and lowered his head. At first I didn't see a connection between the bell and Mr. O'Shea's behaviour. I thought he was responding to something I'd said. But no, it was, of course, the Angelus. Six o'clock. Mr. O'Shea was the only one in the pub observing it. I was moved by this, but Mr. O'Shea was a bit embarrassed.

"It's just the way I was brought up," he said. "It doesn't mean anyone else has to do it."

We finished our pints. He wanted to buy me another. I had to go soon, but there was time for a half.

"A half of what?"

"A half of Guinness. What I had before."

"That's not what you had before."

"Yes it was."

"That is not Guinness." He pointed at my glass.

"Sure it's Guinness. I should know what I'm drinking."

"That's not Guinness," he said. "Look, this is not black, me friend. Guinness is almost completely black. This is pale."

Maybe I'd made a mistake. After all, he was so certain, and he was a Dubliner of twenty years' standing, with a previous thirty-eight in County Kerry, and me only having been in the country a few hours.

But no, it was Guinness; it looked pale because there was only an inch in the bottom.

"Go ahead, have a smell. You'll see it's Guinness. You do know what Guinness smells like don't you?"

"That I do. Guinness smells like the air of Dublin."

He gave my glass a sniff and said, "I'm sorry. It's not Guinness."

"It is so Guinness. Have a taste if you have the courage."

He screwed up his face and took a sip. His face changed.

"Ach, you're right. It's Guinness all right."

A fellow on my left caught my eye and pointed to a ten-pence coin on the bar. He wanted to know if it was mine. I told him I was leaving it as a tip. "Oh, oh, oh," he said, without taking his eye off it. He was mesmerized by it. "Well, well, well." Could he have been coveting it for himself? He had just finished a chocolate bar, washing it down with a good slug of Guinness. With that coin he could get another bar.

"I guess it's not the custom here, is it?" I said, meaning leaving a tip

"Well, it is not. Not really," he said.

"I wouldn't want to start a trend or spoil the bartender."

"Ach, don't worry about it," he said, and went back to his drink.

PHOENIX PARK

In the morning I hopped on the Number 10 bus, took a front seat on the upper deck, and rode past movie theatres showing first-run films from the United States and out the North Circular Road to Phoenix Park. It was early spring, the daffodils and forsythia were in bloom, and the residential lawns were brilliant green, but the trees, though covered in green moss, were not yet in leaf. The Dublin Mountains, looking as if they were covered with violets, beckoned from the end of every street. The sky was blue, the rosebushes were getting heavy with bud, and the occasional ornamental cherry tree heavy with blossoms as we drove toward the giant obelisk of the Wellington Monument in legendary Phoenix Park.

One of the women at the Allied Irish Bank had told me that Dublin Zoo was in a frightful dilemma financially and was operating on a week-by-week basis. When I walked into the bank, there were three attractive women tellers resting on their elbows and staring seductively at me. I paused, and the irony of my predicament wasn't lost on them: I didn't know which of the three to go to.

"Which one of us would you be wanting then?" said the one on the left. All three were smirking.

"I can't choose."

"You have to," said the one in the middle, stamping her foot.

"I can't."

"You can't have all three of us," said the one on the right.

"Why not?" I said.

They looked at each other and smiled.

I bought a bus pass for three pounds from the teller on the right, chatted with the teller in the middle, and presented a money order to the teller on the left for cashing.

"Don't be expecting too much now," said the middle teller, referring to the zoo. "It's in a frightful dilemma financially. It's operating on a week-to-week basis."

From Infirmary Road I stepped down into Phoenix Park. Unmarked paths led in various directions. The bus driver had said just follow the signs to the zoo, but there didn't seem to be any signs. At the side of a large pond a pair of wild swans were skimming along close to each other – but not too close. A tall woman in a black coat, with eyes painted bright green and a broad mouth painted bright red, stood watching the swans and waiting for an elderly man to catch up with her. She was in her late forties. I asked if the zoo was up this way.

"Oh, I don't know, dear. Maybe those workers over there would know. A lovely place here, isn't it?"

In retrospect I wondered if she didn't know perfectly well where the zoo was, but, like the Ulster dairy farmer who would later try to dissuade me from going to Belfast, she would have preferred I not visit the zoo because it was in such bad shape. A visit to the zoo, however, was mandatory, if only to see how things had changed since Morton's triumphant visit a lifetime ago.

The two workmen were checking the roots of an old tree. They had an ancient cart full of well-maintained gardening tools from the previous century. We chatted for a moment about the weather.

"Is the zoo up here?" I said, pointing along a path that wound up a green hill and into a copse of naked trees.

The older man, who apparently hadn't understood my accent, looked at the younger. The younger man paused, then said: "Indeed it is. You go up here then turn right then left –"

"Is it the zoo he's looking for?" said the older man. "Tsk! See that lamp post up there? Go there and turn left."

Uphill from the pond, I stopped at a highly dramatic statue surrounded by low shrubbery. It loomed above me, a fierce-looking man with huge hands hanging down, and with thick Superhero-comic-book veins in them, an intelligent and defeated hero – John J. Heuston, captain of D Company, First Battalion, Dublin Brigade, Irish Volunteers.

To him and his command and to all of his company who in the years that followed strove for the liberation of our country the company erected this memorial in the year of our Lord 1943.

Heuston was one of sixteen men executed by the British on May 8, 1916, for their part in the Easter Rising. The sixteen included the severely ill James Connolly, who was crippled with gangrene from a leg wound and who was shot while tied to a chair. One of Dublin's train stations was named after Connolly, the other after Heuston. The thought of the sixteen martyrs to the nationalist cause still commanded a lot of reverence throughout Ireland.

As for the Wellington Monument, at two hundred feet it was only one-sixth as high as the CN Tower in Toronto, but it possessed such character and strength it made the latter seem toylike and tame. It could be seen from various places here and there around Dublin, and

it always seemed to be making a political statement, all the more so
when one stood dwarfed at its base.

On one of the monument's four faces, above a full-width series of
steps on all four sides, was a Roman-style battle scene heavily sculpted
in dark bronze, as if on the face of a sarcophagus. The battle in question was the most famous of the nineteenth century: Waterloo.
Someone had scrawled under it FREE MARTIN FORAN NOW. On
one of the other sides there was an Indian scene, with palm trees, and
a Moslem commander with long, thick moustaches. A prankster had
climbed up and painted the commander's face bright yellow. It might
have been Amanda, Linda, Rocky, Jay W., Fogey Lee, Noel, or Reno –
all of whom had climbed up and painted their names in block caps.

A plaque indicated that the monument had been built in 1829,
which was the year the British government, with Wellington as prime
minister, passed a bill granting Catholic emancipation following a
bitter century of persecution. Wellington had been born in Dublin
sixty years earlier, although, when people referred to him as being
Irish, he would reply that having been born in a stable didn't make
one a horse.

The park was full of birds. There were black birds with long white
tails and a small bird with green head, brown body, and black-and-
white wings. Wondering why I could never identify birds, I stepped
out into the street, and a passing motorist smiled benignly as he
swerved to avoid me. He probably had me down as the first American
of the season, for no Irishman would be dressed in a Donegal tweed
jacket and a Harris tweed motoring cap. I was even carrying a hickory
walking stick, to ease the pain in my left leg, which had been broken a
couple of months earlier in a fall on an icy street.

At the front gate of the zoo I handed a sleepy fellow my three-
pound-thirty entrance fee.

"They tell me you're in a bit of trouble here at the zoo."

"Oh, I think we're over the worst of it now, thank you."

"You got some funding, did you?"

"We got some money."

This fellow was wishing I'd shut up. This was definitely non-Irish of him. He had me down for the kind of guy who had nothing better to do than go to the zoo by himself on a weekday. They'd have to keep an eye on me, or I might be trying to have sex with the yaks.

"That's wonderful. Where from?"

"Oh, from schools, various places, that sort of thing."

H. V. Morton had been honoured with an invitation to breakfast at Dublin Zoo, an invitation which he considered "not only a compliment, but also a solemn and historic social event." He was met at the zoo gates and was conducted to a room where a dozen men stood around eating porridge from little glass bowls. This would have been the late twenties, and the Council of the Royal Zoological Society of Ireland had been holding weekly breakfast meetings for more than ninety years. Each week attendance was taken, and at the end of the year the three worst attenders were removed from the council. No more free porridge.

My intention was to inquire if the council was still meeting for breakfast. But the atmosphere wasn't quite right for such inquiries. Zoo employees wandered around in a state of agitated somnambulism. They looked as if they would start screaming if anyone went up to them and asked: "What is the difference between an African elephant and an Asian elephant?" Or, "Does the Council of the Royal Zoological Society of Ireland still hold weekly breakfast meetings here?" They also gave the impression they would not welcome any questions about Sita's foot.

At Morton's breakfast, they had handed him Sita's foot for inspection. Sita was an elephant, and had suffered the indignity of having had a foot sawed off, although at the time, presumably, she was dead. The inscription on the foot read: "Sita, who killed her keeper and was shot. June 11, 1903." I wanted to ask if Sita's foot was still in existence and if so could I see it. But every time I tried to catch an official eye, that eye would sadly look away.

Morton's breakfast invitation made a huge impression on him. He effuses about the wonders of Dublin Zoo, and he makes a very broad point of how the zoo began, in 1831, with a big assist from the English, who designed it, organized it, and sent a wolf, a leopard, and a hyena from the Tower of London, as well as some unspecified animals from the royal menagerie at Windsor Park.

To Morton, the zoo was a symbol of both the new Ireland and the new friendship between England and Ireland, a great friendship that would enrich both nations in many glorious ways and lead to a new millennium. His visit to the zoo, and to Ireland itself, came on the heels of the Anglo-Irish Treaty and the setting up of the Irish Free State.

Morton interviewed Christopher Flood, who had achieved international fame as a brilliant breeder of lions. "I've never taken a stick to an animal in my life," he boasted. "I just speak to them. They know. They have to obey me. I developed this power over them unconsciously." James M. Cain, author of *The Postman Always Rings Twice*, satirized this attitude brilliantly in his famous story "The Baby in the Icebox," which (coincidentally?) was written a year after the publication of *In Search of Ireland*, complete with the Flood interview.

In those days Dublin was famous for its lions. There were Dublin lions in Adelaide, Toronto, and Antwerp. Dublin lions "travelled around the world in fairs and menageries," Morton noted, adding that the most famous was Nigeria, "a magnificent creature presented by King Edward." She had twenty-six cubs and they all lived.

But on the way to the lions I passed three snow leopards in a desperately small cage. Two were snarling at each other and the third was silently staring at me with a look of profound concentration, as if trying to figure out some vexing problem.

There was scarcely a bird in the Tropical Hall Aviary, but there was a little colony of squirrel monkeys from South America, and they were sponsored by St. Andrew's College, Blackrock. And off to one side, to the immediate left of the exit from the aviary, as if placed there as an afterthought, two chimpanzees were pitiably cloistered in a small and anonymous glass cage. The younger chimp was sitting up straight and had entirely covered his legs and lower body up to his chest with packing straw. He sat there with a silly look on his face, a very passive look, as if heavily doped on Xanax. The mother was busy draping herself with straw as well, but when she spotted me she pushed her straw to one side and made a leap towards the window. Her dosage was apparently not as heavy. She had one finger in her mouth and another in her nostril. When I held my walking stick up horizontally, she looked at it with interest as if she'd love to be able to jump on to it. She cleverly blew on the glass, made a little fog, then wiped it clean so she could see me better.

Two very handsome giraffes were busy nibbling off and swallowing paint chips from the eavestrough of their little house. A herd of zebras would run in tandem, then slam on the brakes at the last minute and kick up a cloud of dust just before they would otherwise have fallen into their moat.

The elephants – mother and son, like the chimps – were not in leg chains, but they didn't seem happy at all. One thin electrical wire surrounded their tiny space, and there was a moat four feet deep. The mother was exerting considerable pressure with the top of her trunk, trying to push down a heavy metal fence, just for something to do. They had no other elephants to communicate with – just the sounds of traffic coming from the North Circular Road off in the distance to increase their sadness and longing. The elephants were sponsored by Burmah and Castrol.

A large hand-painted sign gave the running speeds of various animals. I gasped audibly when I saw the sign was sponsored by Player's cigarettes. Starting with the giant tortoise (one-sixth of a mile an hour) all the way up to the aptly named swift (106 miles an hour), there was the cheetah at 63, the pronghorn at 61, the lion at 50, the kangaroo at 45, the zebra at 40, the ostrich at 42, the giraffe at 32, the rhino at 28, the hippo at 25, the elephant at 24, the camel at 20, and the buzzard (gliding) at 75. Nothing for a buzzard diving or going full out. But then again it's hard to catch buzzards working hard. In fact the noted author William S. Burroughs claims to have started firing at a group of buzzards eating away at a dead animal, and, before they had reacted sufficiently to fly off, six of them were dead. I don't think this was at Dublin Zoo, though. He probably would have been kicked out straightaway – and with no refund.

Another sign, sponsored by the National Irish Bank, explained "how animals save to survive" and told about squirrels and their nuts, camels and their water, the dung beetle and its dung: "Tiger drags his kill into the undergrowth and hides it among the rocks or under vegetation for future meals. Even the dung beetle saves, the tortoise saves, the beaver saves . . . and you can save at the National Irish Bank."

A "Life Comes in Two Forms – Animal and Vegetable" sign was sponsored by Radio Ireland. There were similar signs when I was a kid visiting Toronto's now-defunct Riverdale Zoo, where kids today hide in the decrepit old cages and sniff glue and gasoline.

A pair of Patagonian cavies, big brown animals that were created immediately after the Big Bang and are the size of overweight Irish setters, were living in a garden shed supplied by Baumann's Doggy World, Stillorgan, 884021. And a deer was peeking shyly out from another small shed at the top of a hill. All of a sudden, like the gangs of little boys in the motion pictures of Hiroshi Shimizu in the late thirties, about forty of them came silently bursting out of the shed, leaping and bounding and running at enormous speed along the eighty-yard-long runway. They got to the end, stopped with sudden grace, then walked back slowly and re-entered the pen. It was hard to see how they all managed to fit in.

Another sign seemed to contradict Morton's contention that the English got the zoo going with a huge donation of animals from the Tower of London and the royal menagerie at Windsor Park. It stated that "Dublin Zoo started in 1831 with one wild boar and now boasts one of the finest collections in the world with thirty acres of picturesque grounds." In 1831 it cost six pence to get in and, since all you got to see was one boar, it would be a much better deal today – especially since in those days boars still ran wild in the countryside, and you could even see the occasional one slinking along a quiet Dublin street after midnight. Members who had paid-up subscriptions could bring two friends and all three would get in for free. But you had to write your name at the gate and leave your walking sticks and umbrellas. People in those days apparently loved to poke the boar in the eye with such implements.

Irish Life (an insurance company, not a magazine) sponsored the Record Ages sign: The tortoise 200 years, man 116 years, cockatoo 108, elephant 69, ostrich 60, butterfly (non-hibernating) one month, hedgehog 10.5 years, tiger 22, giraffe 28, zebra 40, gorilla 54, crocodile 56. Jessie the elephant lived 69 years at the Toronga Zoo in Sydney.

And finally here are the famous lions, three of them, in the Craigie Enclosure, at least ten times as spacious as what the elephants have to endure, and constructed in 1958 through the generosity of the Craigie Family. A male named Rajah, a female named Tina, and another female, unidentified, were sitting quietly, but wide awake. They were at the highest point of their enclosure, towards the rear, as far from visitors as possible, though I still seemed to be the only visitor. Rajah was sponsored by the *Encyclopaedia Britannica* and Tina by New PMPA Insurance. They had their eye on me, but they were not coming down. Both Tina and the unnamed female had grief-stricken expressions on their faces. I later found out the zoo was still in the business of exporting lion cubs around the world. That might explain the grief – and the spacious enclosure.

After leaving the zoo I wandered through Phoenix Park and came across a large pit in the ground with an old heavy metal fence and gate surrounding it and concrete steps leading down into it; there was no indication of what it was all about. It was just after one o'clock, and some business people were eating chocolate bars as they strolled toward the park gate. A hunchback of indefinite age was picking up dried twigs and small branches and placing them in a terribly decrepit baby buggy. There had been something hauntingly familiar about that zoo, as if I had visited it in a previous life. Perhaps I had lived there and, if so, I was probably a Patagonian cavy.

Postcards to my daughters:

Hi Jennifer! My first day in Dublin I go to the zoo. The flowers are coming out but they're not all the way out. The weather is not what you would call warm but not what you would call cold either. It's not what you would call windy and it's not what you would call still. It's not what you would call rainy and not what you'd call dry. The people are not what you'd call friendly and not what you'd call unfriendly. All in all, it's my kind of place.

Hi Alison! I've never seen such a city for chocolate bars. Everywhere you go you see people eating chocolate bars. On the street, on the buses. Poor people. Well-to-do people. Business people. Construction workers. Even in the pubs you see people with a Guinness in one hand and a chocolate bar in the other. And on billboards, in the papers, magazines, and on radio and telly – full-calibre chocolate-bar advertising.

LOURDES BRASIL

I spent an hour watching the urban scenery from my bedroom window. Rush-hour traffic skidded around the Beresford Loop and under an ugly Victorian railway bridge which had been rusted out and reinforced many times. Over the bridge a sparkling new state-of-the-art train jammed with commuters carrying lap-top computers whizzed by every ninety seconds or so. The Custom House glistened, silently reciting its mantra: "Top o' the mornin' to ye." It felt mysterious to be in Ireland. I was stark naked, kneeling next to the window with my binoculars, when the chambermaid burst in to clean the room. I made a mighty bedward leap, my heart pounding with fright, and wrapped myself in the sheets.

Lourdes Brasil was in her mid-twenties, a tall and awkward Spanish beauty of ironic innocence, with an intelligent eye, and she had, about an inch under her eye, perhaps adding to its intelligence, a large shiny black *verruca vulgaris* the size of a beebee. It shivered and glistened. She also had bushy eyebrows that met in the middle, giving her a resemblance to the young Frida Kahlo.

Lourdes had been in Dublin four months, and she didn't mind confessing that she didn't much like it. Her brother had spent some time in London studying English and reported that the English were very stupid. They took a superior attitude toward anyone whose language wasn't English. And now Lourdes was discovering the same kind of stupidity in Ireland. Such an attitude was strong in Canada when I was a child, I told her. People studiously avoided speaking foreign languages on the street for fear of reprisals. But things had improved considerably.

"It's hard to understand," she said. "Ireland is a poorer country than Spain. What makes them feel superior?" She wanted to know why English-speaking people felt that people who didn't speak English were retarded, or savages, or both. Her boyfriend had been visiting last weekend from Spain, and they went up to Belfast together. "The border guards were very rude and upset when they found my friend couldn't speak a word of English."

Trying to make her feel better, I suggested it was a matter of intelligence. I mentioned my neighbourhood coffee shop in Toronto, where the manager is Serbian, the waitress is Bosnian, and her boyfriend, who hangs around a lot, is Croatian. "War is for idiots," they aver when asked how they get along so well.

I also offered her a quote from Padre Blazon, the hilarious old Spanish Jesuit priest in Robertson Davies's *Fifth Business*. "Not all the Irish are idiots. They have a lot of Spanish blood, you know."

When the conversational tone ripened, I tried not to panic. Lourdes said she was twenty-five, had a modest reputation in Spain as a poet, having published in all the hot literary magazines, and she wanted me to know that she no longer had strong feelings about her boyfriend. Her feelings had been spoiled by the intensity of his dependency upon her. It was so even before she left Spain. In fact that was one reason she left.

"An older man wouldn't be like that," she said, with a significant look. When she noticed my discomfort, she laughed with a high-pitched tone, much out of character with her deep, soft, serious speaking voice. "Older men," she added, "they are easier to be friendly with. They are not so much boring; they're neither possessive nor are they perpetually lusty."

Hard-core eye contact was becoming a constant backdrop to our little conversation, me with the covers pulled up to my neck and she sitting on the edge of the bed which she had made so often. Her flirtatiousness was both flattering and embarrassing. She brought in her English-language magazines, Irish and British, and her tattered English–Spanish dictionary with a quick look that said, "Poor me, I need help." I said her English was excellent.

The little hotel had three floors and about eight very large rooms. At tea that afternoon, the entrances of Patricia, the manager, had generally coincided with Lourdes's exits and vice versa. Patricia said she was Dublin-born but "I love going down the countryside of Ireland. I just love going to the local pubs all over the country. Walk all day and at night go into the pubs." Her eyes seemed to be saying she wouldn't mind being asked along, though she couldn't possibly come, of course, for solitude is the poet's only guardian angel.

Patricia had the habit, in conversation, of speeding up or speaking more loudly when her interlocutor tried to get a word in. She was contemptuous of the Irish who go to Spain for their holidays and return sporting new leather coats, only to find out that they could have bought them more cheaply in Dublin.

The magnolia blossoms were out in Saint Stephen's Green. An amorous couple on their lunch break attracted the attention of a pair of Gardai, who kept walking back and forth in front of the bench, as if trying to decide on the appropriate moment to pounce on them and make an arrest. Their moustaches were quivering with anticipation and excitement. The lovers were full of heart-rending sighs, and looked as if they were about to tear each other's clothes off. Even the cops looked a bit steamy.

Saint Stephen's Green, a little park given sheen by history and literature, including a papal visit in 1979, was surrounded by Georgian office buildings, hotels, townhouses, and the occasional glass-and-aluminum monstrosity erected in the 1960s. In one of the latter is housed the Canadian Embassy, where I went to check for messages.

An elderly woman, impoverished and all in black, was pleading with an embassy official for clearance to emigrate, but he insisted she had to fill out forms first. I went up to a wicket, gave my name, and asked if there were any messages. The woman behind the wicket said there were no messages for me.

"But you didn't check."

"I don't have to, do I, *sor*? Because there are no messages, period."

I spent the day wandering around town, buying postcards, buying green underwear, gawking at people. I seemed to have lost my Harris tweed "Irish" motoring cap at the zoo. A man with one eye went by, a large shiny patch of pink flesh, grafted from the buttocks I suppose, having grown nicely over the other, just like the old woman who ran the candy store when I was a kid. People kept calling me "*sor*." I naturally figured that was the Irish pronunciation for "sir." Later I discovered it was the old Irish word for "louse."

"It is the rule of God's providence that we should succeed by failure."
– John Henry Cardinal Newman.

This is one of many Newman quotes posted around the walls of the Catholic University Church, founded by Newman in 1845, built by John Hungerford Pollen, and attended by James Joyce.

A campaign to have Cardinal Newman beatified was in full swing, and there were three slots in the wall for offerings to the Poor, the Pope, and the Altar. I sneaked into a private room, and my suspicions were confirmed: the money all went into the same box.

There was a large alabaster bust in the west aisle. I thought it was some pope I'd never heard of, but it turned out to be Cardinal Newman. "The process for the beatification of John Henry Cardinal Newman has begun. Please report favours received to The Oratory, Birmingham 16." Maybe I've received a few favours in my life, but none I can connect with Cardinal Newman.

I took a taxi over to the Liberties, west of Marrowbone Lane, and proceeded to limp through the narrow streets, with vendors hawking cheap rings, rubber boots, rubber bands, fresh fish, and loose underwear. The Liberties was one of the few shopping areas in Dublin that didn't especially cater to the tourist. Saint Catherine's church was where the great nationalist hero Robert Emmet, aged twenty-five, was hanged after a fake trial in 1803. "Let no man write my epitaph," he said in his final speech. It's said the hanging didn't kill him; his body twisted horribly as he choked to death. But before he died, the hangman removed the noose, cut off Emmet's head, held it up to the crowds, and screamed, "Death to traitors."

Across from Saint Catherine's is the Guinness Visitors' Centre, where one gets to see films demonstrating that the only ingredients in Guinness have always been, are now, and always will be barley, water, hops, and yeast, world without end, amen. They say it so often you begin to wonder.

The money I would save by not drinking Guinness and Paddy's, owing to the fact that I was driving, would pay for the car rental fee and the gas to boot. I had been thinking of following Morton's motor route rather loosely, by a series of short bus and train rides. But accurate schedules weren't available this year, connections were poor, and departures infrequent. And my leg was more bothersome than anticipated.

Someone said they'd read in the paper that all the animals in the zoo were going to be put down after Saint Patrick's Day, unless some funds were forthcoming. In the papers I read about the IRA Provos demanding 3.5 million pounds from the Irish National Bank. Also three County Offaly farmers had gone to jail rather than have their cattle tested for tuberculosis. In the *Irish Times* someone was selling his snooker cue: "Brand new genuine Riley Brazilian seasoned ash. Cost 135 pounds, sell for 35. Will deliver." And someone wanting desperately to sell his Sony video camera resorted to stating that it was an "unwanted gift, seldom used – can be verified." But there was nothing about the zoo.

The next day at breakfast, served in the little hotel dining room by the devilish Lourdes Brasil, I chatted with a fellow who had been having trouble with the United States Embassy regarding his visa. He was booked to fly to Boston for the Saint Patrick's Day parade. He had spent three and a half months in New York last year and because of that the embassy officials were afraid he'd want to stay permanently this time. He said he was almost finished his airline pilot's course, and he figured soon, ironically, the Yanks would be offering him all kinds of jobs and begging him to emigrate.

His name was Tommy O'Toole. He was from Cork City, and he agreed I should rent a car. There were all those remote country pubs I wouldn't be able to visit otherwise, and, as I later came to realize, all those wonderful megalithic monuments.

"People are laid back in Ireland," he said. "Not like in the U.S. In New York it's crazy there."

Lourdes was standing at the door, listening attentively, with a subtle smile on her face.

"Crazier than Cork, was it?" I queried.

"It was awful culture shock I suffered when I got there, I tell you – and just as bad if not worse when I got back here, you know."

I wanted to know more about the visa problem and he was obliging.

"They said how long did you stay last year? I said three and a half months. Well, they didn't like that at all. I said you gave me a visa for a year, what was the matter with me staying three and a half months? They said they were afraid I was going to stay permanently. They wanted proof I'd be going back home. So I went all the way back to Cork City and got letters from the company I work for, my parents, the parish priest, friends, the flying school, and came all the way back to Dublin."

"You do want to get back to the U.S.A., don't you?"

Evelyn Waugh somewhere refers to "the Irishman's deep-rooted conviction that there are only two realities: hell and the U.S.A."

"That I do. And they still haven't given it to me. It's very frustrating. If I didn't want that visa bad enough I'd tell them what to do with themselves, eh? They make you feel like a bloody espionage agent or something like that."

He was training in Cessnas now but he expected to be training in Lear jets by Christmas. Then he started snapping his fingers and saying: "Oh, what's the word? I lose me words sometimes."

"Discotheque?"

"That's right! Eh, how did you know?"

"I took a course in ESP last year."

"Geez, that was amazing. I'd like to take that course."

He said that, in addition to attending flying school, spending a few months in Boston every year, and driving for a construction company, he also worked weekends at a discotheque.

"Doing what?"

"Security."

"Bouncer?"

A look of pain crossed his face.

"That's what they call us," he admitted. "Not a word I'd use though. We're the ones who decide who goes, who stays. Most of the clubs are pretty quiet, but if a guy hits anyone he's out."

I mentioned a recent case in Toronto where a bouncer got five years for beating a guy up in an alley behind the club and the guy died. It was a simple case of a guy not liking getting booted out of the club, deciding to fight back, the fight escalates, and bingo.

Mr. O'Toole plunged into a thoughtful silence. I guiltily sipped my breakfast tea. We were at separate tables in the small dining room. Lourdes looked radiant in the morning sunlight bursting through the curtains. I took some pictures of her. Mr. O'Toole finally spoke.

"Dangerous."

"Dangerous? Taking pictures of Lourdes?" He probably had a point.

"Oh, heavens, it's not that. It's the job I'm speaking of. A guy you kick out can hold a grudge. You can be walking with your girlfriend the next day and he'll say hey you, and start a fight."

I told him I'd promised myself an early start so I'd better get going.

He looked genuinely stricken. "I'll have to find something to do until two o'clock when I go to get my visa."

I flicked on the radio as I brushed my teeth, and Gay Byrne, the broadcaster/author, whose latest book was in all the bookstore windows, was interviewing, with what seemed a condescending tone, an elderly woman who wanted to become a nun. The woman's husband was dead and the children all grown up. When I came out of the bathroom, Lourdes was standing there. She had listened quietly to the conversation about the visa and now had something to offer: "Spain, it is being destroyed by the American tourists," she said. "There's altogether too many of them. They are like Pepe in his own house," the latter being a literal translation of a Spanish idiom apparently meaning rude, crude, and not very shrewd.

Later, when I mentioned that the Irish were always going on and on about how they are so lazy in their own country but become terribly hardworking as soon as they emigrate, she said she had another Spanish idiom that covered that: "In the blacksmith's house the knives are always made of wood."

On all the newsstands today was prominently displayed, on page one of some Irish tabloid, a full-colour head-and-shoulders shot of a girl whose hair had been burned off. The story was she had put gel on her hair and lit a cigarette. The gel contained a high percentage of alcohol. Her face and scalp were terribly burned.

But the story smelled phony somehow. It played a little too well to Irish conservatism and latent snobbery. Any girl foolish enough to put that much gel on her hair deserved what she got, especially if she was also foolish enough to smoke cigarettes. An Irish priest would later offer a more sinister interpretation.

A Murphy Tours bus went by, on a tour of the capital from some remote corner of the Republic. Twenty or thirty school kids were happily jumping up and down in the back four rows. The rest of the bus was empty, except for two elderly schoolmistresses side by side right up front.

THE BRIDGES ON
THE LIFFEY

It would have been better to hire a car from a place with a slightly more Irish-sounding name, or at least less imperial-sounding, but when I called Ray Mills at the Great Island Car Rental Agency it turned out that his cars were not only more expensive but I would have to take the train to Cork City to pick one up. So here I was at the Buckingham Car Rental Agency on Bachelor's Walk on the north end of O'Connell Bridge. The manager, Maeve Bracegirdle, a happy woman, genial to a fault, gigglingly warned me that petrol was four pounds a gallon. But it turned out to be a mere two pounds eighty, one pound more than in England.

They were short of cars just now, but if I came back at eleven she'd try to have one for me. She had one reserved for a fellow, but she didn't think he was going to be allowed to have it because he didn't look as if he would have the proper papers or something like that.

In a store on Abbey Street was Eric Newby's most recent, *Round Ireland in Low Gear*, several curved-stairway-like stacks of them, skilfully executed, seemingly, by a recent transplant from the fresh-fruit section of a grocery store. I'd read the book last year, a book so full of vivid and horrendous descriptions of cycling during torrential rain-storms, hailstorms, sleetstorms, and snowstorms – and getting lost every ten minutes – that it almost made me lose interest in going to Ireland. But here it was in a different edition, the cover featuring a picture of Newby and his wife, two elderly cyclists – very inspiring.

The sidewalks of O'Connell Street were thronged with swarms of mid-morning pedestrians, many carrying a big fat novel – some with one under each arm – and bearing a serious look and an air of knowing where they were going and why. A certain type of woman started to appear over and over again. She was tall, thin, in her forties or fifties, with a mystical and tormented face, an air of cynicism, even bitter-ness. She was dressed entirely in black, and either had no makeup at all or was liberally smeared with rouge, eye shadow, and lipstick. She was neither virginal nor matronly, saintly nor sluttish; her fingers were tobacco stained, her nails chewed. You could imagine her wan-dering the rainswept hills in a "long black veil," like the woman in the song of that title, as sung by the Wolfe Tones. Were these women the victims of tragic love affairs or were they women who could never find a man serious enough to suit them, whose soul had the depth to resonate with theirs? Perhaps they were victims of the Irish male pub culture, for there seemed to be no obvious male equivalents for their kind of stately high-mindedness. Perhaps they were in secret commu-nion with dead martyrs and saints. Perhaps they were the women of jailed IRAers, or perhaps they were women who had been left behind when their men emigrated.

The great mass of women on the streets seemed content to be their own particular undisguised selves in a way that one hardly sees on, say, Yonge Street or Fifth Avenue on a weekday morning – or when you do it seems like eccentricity. Particularly fascinating were the nuns, especially the older ones. Many seemed to have true saintliness in their features: merry, girlish, and sweet, well into their seventies.

The tourist office on O'Connell Street was packed with North

Americans, British, French, and Germans. All the men and some of the women were wearing Irish motoring caps. "What must it be like in the summer tourist season?" I said.

"It's horrible," said a security guard. "People are lined up outside all the way down the block and across all the bridges."

People on the street were wearing sprigs of sagging, tired, lifeless weeds in their lapels.

"Shamrocks," said the guard. "Saint Patrick's Day coming up."

The bridges on the Liffey were nicely spaced so that you could stand on one and look at someone standing on another looking at you. The Liffey was so tame and narrow it had to take a nice little civilized bend here and there to show it wasn't a canal. In old maps the Piddle (also known as the Poddle) flowed into it from the south. But very little of the Piddle remained.

A nicely dressed, well-groomed man had set up a table on O'Connell Bridge. He was wearing a green tie, a white shirt, a grey sports jacket, brown trousers, and black Oxfords, and he was nervously taking things out of his suitcase and placing them on the table and taking other things off the table and putting them in his suitcase. There were rings and chains and cheap little doodads.

He had a sign posted: ALL ITEMS ONE POUND.

"All those items for only one pound?"

"Do you have a big sack?"

Back at the Buckingham Car Rental Agency, Mrs. Bracegirdle was on the phone: "But there are compensations, of course," she was saying. Then she burst into laughter. She was a tall, stout woman, with manic chins, loved her job immensely, and had tremendous vitality and wit. "It's a very nice new sporty car you're getting," she told me. "A Satori two-seater with only, let's see now, 2,888 miles on it. And it's the fourth car I've rented today."

"A Satori?"

"It's all we have now, and we're not charging you anything extra!"

"What colour?"

"Let's see now, deep purple."

She said something about men not usually asking that question. She wanted to know every detail of my leg injury. She said something about it taking longer to heal when you get older.

The phone rang. She pressed a button and it stopped ringing.

"Oh, I feel as if I'm about twenty in my mind but I'm forty-six years old – hee hee hee hee! – and I work here all week and go home and cook and houseclean for my husband and my nineteen-year-old son – and I just can't seem to do it all anymore."

She looked a little guilty, as if she hadn't been working hard enough lately.

"When you're older you don't feel so guilty about lying around doing nothing," I offered.

"Well, I work six days a week and the only day I have off is Sunday. And I spend it looking after the family, cooking, cleaning, and all that. Hah hah hah!"

People who laugh easily are so likable, especially when they laugh at your jokes, so I told her a few, and then I told her about the blatant case of false advertising out there on O'Connell Bridge, which you could see out the front window. "See that fellow standing there? See his sign? Well, I took him up on his offer and wanted all his items for a pound and he refused. He said *each* item was a pound."

"The bloody bastard!"

Another round of giggling and laughing was interrupted by another phone call.

"Hello? . . . That's me!"

Mrs. Bracegirdle handed me a map of Dublin and started telling me how to get to the main highway heading south, which was where I wanted to go, following Morton's happy trail down to County

Wicklow and Glendalough. But the map looked complicated, and we kept lapsing into chitchat.

"We old-timers, we devise ways of coping with stress," I said.

"I try not to worry about anything," she said.

Stress, in Dublin, apparently meant the Troubles and nothing else. A sudden little cloud masked her smiling face.

"Imagine working for the Bank of Ireland right now," I said. "That'd be something to worry about." I was referring to the current IRA demand for 3.5 million pounds or death to bank employees.

"The threat is always there," she said, "it's just a matter of when it's going to happen."

She had a button on her desk and pressed it to let people in after she gave them the once-over through the window. Only people who looked okay got in.

After a few more phone calls, she decided she couldn't have my Satori delivered to the downtown office so she would have to get a driver to drive me down to the other office, way down in the southern-most outskirts of the city. This pleased me, because I had no desire to drive through the streets of Dublin on a busy weekday.

The driver was a sullen forty-year-old spoiled brat who wanted me to know he was busy and didn't have time to drive me and was in fact so busy he hadn't even had his tea this morning. And it was all my fault. He was driving like a Dickensian madman in thick, dense Dublin traffic, taking wild short cuts the wrong way down one-way streets and alleys, honking his horn furiously at lorries quietly parked in the middle of the road to unload huge crates of chocolate bars, and he kept tossing petulant sneers over his shoulder when the opportunity offered itself. He went around a corner so fast at one point, I slid across the width of the back seat, and found myself pressed up against a warm human body I hadn't previously noticed. It was the famous movie actress Meryl Streep.

"I loved you in *Sophie's Choice*," I said.

"That's a good line. Most guys just say dumb things like, 'Hey, you look like Meryl Streep.'"

"You're not Meryl Streep?"

"No, I'm Valerie Sweet."

"Were you here all along?"

"You didn't notice me when you got in."

She was a Canadian, from Toronto, and was going to the same car-rental place to pick up a car. She was a little upset when she found out I was getting a Satori while she was only getting a Koan for the same money, but she took it philosophically. She sighed and said she had come over to Ireland last summer as a tourist and fallen so deeply in love with the country that she returned and settled permanently. She ran the Arbrae Court Guest House in Dublin. And her love of the country was beginning to wear thin.

"It's great when you're a tourist, but it's a different reality when you've come here to live. It's the difference between getting a Satori and a Koan for the same money."

"What colour is your Koan?"

"I didn't ask. What colour's your Satori?"

"Deep purple."

"Geez!"

We were still sliding back and forth across the back seat in tandem, and kept exchanging glances to see who was being more terrorized by this nutty driver. We spoke calmly, not wanting to let on that we were the slightest bit afraid, which infuriated the driver even more. He wouldn't be happy till we started squealing for mercy.

"Everywhere I go I meet people from Toronto."

"Is that so?"

I told her about being on a bus running along a remote part of the west coast of the south island of New Zealand. There were only three passengers on the entire bus, and as we drove along we exchanged stories. Turned out all three of us were from Toronto.

"No!"

"Yes, and what's more the driver was engaged to be married to a woman from Toronto."

My experience with right-hand-drive had hitherto been restricted to less-congested areas. This was going to be a test of skill and nerve. It was hard to judge how far over the left fender pronged. If somebody was hopping into or out of his car and I smashed into him and killed him, it'd be completely understandable. No judge would convict me.

The much-envied Satori seemed to be going in the right direction, miraculously negotiating busy roundabouts and heading further and further south through the Dublin suburbs, with high crosses sitting prettily along the green medians and with blue mountains way off in the distance. I wanted to travel south along the coast to County Wicklow, but the Satori seemed to have a mind of its own and preferred the mountain route. It had a distant violet pyramid of a mountain in its purple gunsights and was shooting along towards it. "Ravished to blue by the sunlight, turning to slate under the shadows of passing clouds," Molly Keane writes in describing these mountains in her novel *Time After Time*.

Gay Byrne was on the car radio, chatting with some experts about divorce, a hot issue in Ireland. The talk swirled around their reaction to the U.S. film *War of the Roses*, which had just hit Ireland amid a heap of phone-in controversy. They were talking about divorce the way Canadians talk about racism in the police force or first-nation self-government.

"Only a lunatic would think that divorce is never a good thing," opined Byrne, wisely summing up the discussion. "And only a lunatic would think that it's going to solve all your problems."

I'm looking down into a deep, boxlike, four-sided valley bordered with numerous barren hills. Cultivated land inches up the slopes, a third of the way here, half the way there. Above the cultivated fields can be seen the traces of old agricultural land that had been taken out of commission long ago, owing to erosion and harsh weather. The tops of the hills are thinly bundled in mist and low-lying clouds.

Rivers here and there are silently falling down into the valley, the source of the Liffey apparently, or one of its sources.

The hillsides are speckled with small clumps of farm buildings, but no villages are visible in all that vista of valley. It's as if I'm standing on the same spot where, decades or maybe centuries ago, a man stood and heard faint gunfire coming from his house way down in the valley. When he arrived he found his wife and children dead, killed for having refused to divulge his whereabouts.

The wind was cold and heavy and I was lost somewhere up in the Sally Gap. I stopped to chat with a hitchhiker and get directions. I told him right-handed driving wasn't my cup of tea, and so I hesitated to give him a lift. He looked in my eye to check my sanity.

"Ach, I'll take the chance," he said.

He climbed in. He was a thin man about thirty, with the prematurely weary look of a poetic recluse, a mix of intelligence and poverty, humour and sorrow. We drove along the narrow curving road down into a wooded hollow in the foothills of the Wicklow Mountains. He said he lived alone in a one-room stone cottage up in the hills with his dog and his cat.

I sniffed and wiped a tear from my eye. He noticed.

"But they don't say much," he said, comfortingly.

"What do you think of the theory that a dog regards its master as the pack leader, while a cat regards its master as its mother?" I asked, after recovering from my melancholia.

"No wonder they don't say much."

Did he know how to get to the R755?

"The R755? Now what would that be?" He said Irish people didn't know the roads by numbers, only by their ancient names – the Dublin Road, the Glendalough Road, and so on.

"It would be the Glendalough Road."

"They're trying to get the metric business going here, too, but nobody pays much attention to it."

He seemed to enjoy living in the hills, immersed in the ages. He wanted to be dropped off at Enniskerry. He said he usually walked the few miles, but if a car passed he'd try to flag it down. He said he couldn't afford even an old wreck because he had to pay five hundred pounds a year comprehensive insurance on his house. I asked why so much. He said he had a long record of arson convictions.

"Not connected with the IRA at all?"

"Oh heavens no. That's funny, that is. No, I'm afraid I'm just another certified pyromaniac."

Enniskerry, a tourist centre billed as "one of the prettiest villages in Ireland" and the site of the vast gardens and high waterfalls of the Powerscourt demesne, was where he went to have a pint and "a bit of crack" in the local pub or else to get the bus to Dublin. This time he was just going to the local pub, and he invited me to come with him. But I didn't feel up to it just then. I told him I had to keep moving south. I felt a touch of anxiety and wanted to get used to the car.

The anxiety disappeared and a sense of timelessness built up on the drive south along the R755, the Glendalough Road, which starts just south of Dublin at Bray Head, described by James Joyce as lying on the water like the snout of a sleeping whale, and the locale of that wonderful Irish movie *The Miracle*. It was probably just my suggestibility, but I seemed to be sinking into the centuries.

"If anyone will see a leprechaun, you will," said a friend when I left. He was probably being sarcastic. But I wasn't in search of leprechauns. I was in search of Morton:

> There is something in a minor key that a man never quite hears. Perhaps no stranger ever hears it. But I think the Irish do. . . . If a man could hear it he would know all there is to know about Ireland. . . .
>
> And down the country roads of Ireland walk some of the best-looking country girls in the world. Some are small and red-faced, with dark eyes; others are fair and freckled about the nose, with blue eyes. They possess great dignity of bearing.

A herd of sheep was taking up the entire road. A tractor putt-putted along behind the herd like an outboard motor on a boat. On the back of the tractor was a large metal basket holding about eight lazy sheep.

A shepherd, wearing blue coveralls and black rubber boots, walked beside the tractor, looking for sheep who had decided against walking another step. When he found one he would pick it up and put it in the basket. If the basket was too crowded and the sheep too squashed, one – presumably the least exhausted at the moment – would mindlessly volunteer to hop out and resume walking.

Each sheep had a blast of green paint sprayed on its rump. Two dogs were following, making sure all the little details were taken care of, making sure that there were no sheep with the wrong colour of paint on their rumps, making sure that the shepherd hadn't overlooked any sheep playing possum and being left behind.

"It is these whispering things that are never far away from you in Ireland."

Morton was referring to a line in a poem by Francis Ledwidge.

"But you cannot hear what they are saying."

Morton could make an excellent living today writing ad copy for Aer Lingus. And yet – confession time! – I am not all that different from Morton, for I was feeling those whispering things too.

GLENDALOUGH

There was a vast and empty parking lot, with white lines so fresh and black pavement so shiny it was easy to forget where you were. And off to one side was an ugly, modern, brick-and-timber low-slung tourist centre, rare in Ireland, the sort of thing you'd expect to see in Aspen or Banff. It housed a modern museum, a movie theatre, the administrative offices, information desk, and so on. There would be nothing like it at Cashel, Tara, or Newgrange – though there would be a smaller version of it at the Cliffs of Moher.

This was the entrance to the extensive ruins of the complex ancient monastic settlement of Glendalough, Morton's first stop upon leaving Dublin. Neither the parking lot nor the tourist centre existed in Morton's day, but everything else had existed for centuries. I told a uniformed man with a kind face behind the counter that I thought it would be nice to visit Kevin's Bed.

Kevin was the most unpleasant saint imaginable, the patron saint of misogynists, famous for abusing women, particularly the passionate

Kathleen, by pushing them off cliffs into the water, only because they were in love with him and wouldn't give him any peace. A popular old ballad ends with these lines:

Oh! – cruel Saint Kevin! – for shame!
When a lady her heart came to barter,
You should not have been Knight of the Bath,
But have bowed to the Order of Garter.

It was difficult to keep the eye off the mountains surrounding Glendalough. We were in a deep valley, with two lakes and a multitude of lovely rocky gurgling streams. Kevin's Bed, thought to be a Bronze Age burial site, was a little one-person cave, thirty feet up the side of a perpendicular rock rising out of Upper Lake. When Morton visited Glendalough, a boatman rowed him to the shore directly below the cave of the solitudinous and obnoxious sixth-century saint, and Morton climbed straight up to it, though not without wondering how he was going to get back down unscathed.

"The only access would be by boat," said the uniformed man behind the counter. "And boats don't go over there any longer. They stopped some years ago." Apparently someone had been hurt, and perhaps he or she had sued. It's quite dangerous, he said, but a little light in his eye said that, if I really wanted to get to Kevin's Bed and was resourceful enough, I could find a way.

Morton had asked his boatman how deep the lake was. The boatman said it was so deep that, when his sister disappeared while swimming, they got a letter from her a few weeks later from Manchester asking them to post her some dry clothes.

Such tall-tale tourism is frowned upon today. If I'd asked this man for the depth of Upper Lake, he'd have told me to several decimal points. Instead he invited me to view the special film on Glendalough. Since I was the only tourist on hand, he could start it up whenever I was ready. I told him I'd read a little about Glendalough, so I'd forgo the film. He seemed pleased. His name was Kenneth Dignam.

"Sometimes," said Mr. Dignam, "you can have too much information. It gets in the way of simple awe."

It had been early spring in Dublin but here in this deep valley, liberally
nuggeted with relics from different points around a great cycle of time,
it was late winter. If Saint Kevin – Caoimhín in the old spelling – had
been pursued by women, it might have been because not only was he
young and handsome but also he could perform miracles. Kevin had
studied with three wise men who taught him the secrets of performing
miracles, just as Jesus was said to have picked up some tips from the
Druids during a visit to Glastonbury as a young man. I'm not sure what
Kevin's miracles were just now. Maybe he could make scrambled eggs
whole again. Or make squashed birds come to life.

According to the twelfth-century travel writer Gerald of Wales,
Kevin had a student who fell ill and asked for fresh fruit. Kevin prayed
for the young fellow, whereupon a willow not far from his church
brought forth fruit that was health-giving to the boy and to others
that were sick. And to this day both the willow and others planted
from it form a wall of trees around the old cemetery and bring forth
fruit each year. This fruit is white and oblong in shape, health-giving
rather than pleasant to the taste. The locals have a great regard for it;
it gets transported to the farthest parts of Ireland to cure various
diseases, and it is called the fruit of Saint Kevin.

Gerald of Wales is still resented today for being viciously slander-
ous of the Irish, but he becomes temperate when he speaks of Kevin.
One of Gerald's stories is familiar from the tales of the saints of India.
It seems Kevin held his hand up to heaven one day, as was his custom,
and a blackbird flew down and perched upon it – and then started lay-
ing eggs in his palm. Full of pity and patience, Kevin stood there night
and day with his arm upraised and his hand still until the eggs hatched
and the fledglings had all flown away. That is why Kevin is often pic-
tured with a blackbird in his hand.

Performing miracles has always brought fame, and there's nothing like fame, or even a bit of notoriety for that matter, to cause a serious person to seek out solitude, which is what Kevin – definitely no crass publicity hound – came to Glendalough in search of. At first he slept in the trunk of a tree. But his admirers caught up with him and he gradually retreated to more remote quarters, until he found the little Bronze Age grave in the wall high above the lake.

But still the admirers came, and stayed. Kevin was reluctantly made abbot of the monastery at Glendalough in A.D. 570, and the community grew in size and in fame until people from all over Europe were arriving to study. "All these the Irish willingly received," wrote the pro-Irish Venerable Bede, four centuries before Gerald of Wales and the arrival of the detested Normans, "and saw to it to supply them with food day by day without cost, and books for their studies, and teaching, free of charge."

Nothing of that was left, but nothing of the general layout here has changed since English forces destroyed the buildings in 1398. What was in ruins now was in ruins then – except for the round tower, the conical roof of which had been somewhat rebuilt in recent years, with the original stones. And of course the tourist centre and parking lot.

The round tower was 103 feet high and, like many such structures all over Ireland (to which they are unique), was used for tintinnabu-lation, meditation, and protection from Viking raids. Word of an imminent raid would reach the settlement, and everything stealable, killable, or eatable would be jammed into the round tower, the rope ladder would be pulled up, and everyone would be safe and sound, although probably shivering with fear. And a thousand years after its erection, the tower still neither sagged nor leaned, nor had it settled. It just stood there, as handsome as the day it was built.

Inside the ruined churches and monastic buildings of Glendalough were numerous tombstones from the seventeenth and eighteenth centuries, many propped up against what remained of the smashed walls. There was a fellow who died at the age of 102. There was also a beautiful gravestone commemorating a young fellow with such elo-quent brevity I closed my eyes and saw him standing there. I saw him as the village idiot, but one who was dearly loved and the subject of much good humour: "Here lyeth ye body of TODESTOOL died happily 1763. 17 years old."

Morton apparently didn't have to endure the roar of straight-pipe track bikes or the sound of rock music from the adjacent campgrounds at Glendalough, famed for its atmosphere of peace and spirituality. The campers and motorcyclists were here today for the annual motorcycle races.

A bright green meadow was scattered with numerous ancient stone crosses, each of which had had one of its arms lopped off, probably by fourteenth-century English swordsmen. A herd of grazing sheep was keeping the grass green and short. Also, there was the occasional seemingly random bump in the ground, a grassy pimple-like earthwork a few feet high, topped off with a stone cross, or sometimes by a curiously twisted tree. I'm sure dowsers would have something to say about these modest bumps, that they gave off spiritually nourishing electromagnetic pulses, or that they represent places where subterranean streams intersect, alluding to the lost wisdom of antiquity, a wisdom that only dowsers are in touch with today.

A giant mahogany cedar at least five hundred years old was trapped in the shadow of its own immense drooping branches. I stood inside the thick circular screen they composed; it made a wonderful hiding place. You could have stashed an entire kindergarten class in here, along with the teacher, the principal, and the support staff. One strangely curved branch, as thick as a man's chest and amazingly smooth on top, seemed to cry out for couples to make love on it. Hundreds of couples over the centuries had taken advantage of the inviting shape of the branch and the wonderful privacy. The branch had been worn smooth by all the lovemaking, or else made love on because of all the smoothness.

Adjacent to the tree, and much more ancient, sat a small *rath*, or *caher*, a perfectly round circular stone enclosure, about twelve metres in diameter. It might have been used as an animal enclosure, but it was more likely a circular fortification and dwelling place. The walls were about three feet high and covered with grass and several inches of soil all the way around. There were some flat stones lying at the centre of the circle, and just inside the circumference was another circle of small stones. "The rath survives, the kings are covered in clay," says a scrap of verse from the fifth century.

An old man about eighty strolled by in the silence, deep and spiritual in spite of the distant motorcycles, and I experienced a premonition of myself returning to Glendalough at that age. He knew his way around, he'd been here before – when he was my age, perhaps. He seemed to skim, his feet an inch above the ground, his hands behind his back like a speed skater, but unconscious and unreal. Maybe time plays tricks on us at places like Glendalough, and this ghost was a signal from myself, beaming back from decades in the future.

Up a small hill sat a low-set, well-designed, and perfectly preserved eleventh-century building called Reefert Church, *reefert* being a corruption of a term meaning "burial place of kings." It had an unusual shape for the eleventh century, and was reminiscent of the low-slung tourist centre adjacent to the parking lot. Before the days of Kevin, the pagan O'Toole chieftains were buried here. This church had been the site of great lamentations from time to time. How horrible it must have been when a king died!

Back at the tourist centre, Mr. Dignam looked at me tenderly and said: "I hope, sir, that you haven't come all the way from Dublin for the peace and quiet of Glendalough only to find the motorcycle races going on." He said the hotel down the road sponsored the world-championship races every year. "Our only hope is they'll come up for the races and discover the antiquities."

"I suppose it's terribly crowded here in the summer?"

"That it is."

"Even without the motorcycle races to attract people?"

"Even without the races, it is."

THE LONGEST ARMS OF
ANY MAN

Mrs. Kitty Ricketts was one of those darling little white-haired grannies you see here and there on your travels. She just wanted to talk about the high crime rate these days. She ran a lovely little bed-and-breakfast on the busy main street of quiet Kilcullen. It was a busy main street because it did double duty as the high-speed N9, a major southern route out of Dublin, connecting with Kilkenny and Water-ford. Further, this was the Friday night of the Saint Patrick's Day weekend, and the roads were so busy with traffic streaming south out of Dublin and I was so tired that I was very happy to be able to pull up the narrow lane and park in the back yard, next to a neat little com-munity of Tinkers' bunkies, shacks, and caravans, each with its little gas light burning away.

"Ach, the robberies in Dublin," said Mrs. Ricketts. "They don't care, they don't care one whit. I had tourists in here, Americans they was, and they had all their money and their passports robbed. They were just beside theirselves with worry. Your heart just went out to them, the poor things, it did."

I muttered something about poverty and social injustice.

"Ach, it's not the poverty. It's just people nowadays, they're all on the make."

I said I'd have to be really poor before I'd think of robbing anybody.

"That's because you're a gentleman," said Mrs. Ricketts. "Isn't it?"

"I guess so, ma'm."

"Well sure you are. But these people now, they're smart alecks. That's what they are. That's their way of living, don't you know? Beats working. And every once in a while they get to have a holiday in jail. They don't mind that at all."

Had she spent her entire life in Kilcullen?

"I lived for years in Kildare," she said. "But I'm originally from Hollywood. That's where I went to school."

"Hollywood? Did you ever know any movie stars?" I was dozing off on my feet.

"Oh good heavens. You're kidding me now, aren't you? Hollywood, it's, well, uh, not the one in America. You must have come through it if you drove up from Glendalough."

When she asked what I would like for breakfast, I told her just about anything would do, but if there was any possibility of kippers that would be splendiferous. She seemed thoughtful.

"Now I don't have any on hand just now, but I'll see if I can get some."

"Now don't you go to any trouble, Mrs. Ricketts."

The night before, I had slept poorly thanks to Lourdes Brasil. She knew I was leaving in the morning, so she made a big pot of tea and kept me engaged in conversation till all hours. Nothing worth relating here, except to say that she was going to be having a month off starting the following week and hinted that she wouldn't mind being invited to join me in my travels. Truthfully, she more than hinted. She grabbed my shirtfront, punched me on the shoulder, grabbed me around the neck, and pinched the back of my hand with all her might till I almost hollered. And then she put the pillow over my face to shut me up. She wouldn't stop till I promised I'd call her. It was reminiscent of the haystack scene in *Smiles of a Summer Night*.

But now that I'd had a nice little chat with Mrs. Ricketts, I wasn't so tired. I wandered down the main street and had a pint of Guinness in the local pub. There didn't seem to be any natural openings at the crowded bar, and naturally I felt too self-conscious to elbow my way in as if I belonged. So I sat by myself at a little table in a lonely corner and watched a polo game from Argentina on the telly.

Morton never had moments like that. He would have squeezed in at the bar, then expanded his chest and made sure everyone knew he was the very same H. V. Morton they'd been reading about in the papers and that he was writing a book that was going to make Ireland famous. His first night in this area he went to the races on the Curragh, where the Irish Derby is run every summer, and won a bundle. The next day he even did some riding in the morning air, which was, and we have to take his word for it, like "iced wine."

From my bedroom window on the second floor of Mrs. Ricketts' place I could look down and watch the Tinkers playing gin rummy on card tables in their little caravans. Also I could hear someone vomiting in the bedroom next to mine. I fell asleep and dreamt I was having trouble breathing, and had gone to the hospital for tests. The doctor, who looked like Lourdes Brasil, was very thorough, and when she had finished she asked me to come back the next day for more tests. But the doctor wasn't there when I showed up the next day. I sat at a typewriter and started to type out the story of my life. Several other doctors came in. They looked like Tinkers. They sat down at a large table and started playing gin rummy.

"No more conferences in Dubrovnik," one of them said. "Let's face it, it's not much longer we're going to be able to put up with greasy kippers and computers with right-hand drive."

They went on and on rather surrealistically, then looked at me and indicated that my typing was bothering them. They wanted to know what I was doing there. I told them I was waiting for my doctor.

"Didn't she see you yesterday? What makes you think she'd want to see you again today?"

In the morning I stumbled downstairs and into the front room. The table sparkled with silver and fine china. "Tea or coffee?" said Mrs. Ricketts, who appeared from nowhere, looking bright and fresh.

Mrs. Ricketts placed a large steaming stainless-steel pot of tea on the table. Then she brought in a plate of kippers and fresh sliced tomatoes. "I hope this is to your satisfaction," she said, with the cutest little smile I'd seen outside of Hamilton, Ontario.

"My goodness, Mrs. Ricketts. I certainly hope you didn't go to any trouble."

"Oh, it was a pleasure. I just sent down to the butcher's and green-grocer's they have down the street and they had them there in stock."

"Thank you so much. They look . . . scrumptious."

"Well I hope you enjoy them and that you slept well – and weren't bothered by any noise."

I wondered if by that she might have been alluding to the vomiting in the next room. Probably a drunken guest, or one who had been eating too many kippers, who had gone back to sleep and hadn't awakened yet – or perhaps he had been up for hours and had already left. I poured myself a cup of tea – loose, not bags – and dug into the kippers. They were a little greasier than I remembered them. Geez, I sure hope she doesn't read this.

Mrs. Ricketts had laid out a few papers for me. The big thing in Ireland was the World Cup. For the first time in history a team from the Republic was going to be in it, much to the dismay of some. An electronics store in Kildare had taken out a full-page ad in the local paper, stating that, if you were to buy from them a "Grundig TV, satellite television, or video," you would get all your money refunded when Ireland won the World Cup.

"A great sales promo and a great gamble," I said. "He could go broke."

But Mrs. Ricketts figured the Irish chances were pretty slim. "It's a miracle they got this far."

She began chatting about the recent death of an old man who had been in his time well-known in local spiritualist circles. On the day before the funeral, violent knocking was heard from within the coffin. The day after the funeral Mrs. Ricketts bumped into the daughter of the deceased man and they had a little chat. I think they bumped into each other in the butcher's and greengrocer's. Mrs. Ricketts asked her about the knocking. The story was all over town.

The daughter said the whole thing was obviously something to do with her father having been interested in spiritualism all his life. Mrs. Ricketts wanted to know if anyone had thought, given all the knocking and banging and scratching from within the coffin, to open it up and have a look inside.

"How could we have done that, now?" said the daughter. "The funeral was all arranged."

I gave Mrs. Ricketts a big smile and she smiled back.

"That wouldn't be a bit of a tall tale for trustful tourists by any chance now would it, Mrs. Ricketts?"

She had the cutest little look of wounded innocence.

"Every word is true, so help me."

The Tinkers had a good relationship with Mrs. Ricketts. They grew flowers in flats and gave them to her in exchange for being allowed to park their caravans and build their bunkies in her back yard. She subsequently sold the flowers to amateur gardeners in town.

With Mrs. Ricketts in the kitchen, I got up and strolled around the large living room, admiring the doodads, knickknacks, and whatnots here and there on little tables and mantels and windowsills.

There was a framed picture of Will Rogers on the wall.

There was a thermometer bracketed by two brass kangaroos.

There was a reproduction of "Irish Cottage" by André Zorbenis.

There were several framed black-and-white photos of a beautiful-but-unsmiling young woman in her twenties marrying some military officer in his fifties. This might have been Mrs. Ricketts in her youth.

There were several china teapots and some lovely sherry glasses.

There was a framed clipping from the 1965 *Sporting Calendar*, an article about a horse, owned by the Duchess of Westminster, winning a gold cup.

Sitting on a card table was an early version of a computerized type-writer – an IBM 6787.

"Gathering Towers" was the title of another André Zorbenis, showing a meditative woman at the side of a river full of swans.

There was a ceramic statue of a Roman chariot with two rearing horses on a dangerously narrow base.

There were scores of Japanese vases filled with tons of silk roses.

Mrs. Ricketts had told me the previous evening, just as I was going down to the pub, that the right arm of the nineteenth-century Irish boxing champion Dan Donnelly had been preserved and was on display at the Hideout.

"He had the longest arms of any man," she said.

This morning she wanted to know if I had seen it, and if so what I thought.

I had to tell her that the Hideout had been closed and I had to go to another pub. She was terribly disappointed to hear that, but she said if I wished I could see a giant statue of Donnelly. It was out on the road to Kildare, with both arms intact.

"It's just past where the ditches end," she said. "You can't miss it."

Mrs. Ricketts kindly cashed a traveller's cheque for me. I gave her fifty dollars Canadian and she gave me twenty-five pounds Irish. And then I gave her ten pounds for the bed-and-breakfast. And when I gave her an additional two for going to the trouble of getting the kippers, she seemed very pleased indeed. She was beautiful when she smiled, as most people are.

Back in Canada, to which I was eventually to return, I couldn't remember if the pub in question was the Hideout or the Hangout. It appeared both ways in my notes. So I dialled Irish directory assistance, rather than make a special trip back.

When the Irish operator said just a moment, and I thought he was temporarily disconnected, I said to the Canadian operator: "He's right now flipping through a huge book. They're a little backward over there and they're not computerized yet."

Well! I could have died! You guessed it, a few moments later the Irish operator came back on the line with the number, and he said, "According to our brand-new up-to-date state-of-the-art computer –"

"Oh, that was just a joke. I hope you didn't take me seriously."

He knew it was a joke, an affectionate one at that. The Irish are, as is well known, justifiably proud of their technological backwardness, relatively speaking, such as it is, even if it *is* only in the minds of distant admirers.

He told me it was the Hideout, not the Hangout, and when he hung up the Canadian operator came back on the line.

"You noticed I didn't say anything," she said.

"Oh, you knew he was still on the line, did you?"

"Oh sure. I deal with Irish Information all the time. The United Kingdom and Ireland. It's always such a pleasure to deal with them."

"Have you ever been over there?"

"No. But some day when I have a good long vacation. And Australia too. I want to go there. The operators there are just as nice to deal with, really."

Meanwhile, back in the Republic, the Hideout was still closed. I was neither destined to see this long-dead pugilist's massive and incredibly long arm, nor the statue, as it turned out. I walked across the bridge and looked down to the strawberry fields sweeping down to the Liffey – the Upper Liffey it would be called at this point. It was banked on both sides with a landscaped park, little pink strawberries in the grass, early spring flowers, a standing stone or two.

A couple of teenage Irish louts, in the style of Johnny Rotten and Sid Vicious, were leaning against the front door of the locked-up Hideout as I walked back to Mrs. Ricketts' place.

"Do you know what time it opens?" I said.

"Haven't got a clue," they said, loutishly.

"And that statue of the famous old boxer, where would that be?"

"Famous old boxer? Haven't got a clue on that either."

"You fellows are graduate students in Joycean studies at Trinity College, just home for the long weekend, am I right?"

They looked at each other. One made a circle around his ear with his finger.

And so I drove out the Kildare Road, looking for the statue of the Irish boxing champion Dan Donnelly. I found where the ditches ended all right, but that was about it. Mrs. Ricketts said that there were large concrete footsteps leading up to the statue, commemorating the time Donnelly walked away from a fight, even though he could certainly have decapitated the adversary with one lazy punch. And the adversary certainly deserved such a fate, for it was obviously a suicidal act picking a battle with the mighty Donnelly.

✦ ✦ ✦

Extensive research on this subject subsequently showed that the statue was not a statue but a standing stone, on which had been engraved the words: DAN DONNELLY BEAT COOPER ON THIS SPOT 13TH DEC. 1815.

Donnelly did not walk away from the fight. On the date in question twenty thousand gathered on this spot to watch Donnelly take on the Staffordshire bargeman George Cooper, the pride of England. In the eleventh round, after twenty-two minutes of furious fisticuffs, Donnelly connected with Cooper's jaw and broke it. The fight inspired a folk song, "The Ballad of Donnelly and Cooper."

Five years later Donnelly dropped dead in a Dublin pub after drinking, so it is said, several gallons of ice water.

His body was subsequently stolen by grave robbers, but it was recovered and re-interred – with the right arm missing.

A photo of the arm, as it appears today, can be found in the February 20, 1995 edition of *Sports Illustrated*, accompanying an excellent article by the well-known Toronto writer Allen Abel.

THE BROWNE'S
HILL DOLMEN

It was a wonderful day in Ireland, with blue sky and puffy swirly white clouds, with blossoming croci, clematis-covered condominia, tulips, daffodils, forsythia, magnolia, morning glory, hollyhocks, horse chestnuts, buttercups, snowdrops, and little pink flowering cherries or whatever, and flocks of warblers, wrens, bobolinks, sky-larks, the unique Irish bats that fly all day and sleep all night, and those beautiful vivid green Irish miniature flamingos (about the size of parakeets) all whistling, warbling, screeching, and cooing at the top of their lungs, and Irish thoroughbred stud farms reaching all the way to the petunia-covered hills on the horizon. And wherever you looked, whether you were driving through the country or the town, you saw doom-laden teenage girls pushing squealing vomit-stained babies in squeaky hand-me-down buggies.

The mood of the people didn't seem to reflect the rigidity of the laws governing reproduction. Sunday, for instance, was much more open and merry than in hard-core Protestant countries, particularly certain islands off the coast of Scotland, where a traveller literally has to give a secret password to get a cup of tea on that particular day of the week.

The sheep are keeping the grass nice and short for the golfers. If the greens fees are low it's because they don't have to pay greenskeepers.

"Do the sheep ever get bonked by balls?" I asked someone.

"Not as often as the golfers would like."

"Meaning?"

"Well, it's this way now, see? It's not widely known, and we don't want it to be, see? But if, say, in a foursome a golfer tees off and bonks or boings or bops a sheep on the noggin, causing said sheep to expire, the other three have the right to kick in a pound apiece. And all four get to take the sheep home and have enough meat for the table for a month of Sundays."

"Keeps things exciting, I suppose. Gives the player a little extra to play for."

"It does, that. And the one who does the actual bonking, why he doesn't have to kick in a pound, you see?"

The highest accident rate per capita among motorists in Ireland belongs to the Irish, who are by and large reckless bloody fools behind the wheel, if I might be allowed a vulgar generalization, backed up as I am not only by my keen observation but also by statistics duly published in the *Irish Times* and discussed on the air by none other than the insightful and incisive Gay Byrne. Among visitors, the British have just a slightly lower rate, followed by the Australians and the New Zealanders, who come over to search out their roots and only occasionally get killed in a flaming wreck.

North Americans and Europeans apparently seldom get in crashes while visiting Ireland, according to the stats, though presumably, because of the amusing novelty of driving on the left, they inadvertently and often even unknowingly cause a lot of pileups.

With great excitement, I stopped at Saint Brigid's Well, not realizing it was merely the first of thousands of Saint Brigid's wells around the country, each featuring a set of Christian images superimposed on an ancient holy pagan well. This one, however, was special, because it was just outside Kildare, and Brigid (also known as Brigit, Bridget, Brigida, and Bride) had been the abbess of Kildare, in the early decades of the sixth century, just a little before Saint Kevin. One of the four great pagan festivals of Ireland was Imbolc, February 1 – and it has now become known as Saint Brigid's Day. This particular well featured a plastic-and-cloth Brigid in a glass case. In one hand she was holding a crozier with the top missing, and in the other a beautifully carved miniature wooden church.

A stream flowed by, so narrow a dachshund with three broken legs could have hopped across without getting the tip of its tail wet. It descended from a hilltop spring, with a dam or two, a little waterfall, and a series of little sluices to give it depth, show off its clarity, and present a miniature Italianate touch – all to the glory of Saint Brigid. Along the little stream were the stations of the cross, represented by dabs of paint on little stones in a row. Unfortunately, the place was deserted. There were no amateur historians to fill me in on local legends and miracles.

For a while it was T-shirt weather, and then a big black cloud insisted sweaters be put back on. Off to one side fifteen swans floated in a larger river, which was slowly flowing between bare green hills studded with croci. The swans appeared to be hoping for a handout. Like all animals, they'd rather be fed than find their own food, but they were so lustrous one could only compare them to poets seeking a patron.

A car went by with a bumper sticker reading: "If this was a horse, I would shoot it." In Kildare I saw a panhandler, the first I'd seen in Ireland, and, I believe, the only one I was to see. He was sitting on the step of a shop that was closed for the day. I stopped and stared at him rather rudely for a moment, I'm afraid, because he was a dead ringer for the actor Jeremy Irons. He looked at me mildly and said, "What's the matter?"

"Nothing," I said. I gave him a pound, in atonement for my rudeness. He looked at me in disbelief, then broke into a huge smile.

There wasn't much traffic, but once every mile, it seemed, I was being forced into a ditch by an approaching speed maniac who refused to relinquish the centre of the road. The ditches were dirt shallow, yet each time an approaching vehicle appeared, I thought this could be it.

In Callan, with its lovely eighteenth-century bridge over a broad, swirling, surging section of the Munster River, I bought some supplies, including some matches that turned out to be in the family way. The box said: Impregnated Safety Matches – Criterion – Made in Estonia.

The old cemetery in Callan was filled with people who hadn't known they were about to die, at least a lot of them hadn't, and I wondered if I would get through the day, given my inexperience on Irish roads, without joining the majority, as the ancient Irish bard put it. It was my solemn responsibility to get used to the Irish style of driving before being joined by Lourdes Brasil.

An old man in a black suit and tweed cap was pushing an old bicycle across an empty field, and I became gripped with sudden envy and a feeling of regret that I hadn't been living in some remote corner of Ireland for ever. Even the dogs have a special Irish quality about them, with stray mongrels rolling over like two-bit floozies at the approach of a stranger and wiggling their legs in the air. I stepped into a pet shop in Carlow to ask for change for a fiver and ended up complaining to the sales clerk about the obnoxious overfondness of Irish mutts.

"Well, that just shows the special Irish affection for domestic animals," she said, then laughed as she could see me trying to figure out what she meant.

Carlow Castle is an awful mess. A local physician, somewhat eccentric by nature, possibly a shell-shocked veteran of the Battle of
Waterloo, bought the thirteenth-century castle in 1814 and decided
to convert it into a lunatic asylum. He was undoubtedly certain he
was doing the right thing. Apparently the town was badly in need of
such an institution, and if there weren't enough lunatics in town to fill
it up, they could intensify their search throughout the entire county,
though it must be admitted County Carlow was then, as now, the
smallest in Ireland.

At any rate the doctor, Middleton by name, figured the walls were
too thick, and so he sought to make them thinner by the liberal use of
explosives. But in determining the dosage, he erred on the heavy side,
in spite of, or maybe because of, his extensive war experience.

The ruins are just as they were left after the huge explosion that
rocked three counties.

No lunatic was ever given asylum in that pile of rubble.

Dr. Middleton lived in shame for the rest of his life, for what had
been one of the most glorious and well-preserved Norman castles in
that part of Ireland, one that had survived Henry VIII and Cromwell,
one that had soared three storeys high with stout round towers in each
of the corners, was now unrecognizable.

You can imagine how badly the poor doctor must have felt.

Ireland loves its lunatics, and there is a wealth of similar stories,
many of them involving the English. There was the castle intended
for construction on the northwestern frontier in India that by a
strange set of circumstances – involving, one suspects, incest and
opium – managed to get itself erroneously erected in the lovely town
of Cahirciveen, County Kerry.

And during the Easter Rising in 1916, the rebels were scheduled to
meet a German ship in Tralee Bay. The Germans were running
twenty thousand rifles, ten million rounds of ammunition, and ten
machine guns past the British blockade. But there was a mixup in the
date, the rebels failed to show, a Royal Navy gunboat showed up
instead, and the German captain had to scuttle his ship.

A couple of decades later, a General Eoin O'Duffy gained immortality when he raised a regiment for the Spanish Civil War. There was a ship waiting for them at Limerick in the west, but O'Duffy, a tad confused, took his men to Cork in the south. When this honest mistake became apparent, the regiment voted unanimously to go home. If it hadn't been for that little error, who knows? The Spanish Civil War might have gone the other way, and in the former case the Easter Rising might have succeeded.

In downtown Carlow, while trying to make my way out to the Browne's Hill Dolmen, I became trapped behind the local Saint Patrick's Day parade. It was a bit like a play by Jean-Paul Sartre.

It wasn't a very colourful parade. It was downright solemn actually, with men, women, and children walking slowly, heads bent, along the middle of the road, in an atmosphere of great sorrow. No bands. No flags. No colours. No hooting. No hollering. No exit. Everyone was dressed in shades of black. Cars were doing their best to make quiet, unobtrusive U-turns and slip away down side streets.

I pulled into a gas station.

"Could you please tell me where the R276 would be?"

"Which is to where?" said the thin man pumping gas into his car.

"To the giant dolmen."

He was obviously a rock-fancier. In fact he had, attached to his car, a flatbed trailer full of fresh-dug rocks. I wanted to ask him if he had dug them all up himself and what he was planning to do with them, but I felt shy. He probably would have told me a good story, too. Or he was maybe just trying to mend a wall ten centuries old.

"You go down here, then just turn left and go out one and a half miles and it's on the right." The Irish take such pride in giving excellent directions to tourists.

The Browne's Hill Dolmen is thought to be the largest known dolmen in Europe. Certainly the largest known tomb of its type. I passed a little subdivision called Dolmen Heights. And then there was a Dolmen House.

I walked along a footpath, across the long edge of a large green polygonal field. The dolmen was visible way off in the distance. I was the only human being around. Remembering Morton's comment about "historical perspective," I told myself that, although the dolmen was more ancient than the pyramids of Egypt – in fact older than human history – it wasn't as old as the surrounding hills. Nor was it as old as the water lying around in little puddles.

The dolmen was composed of an immense whale-backed capstone, said to weigh a hundred tons, that had been somehow lifted up and laid to rest on the heads of eight broad and stout upright stones, two parallel rows of four each. But over the millennia one of the rows had collapsed, and the huge capstone had perforce collapsed with it, no doubt at exactly the same moment, although it was still supported fully by three of the four stones in the other row. One end of the great capstone hovered above one of the end stones of the good row owing to its downward tilt on the other side.

This particular upright end stone had over the centuries exercised its newfound freedom by gradually assuming a tilt of forty-five degrees toward the low hills to the east, which were the same height as Browne's Hill. In fact the only uprights to remain upright were the three that were bearing the great burden of the capstone. Nothing like a little pressure to keep you straight. These stones seemed alive.

The dolmen resembled a massive stone tent collapsed on one side. The capstone was humped in such a way that it appeared to be heavier on the side that had collapsed, and this circumstance probably contributed to the collapse. The capstone was smooth and of tremendous beauty, like a seashore pebble enlarged several hundred times and heavily veined. It enthralled the eye. There was a curious V shape to one side of the stone, the humped side that had collapsed, and I wasn't sure if this V was natural or not. It looked as if it might have been cut to accommodate the support of the standing stones, and the aeons –

maybe ten thousand winters – had worn the cut so smooth it looked natural. The V took away the otherwise perfect symmetry of the capstone and gave it a wonderful Picassoesque resonance.

Would it be possible to determine when the collapse had taken place? It might have collapsed at the death of the Great God Pan, or at the moment of Christ's death. It might have collapsed on the day Saint Patrick arrived in Ireland. One day people around here might have heard a tremendous crash and come running to see that the capstone had suffered a great fall. Maybe it had collapsed at other times in the past, and had previously always been repositioned.

A large black bull was staring at me as I stared at the capstone, the collapse of which had tilted it so that, for the moment, it looked like a stubby rocket about to take off. The rocks didn't mean much to that bull. And yet he and the other members of his herd were huddled right next to the dolmen, even though they could have been anywhere in a rich pasture of at least fifteen acres. But there they were huddled against the stones. It made one think of the ancient legend that said that if you let a cow wander freely, where it lies down, that's the place to build a church – that is if you want to build a church.

The bull's eye stared at me, in focus for a while, then slowly, without expression, the eye turned away, like a cat's, but with less depth. Not a real look, a vacant surface stare with a touch of meanness. Not like the warmth and sad dignity of a caged elephant's look, the eager anticipation of, say, a possum, or the quick devilish glance of the snail.

This had to be the burial place of a once-renowned and highly feared king, or a line of great kings. Who knows who is buried here? It would have been a greater honour for a poet to be buried here than at Westminster Abbey, for dead certain.

Whether the visitor invests the dolmen with a magical aura or the dolmen possesses one of its own, it's hard to say. But somehow the latter explanation is preferable. Maybe the space on which the dolmen was erected had that aura before the dolmen was dreamt of. Maybe it has something to do with underground streams crossing. Maybe the mysterious ancient folk who built this dolmen, some time in the third millennium before Christ, at least a thousand years before the arrival of the Celts, did so to consecrate a sacred spot that had had a perceptible aura of its own since the glaciers retreated. Ley-lines, acupuncture points on the soul of the world – these stones certainly retained the power to stir the imaginations of a lot of people, many of them considered madcaps and zanies, sometimes because of their habit of solemnly gathering at the stones, at the full moon, dressed in hooded white robes. Locals would often spy on them with telescopes to make sure they weren't engaging in anything taboo.

From the stones you could see to the horizon in all directions. It seemed a likely place for a church, but the powerful aura of the dolmen had probably scared the church-builders away. The unwritten rules forbidding tampering with these stones have been respected more fully in Ireland than elsewhere. As with the sites of other megalithic monuments all over the world, this site would have made an excellent place for determining the exact time of the rising and setting of the heavenly bodies. The sky was a perfect bowl.

There was nothing frivolous about this dolmen, or any true dolmen for that matter. This one certainly was not put up on a whim. It's a magnificent work of art that speaks of an immeasurable solemnity and deep purpose. There may have been tremendous astrological significance, but these stones have been sitting here like this for so long that they must have meant a lot of different things to a lot of different people at various points along the rim of the great wheel of time.

Even from the car the dolmen had looked immense and seemed to radiate a great sadness into the atmosphere. The cattle, still huddled against the stones, looked like aphids. The devout wouldn't be visiting these heathen stones today, it being Saint Patrick's Day, and there was a blessed scarcity of tourists so early in the year.

Next to the dolmen was a post bearing the standard plaque stating that injury to this National Monument was punishable by law. But there was no historical plaque identifying the site. This is normal in Ireland, where there has never been any money to spend on history. Though it appears in all the guidebooks, this site is not all that well known. It's as if its power should only be for the few. The feeling that the stones themselves had drawn me to this spot was one that was to recur often at different places in Ireland and with ever-increasing intensity.

I jotted in my notebook that the Callanish standing stones seemed older than the Browne's Hill Dolmen. But I don't trust that feeling now. It's just that those strangely whorled blade-like stones at Callanish, on the Isle of Harris in the Outer Hebrides, seem much more ancient because of their strangeness. The Browne's Hill stones have a more familiar shape, somehow, aesthetically. A less severe, more comforting shape. Not all these places are alike by any means. There's nothing anywhere that resembles Callanish for instance, with its two avenues of thin broad stones, each seeming to have been chosen for the grotesqueness of its shape and texture. There, the avenues, both with a double row of stones fifteen to twenty feet high, intersect at right angles in the form of a perfect Christian cross, though the setup predates Christ by three thousand years. Strange stories are still being invented about it, including my favourite: it points directly at the position of Polaris five thousand years ago.

Morton never mentions this sort of thing. He was more interested in the future than the past, in goodwill than in mystery. He was blind to these stones; he felt interest in the past was not all that conducive to the sort of peace and goodwill he was single-handedly trying to establish between Ireland and England. It would be easy to mock his feelings in that regard, but in a time when inter-racial understanding was practically non-existent, Morton was a good guy, a moderate. Maybe he changed later on, I really don't know anything about him other than what is revealed in his book on Ireland. *In Search of Ireland* was written before Hitler's rise to power. Yet it was a time when anti-Semitism was decidedly fashionable everywhere, like a cloud of gas waiting for a spark. And then there were all the other forms of racial prejudice. Morton didn't pretend to be in the league of Yeats and Eliot and Pound and all those inspired cads. He was just a normal hack writer with a popular touch, and he knew it. Those were difficult times, but he had a certain spirit. He was of the age, an Englishman, but he had a bit of a humane vision about him. He's never unpleasant, and that's something.

DUNBRODY ABBEY

During a day visit to Ireland a few years back I was dozing on a train and opened my eyes to catch a vision of a ruined abbey in a beautiful valley veined with a broad tidal river. The view haunted me, and I later spent hours trying to identify it. From the location, it must have been Dunbrody Abbey, but the pictures of Dunbrody weren't a very good match for the vision I had at this juncture between waking and sleeping.

I probably wouldn't have been so ready to return to Ireland if I hadn't awakened in the train at that precise moment. In fact, if I hadn't taken the wrong train, I wouldn't have seen the abbey. On a bitterly cold morning I'd hopped on a Waterford train full of uni-formed schoolkids instead of the commuter train to Dublin. In the Waterford station, while I was waiting to connect with the later Dublin train, a young man engaged me in conversation. He kept say-ing there were an awful lot of popes in Ireland.

Finally I broke down and protested, saying that surely there was only one pope and he was in Rome.

"Not popes," said the young man. "*Popes.* I'm saying *popes.* Do you hear me?"

Turned out he was saying pubs.

So I was back on the scene, after a twenty-five-mile detour from Morton's route brought me to what *Baedeker's* calls the "imposing remains" of Dunbrody Abbey, a twelfth-century Cistercian house. It had been sitting gracefully among tall trees in a broad flat valley on a tidal river just east of Waterford Harbour since the days of Strongbow.

I circumambulated the ruins several times, climbed up ancient staircases, peered into empty rooms, and fantasized about having a wall collapse on me. I climbed up to the nearby railway and walked along the tracks, checking the various angles of vision, trying to determine the exact spot where I opened my slumbering eyes to this scene of sublime beauty. But the angles didn't match exactly and I began to think again that I had the wrong place.

"We've never been to Tintern Abbey, but maybe that's the one you're looking for. Just take the Fethard Road down this way. There's another place called Fethard in County Tipperary, that's why this place is called Fethard on Sea."

The speaker was a short man from New Ross, a few miles north. He was with his tall wife and even-taller son.

"There's another Tintern Abbey too," I offered.

"Is there now? And where might that be?"

"It's in the Wye Valley on the border between England and Wales. Wordsworth wrote a poem about it."

"Well, I should know that. Did you know that, dear?"

"Oh, don't ask me. I'm just an ignorant housewife."

The family name was Kinsella, pronounced with the accent on the first syllable. I mentioned the Canadian writer W. P. Kinsella and how he put the accent on the second syllable.

"Oh," said Mrs. Kinsella, who was one sharp-witted lady, full of dark irony. "They do that in England too. As soon as they get out of the country they change the pronunciation of their name to make them sound classier."

Turned out the Kinsellas ran a little company together, manufacturing cotton tracksuits for all the schools in New Ross and the surrounding counties of Waterford, Wexford, Carlow, and Kilkenny. They did the different school colours and logos, everything to order.

The son was silently beaming down at me. He was about twelve, but very tall, about seven-one, and with bright red hair.

"Our children are just coming of an age when they'll be interested in antiquities," said the father. "Before that, they were not, not at all."

The beaming young giant broke his silence. "I went to Cahir Castle," he enthused.

"Now Waterford is a very interesting city," said the father, still smarting a bit because of the Tintern Abbey thing, "because it's an old Norman settlement – originally Viking but essentially Norman – and there's a very good well-preserved Norman tower on the quays. A good example of Norman —"

"And you'll have to see the glass factory," interrupted Mrs. Kinsella, much to her husband's almost imperceptible annoyance.

"But they're on strike, dear."

"Ach, I forgot."

I told them I was going to seek out Tintern Abbey while it was still light and to take advantage of the good weather, but they didn't want to let me go just yet.

Mr. Kinsella started complaining about modern architecture.

"Some modernistic, gauche structure that takes away from the historical impact —"

"Couldn't he still get in, dear?" interrupted Mrs. Kinsella again. "It's just the workers on strike after all."

Mr. Kinsella, who didn't even try to pretend he found this interruption amusing, was silent for several seconds, while I tried to resist a smile. Before I could decide whether I should ask Mr. Kinsella to continue, he started insisting I check out Holy Cross Abbey, between Thurles and Cahir on the River Suir. It was a Cistercian abbey, like Dunbrody, but had been all fixed up in recent years.

"It's just an ass's roar from the Rock of Cashel."

"Ass's roar? I have never heard that one before."

"You probably don't have too many asses in Canada."

"There's one less for the next little while at least."

"Hah, hah, hah. That's funny, that is."

The only thing worse than looking for your glasses when you're wearing them is trying to put your seat belt on when it's already on. I took off for Tintern, noting that I'd gone 206 miles since picking up the car, though it seemed more like a thousand miles in Canadian terms.

"The west of Ireland, of course, is more interesting in every respect," Mr. Kinsella had said.

He didn't seem impressed that I was looking forward to visiting Newgrange, or that I'd been to the Browne's Hill Dolmen. In fact he looked as blank as when I told him there was a Tintern Abbey in Wales.

The Irish Tintern Abbey had been named after the Welsh one, and a group of Cistercian monks from that one had come to this one shortly after it was built in 1200 by the devout imperialist William Earl Marshall, the Earl of Pembroke.

Pembroke had been caught in a storm in Bannow Bay and made a deal with his gods that, if he survived, he would build an abbey at the point where he came ashore. The little story is a snapshot of the English psychology of the time. The colonization of Ireland was an idea that had arrived. There was no questioning it. God wanted the English to colonize Ireland. It was in the books. Otherwise Pembroke wouldn't have made such a deal. He would have said something like: "God, if you spare my life in this horrible storm, I promise to go home and never return to bother the bloody Irish ever again."

So Tintern was the result of a storm at sea. A modest little structure, it lacked the grand sweep of its namesake on the River Wye.
Directly in front of the abbey was a rare old crenellated stone bridge
over a tidal inlet, ideal for defending against attacks coming upstream
on the tide from Saltmills on Bannow Bay. The bridge was more interesting than the abbey, but this Tintern Abbey was in a far better state
of repair than Wordsworth's.

In 1566 the young Queen Elizabeth granted the abbey to William
Colclough, whose tomb was in the chapel to the southeast of the main
building, and whose family, still with the name Colclough, resided
here until the 1960s, having survived a siege by the Irish in 1641.

Tintern wasn't what I had seen from the train. What I'd seen was
Dunbrody all right, but a Dunbrody transformed in a moment of
enchantment when I was weary from travel and lack of sleep.

The drive around the Ring of Hook presented many views of the sea
during a brilliant sunset. The English in the early years used to sail up
Tramore Bay, with its Hook Head, instead of Waterford Harbour, with
its Crook Head, and this is where the term By Hook or by Crook came
from. So many people told me that story, it must be important.

Churchtown was wrapped in a sunset mist of rose and purple, with
rose and purple waves crashing on the black rocks and sending up
sprays of silver foam, and with a blinking lighthouse, said to be the
oldest in Europe, standing there a quarter of a mile to the south in the
slanting rays of the setting sun.

Nights are dark in rural Ireland in the (late) winter, and after stopping at pubs in Duncannon, Ramsgrange, and Arthurstown in an
attempt to locate a place for the night, I took the Ballyhack Ferry
across Waterford Harbour. Cissy O'Quinn's place on the Waterford
Road was lit up on the inside, but the night was so dark it was hard to
find the door.

The family was watching television, and they couldn't hear me knocking at the window. I went all around the house, knocking on windows, knocking on doors that had signs on them saying Please Use Other Door, pressing doorbells that didn't work. Mrs. O'Quinn finally noticed me and let me in.

She stood in the living room with my coat over her arm and tapped on the window.

"Double pane," she said. "That's why we couldn't hear you." She looked around. "My husband now, he says it would be double *pain* if you accidentally tripped and fell against the window."

"Hah, hah, hah. That's funny, that is."

"My husband, he's a real comic, he is. Any chance for a little joke."

Double-pane windows weren't the only thing up to date about the house. Mrs. O'Quinn waltzed me through every room, pointing out all the items of up-to-date interest. I finally broke down and told her I needed to wind down from the road, and a drink would be nice. She offered me her torch and told me there was a pub about a ten-minute walk down the intensely dark lane.

It was a crowded pub. There was a lone accordionist upstairs, but the staircase was so jammed with drinkers it was impossible to get up to see him. The bartender was an ancient mariner; he looked as if he should have died thirty years ago, with big heavy eyelids and sagging lips and liver spots and the look of a man who had been drinking heavily since early adolescence. But he wasn't saying anything, and after my pint I squeezed my way back out into the darkness. I'd forgotten darkness. It was comforting; it reminded me of childhood.

In the morning I woke up to Mrs. O'Quinn pounding on my door. She wanted to come in to strip the bed. This probably meant they were anxious to get breakfast over with and me out of the way.

But no, for breakfast was a leisurely affair. Cornflakes and cream. A single egg nicely fried sunny-side up. Two strips of sweet Irish bacon and two of those little sausages that always taste like sawdust and old engine oil.

After my little display of appreciation, I asked if she might have anything besides cornflakes. She said she had this cereal she didn't know the name of but she doubted that I'd like it.

"It's full of chopped-up almonds, and oats, and —"

"Granola!"

Mrs. O'Quinn, after patiently listening to my extensive lecture on the semiotics of Crunchy Granola, expressed surprise to be hosting a single man.

"You are not just now travelling all around Ireland on your own, like, are you?"

"Yes, I am. Is that all that strange?"

"That's very unusual indeed," she said in an admiring tone.

I told her I was too pigheaded and selfish to travel with anyone.

"Isn't it the truth," she said. "It can take a lot out of you."

When she found out I was Canadian, it seemed to explain my disposition towards quietness, politeness, respect, and it inspired her to let out a harmless little complaint about Yankee tourists.

"A lot of the tourists from the States seem to be disappointed that we don't have pigs rooting around in the living room."

"And if you did have, they'd be scandalized, right?"

"The tourists or the pigs?"

She couldn't resist confessing she hated it when the tourists made fun of her small tomatoes at breakfast time and told her they grow them ten times that size in Texas or wherever. I told her I'd once overheard a tourist from Texas telling a Welsh farmer he shouldn't under any circumstances accept subsidies from the government.

Cissy O'Quinn wanted to know where I was planning to go today, what I was going to do, and what my "speciality" was. She told me all about what her husband did for a living and what time he would be home that night. He apparently worked twelve-hour days in distant Waterford and was a bit of a bore to boot. Her kids had been fighting, and she wanted to know if I did that when I was a kid.

"Yes, we fought."

"Sex goes out the window when you have kids," she said.

The place was immaculate. It might have been a Victorian farmhouse restored to perfection and then some. Everything was beautiful. The wine racks displayed all the best vintages. There were expensive antique-furniture replicas and all the best appliances available in the most expensive models. The place was scrupulously clean and neat, as if waiting for the photographer from *Waterford Life*.

There were two bathrooms, one with blue toilet paper and the other with pink. One featured a top-of-the-line computerized shower. All of Western Europe was awash in a sea of computerized showers, and they were always malfunctioning. I'd never seen one in North America. At their best there were two temperatures: too hot and too cold. A lot like life.

Some things should not be computerized. You heard it here first.

STAINED GLASS, SWANS, AND GREYHOUNDS

Tchaikovsky's Fifth Symphony was perfect for the late Sunday-morning mood on the slow drive along the Ardhean Road towards Waterford. People walked along the road in their Sunday best, little groups chatting, older men in grey suits, dark brown fedoras, and gleaming black shoes, young men on pushbikes, slow-pedalling next to romantic-looking young women on foot, people inside their homes drinking mugs of tea and listening to Tchaikovsky on the radio.

Nine miles south of Kilkenny, in green rolling countryside, Kells Priory sat, as it had since its founding in 1193, on the right bank of the beautiful Munster River, just as it straightened out before flowing into the River Nore. Once an important religious, military, and commercial centre, it was now in ruins, and surrounded by grazing sheep.

"How was the fishing?" I said to a boy and his mother who were carrying their rods up the hill and back to the car.

"All right," said the boy. The mother smiled.

"Catch anything?"

"Nothing to speak of."

The father jumped out of the car and began speaking earnestly to the son. He was telling him it was the Irish who built Kells.

I walked along the north wall of the priory, on the narrow grassy bank of the river along which flat-bottomed barges for centuries brought building blocks down from the hills, and lumber, and supplies, and visitors. Tiny clumps of fresh violets were growing in the chinks of the wall and swans were sailing on the river. And along came three greyhounds on a leash, being held by a man who introduced himself as Michael Molloy. He was in his early thirties, medium height, glasses, handsome, studious-looking, with a long slender nose, slightly hooked. He was dressed in rubber boots and a greasy brown jacket all torn to shreds. He was eager to stop and talk.

"Do you think the river would have been broader in those days?"

"I don't imagine so, I don't," he said. "You see here, the banks are not high, but they have an air of permanence."

The dogs were standing there patiently. The silence of the place was so profound it was as if there had never been anything other than such peacefulness anywhere on earth.

"Do you have any more dogs at home?"

"Ach, we have about forty."

"It's a business then, is it?"

"Ach, more or less. I race them, you know."

"I think they wish they were racing right now. They're the fastest dog, greyhounds, right?"

"Ach, they are for dead certain."

"They certainly look it. I bet they're as fast as a good racehorse."

"Ach, Jesus. They're terribly fast, no horse in the world can touch them. Mind you now, there are a lot of terribly slow ones, too. More slow ones than fast ones, to be truthful wit' ye."

Thousands of birds were chirping away in the great oaks and bright willows overhanging the stream.

"Any big meets coming up?"

"I race them Wednesdays and Fridays in Kilkenny and Tuesdays

and Saturdays in Waterford. It's a big business; lots of money
involved."

"How good are these fellows?" All three were sniffing the open
palm of my hand.

"Ach, I don't think these three are much good."

"Not of championship calibre?"

"Not at all."

"They look all right to me, but what do I know? Are the females
faster than the males?"

"Not necessarily. When they come in season you have to leave
them off for three months, like. You know, till they come back. A lot
of people put their bitches on hormones to stop them. They won't
ever come in season then. They inject them. Anabolic steroids."

"You breed them yourself, right?"

"That I do. But I don't make me living out of me dogs primarily. I'm
into glass."

"Glass."

"Stained glass, it is. All leaded glass. Church windows."

"Original designs?"

"It would be. These church windows now, they're all after buckling
and that – ach, and they're in bad shape."

"Be wonderful if we could see the windows from old places like this.
I guess there are records though, if you were into doing research."

"Well, it's a terrible life, because over the years all these churches,
they were knocked down. Beautiful windows, they were just thrown
away. There's some dreadful-looking churches around the country.
There's one just up here in Dunnamaggan and, oh my God, it's a
terrible-looking thing. And the older one, they knocked down. And
there were beautiful windows in it, and they were just abandoning
them and letting them break, you know. Ach, different people."

"Disgraceful it is."

"I have different ideas, myself. They're going back now to the old
way again. Kilkenny now, it's supposed to be one of the nicest cities in
Ireland for shop fronts and that type of thing."

"You're into two very traditional things. Greyhound racing must be as old as stained glass."

"It would be, sure. Going a long time in the country, that."

"It probably predates horse racing."

"I don't know how long it goes back, to be honest wit' ye. It's something I didn't ever study. I read about it, but I can't remember."

"Is it something that runs in the family? Your father did it?"

"Oh he did, they all did. The relations bred some of the best lines in the business, even down to today, you know. My first cousin, he bred a dog called Black Spring – ach, there must be ten top dogs in Ireland now that all go back to him. This other cousin of mine, he had a good pedigree and it continued on down the lines."

"Hmm."

"Problem you get in Ireland, you get to the stage where they're too closely bred. Like I had a bitch and could not find a suitable dog for her, ended up having to go through a dog brought home from Australia. He was a total outcross article. He wouldn't have any bloodline connection at all in Ireland. Didn't get any pups though."

"What a shame."

"I've been to him twice now. I brought another bitch to him then, and she had only one litter of pups and she had her first runner last Friday night week and he won and made eight thousand pounds."

"Congratulations!"

"Thank you. There's big money for dogs that are good. A dog can sell for twenty-five thousand pounds. Lots of people in England has plenty of money for this game right here. They'd like to have the Derby winner, so they don't mind spending some money on it. They obviously have it to spend though, you know."

Morton doesn't have much to say about racing dogs. But he might have been thinking of someone like Michael Molloy when he stated, with a touch of unintentional unfairness:

An Irish farmer will starve himself and his family to mate an indifferent mare with a famous sire. . . . Who knows? The colt may develop into a famous horse. This is the greatest gamble in the life of the Irish countryman.

One dog had a dark brown circle on its left rump and a pointed curve of dark brown running from it down the tail, so the patch looked exactly like a comma. I commented on it.

"Oh geez, ye see some peculiar ones. We had a pup born and it was pure white, with a round black figure 8 on its side. The 8 was on its side as well. The pup though, she died on me. And snow white —"

A fish jumped. The dogs twitched. I looked at Michael.

"Any little noise at all," he said.

"Finely tuned."

"They have great sensitive hearing."

I stepped back to get a good shot of the man and his dogs, with the swans in the background, and a corner of the ancient stone wall, and the weeping willows mirrored in the surface of the river.

"Come around, boys," he said. "You're going to get your photos taken."

Michael Molloy wanted to know what I was doing in Ireland. I didn't seem to be a typical tourist, because I was taking the time to chat with people and I didn't seem in a hurry to get to the next place. He wanted to know where I'd been, where I was going, what sort of places I was staying at, what sort of people I'd been meeting. He'd never heard of Morton. I told him I was interested in viewing ruins such as the one where we were standing, Kells – just for the poetry of it, the sadness, the beauty. I had no problem talking like that to him, or to anyone in Ireland actually. He understood; they all did.

He criticized the Irish government for not giving higher priority to restoration and excavation. Some excavation was going on at Kells Priory, for instance, "but it's as slow as a funeral. They're digging with little spoons, sifting stuff out, you know."

Michael's greyhounds had been so well-behaved throughout our chat, silent and still as the ancient landscape, making the occasional gentle tug on the leash whenever a swan sailed a little too close.

"They're so amazingly patient!"

"Ach, they're amazingly good."

"If you have an extra one, I'll take him home with me."

"I'm a little low on them at home right now."

He started talking about a gadget he'd made, rather ingenious. He'd been trying to develop it for commercial sale. He claimed he'd made it from the starter motor of a motorcar and put six hundred yards of cable on it.

"Just tie a bit of foam or anything that's colourful on the end of it, you know. And you have a battery to power it, and it's all operational on a switch."

"Something for the dogs to chase during training sessions, is it?"

"They chase anything that moves. That's the big problem with them. There's not much moving around here. Oh, but if they saw something. . . . That's why they were watching the swans just now. Oh, anything at all now – they'll fly after it."

When Michael spoke to the dogs he spoke in an English so heavily accented it might as well have been Irish. It seemed to be the kind of native English not used when you talk to tourists from other countries. Right now he was kneeling down, talking to them and giving them a little massage.

"You're always rubbing up their muscles." He stood up. "The thing about it is, if they're good they're good, and you can get them to be competitive. But if they just don't have it, there's nothing you can do. You can be rubbing them up all day and giving all sorts of vitamins to them and you can give all day to them. But you can't put the speed into them. You have to do a lot of smart breeding, that's the most important thing."

One of the dogs turned in a flash and gave a tug on the leash.

"What do you see, Lady?"

THE VERGER OF
SAINT CANICE

Just out of Kells a cruiser with flashing lights sat parked at the side of the road and a terse Garda officer flagged me down. "Hello. There's a cycle race just up there. Youngsters on pushbikes. So just be careful." A mile later, there were the cyclists. Another mile and automobile traffic began to thicken on the approach to Kilkenny. It seemed strange that about 95 per cent of Irish automobiles were Japanese, but there were no sushi bars in Ireland yet.

Three boys were sitting on a bench in the grounds of Kilkenny Castle, on the site of which Strongbow had built a fort high over the broad, black River Nore when he first came to Ireland in 1169. Coincidentally, three girls were going by with a dog on a leash, one of those high-priced Chinese mutts you see paintings of, usually on black velvet, at yard sales off Church Street in Toronto.

"Hey, no dogs on the grass," said one of the boys.

"Sez who?" said the girls.

Morton writes about the great packs of dogs wandering the streets of Kilkenny, but this particular dog was the only one I saw all the time I was there. Maybe the townspeople were so stung by Morton's book they got rid of all the dogs.

Strongbow's real name was Richard fitz Gilbert de Clare. He was the first of the Anglo-Normans to attempt to conquer Ireland. He came armed with the authority of the only English pope in history, Adrian IV. As Cortes was to Mexico, so Strongbow was to Ireland. His stone effigy can be seen – Morton saw it, I saw it – in the nave of Christ Church Cathedral in Dublin. Legend has it that he was so cruel that, when his son showed cowardice in battle, Strongbow took a swipe at him with his sword and cut him in two, as a warning to all cowards. "With him," says Morton, "Ireland's troubles began. He held Dublin for Henry II, and founded the Irish problem."

Sunday afternoon in Kilkenny is impregnated with the kind of atmosphere one remembers from childhood. Everything is slowed down, there's no rush, nothing will ever change. All the fights have been fought and forgotten. I felt like heading over to Grandma's place for Sunday dinner. All my uncles and aunts and cousins would be there.

Regarding the group tour of the wonderfully maintained Kilkenny Castle, along with about fifty Irish tourists, I'll just mention the spectacular neo-Celtic wood-carved ceilings, designed and installed by John Hungerford Pollen in the days of William Morris, and an extraordinary marble twin-hearth fireplace designed by the same man.

After a long treatise against snorers, Morton states, "Kilkenny Castle is as feudal as any castle I know and contains many fine pictures and the signature of every English king since Henry II."

It was considered bad luck to touch a certain large marble table, because for centuries it had been used to lay out the dead. I touched it, and suddenly felt doomed. The only cure was to caress thrice the cheek of a nearby marble bust of a certain lady, probably one who had died and been laid out on the same table. I did so and felt better.

Kilkenny is an anglicization of *Cill Chainnigh* (Canice's Church), and the town takes its name from the massive Saint Canice's Cathedral, built in the thirteenth century. It was a mile or so to the west of the castle, on the other side of town, looming above the River Nore. The verger was a friendly man who spoke sadly about the day in 1650 when Oliver Cromwell brought his horses into the cathedral and up to the baptismal font to water them. Then he had the font unceremoniously removed and dumped in the grounds outside.

"A new base is on it. They couldn't find the original base after Cromwell had cleared out. But only about ninety years ago we found the base and it's over there against the wall as a memento to his . . ."

His voice faded.

I asked him about an ancient bishop's chair to the left of the chancel at the entrance to the vestry. It looked as if it had already been a hoary old relic at the time of the building, in the sixth century, of the original monastic settlement, of which only the hundred-foot round tower by the south transept remained.

The smooth marble chair looked more like a stool of repentance, but it shone with ancient mysteries. What great king – probably long forgotten – had it been built for? What miraculous stories had been told about it?

"There is a story that that is a wishing chair – but only for the ladies. Not for the men. Only for the ladies. At least that's the way I've been told."

"They didn't tell Morton that."

I showed him the passage: "There is an ancient stone seat in which the verger persuades you to sit and wish. Ireland seems more full of wishing-stones and wells than any other part of the earth."

"They mustn't have," said the verger. The current verger, that is. He smiled at a thought. He was a short, chubby, likable fellow in his early fifties. He didn't look like a big drinker but rather like one who could occasionally get carried away, and have to be carried away.

He said someone had shown him the Morton book years ago, and he wrote down the title, but he hadn't gotten around to getting a copy. I told him I would have given him mine, but it was still in use.

He said one of his jobs was to cut the grass around the cathedral. As he cut he would read the headstones and try to memorize them.

"I'm researching the Butler family of Kilkenny. They were an awful family for . . . They were a great family to read about, but . . ."

He sneaked a glance at his watch.

"I could cut the whole grass in one day if I didn't get any interruptions. But there are always interruptions. Particularly in the tourist season. I'm never done learning. Someone asks you something and very often I don't know the answer, and that night I'll go to the books and look it up so that I'll have it the next time someone asks."

He said he could never get done what he had planned.

"It never works out. If you plan today what you're going to do tomorrow, no way will that work out right for you at all."

"The fairy curse."

"Funny you should say that. I've often thought that myself. They read your mind and make sure your plans come to naught."

He said there was a clergyman who used to come in for prayer at eight every morning, and perhaps, he thought, to spy on him a little.

One day the verger had done too much celebrating at a reception the night before. When he finally staggered in, the early-bird priest asked him what he had planned for the day.

"Bugger off!" said the verger.

The priest, now long gone, never bothered him after that.

I sat in the bishop's chair, fantasized that I was a woman, and made a wish – for global peace, perhaps, or at least peace in Ireland.

Smoke started rising from the floor. I got down on my hands and knees and tried to figure out where it was coming from. The verger ambled over. A slow-moving man, he got down on his hands and knees too, but he couldn't see the smoke, even though I was pointing right at it. He tactfully suggested it was some illusion caused by light and shadows.

The verger said the current floor was new, having been laid in 1897, and it was difficult to keep clean, particularly on a wet day – as most days are in Ireland – or after a heavy day of tours. He seemed to want me to feel sorry for him.

"I'm the verger, but I'm known as the sexton. For some reason there was no house built for the verger, so when I came here they gave me the sexton's house. There's a notice over there on the notice board saying that the verger is available for guided tours. So I wear this badge – I don't have it on today – that says I'm the cathedral sexton. So these people are always going around looking for the verger. Heh heh heh. So it confuses people. Ah, but it's an interesting life."

CORMAC'S CHAPEL

In the Irish countryside, even in March when the tenderest blossoms have to suffer the coldest blasts of wind and rain, the sunsets seem to go on forever. Everything's still and dreamlike. The lights are not yet on in the houses, but on the road the traffic's heavy.

Everywhere you go in Ireland you see people just sitting there doing nothing, as if in a state of blessed enchantment. In more advanced countries you have to fork over two hundred bucks for a mantra before you can get away with doing that. In Ireland peace still does come dropping as slow as a poem by Yeats – low crime rate, no military to speak of, just a little IRA activity now and then to keep things interesting, though it's not so interesting for the victims, of course, or for the poor souls who have to clean up the mess.

I'm scribbling in my fat green notebook at a small round table in a crowded barroom in the Hayes Hotel in the busy little city of Thurles, upon the plan of which St. John's, Newfoundland, was modelled, according to the night clerk. The beehive corridors of the hotel are lined with framed photos and drawings of Thurles in times past, and it's obvious at a glance the place looks as it did in the nineteenth century anyway, except that it's now busier, noisier, more prosperous.

I slept poorly, and in compensation had kippers for breakfast again, two mornings in a row. I was feeling a bit distracted by four things: a persistent toothache, a sore leg, bad dreams, and Lourdes Brasil. The toothache and the leg were getting worse, the dreams were staying about the same, and, as for Lourdes, I had promised to phone her but I was torn between the pleasure of having her join me and the pleasure of continuing the tour in solitudinous selfish splendour.

Thurles is the sort of town you think about when you return home, a town destined to pop into your mind at odd moments, without warning, for the rest of your life. When a stranger walks down the street, everyone ignores him till he passes, then they stare after him. In the old photos the broad town square has two statues and three horse troughs in the centre. No statues or horse troughs now, but there's an air of vitality, with newsagents, pubs, sweet shops, and hotels all humming away. This morning the lorries were busy delivering bread and chocolate bars.

On the street I was stopped by a man with a clipboard who wanted to interview me. I had a feeling he was an Irish Scientologist. "If you could be anywhere you wanted to be, where would that be?"

"Right here," I said. "That's why I'm here, because I want to be."

He scampered away without taking any notes.

A few miles south of Thurles, at the intersection of the Cashel and Tipperary roads, on the bank of the River Suir, sits King Dónal Mór O'Brien's Holy Cross Abbey, as recommended by the Kinsellas of New Ross. The unfortunately named Suir, famed in song and poetry, is quite splendid at this point, oak-lined, sun-dappled, broad, and full of swans and leaping fish, as it takes its millennial and mythical route south past Cashel and through Cahir, where it takes a left turn and broadens, rolling due east to Waterford before emptying into

Waterford Harbour. Morton refers to the exquisite Suir winding through woodland. But he ruins it all by saying it reminds him strangely of Stratford-on-Avon. Even today tourists from the imperial centres are forever finding things that remind them of home, and becoming irritable when they find something that doesn't.

The restoration of Holy Cross was intended both to replicate its twelfth-century glory and to reinstate it as a place of public worship, a parish church. But it was hard to tell what state of ruin it had been in before the restoration. The tourist office was closed, and I couldn't get a guidebook. The people connected with the church were exhibiting do-not-disturb signs on their faces. My devious mind said they'd be much friendlier if the lovely Lourdes were with me.

But I managed to figure out that Holy Cross was founded in 1180 and houses a splinter of the True Cross of Jesus, which had somehow happened to meander its way along the long way to Tipperary. In 1110 Pope Paschal II gave the splinter of the True Cross to Dónal Mór O'Brien, the king of Munster, who willed it to Holy Cross upon his death. Over the centuries, if the church wasn't too far off their route, warriors going to battle would stop off to venerate the relic.

The restoration of the abbey, which had been left derelict for four hundred years, was carried out between 1971 and 1985. The photographs before the restoration, according to Ireland: The Rough Guide, suggest that every other ruin you've seen could as easily be converted – especially now that Ireland has a pipeline for funds for such projects from the European Economic Community. Such projects, however, have their down side: they dispel what the late photographer Roloff Beny called "the pleasure of the ruins."

And there, in the left transept, was the splinter which was said to have drawn pilgrims from all over Europe in the Middle Ages and which had won charters of protection for Holy Cross from five English kings: Henry II, John, Henry III, Edward II, and Richard II. Much later, Henry VIII quipped, as the monasteries were being destroyed at his command, that there were more fragments of the True Cross in England than it would take to make a whole one.

This splinter looked like a baby toothpick in a small glass case, which had been built into a gold cross from the fifteenth century, which in turn was inside a twentieth-century glass-and-metal container. The interior walls of Holy Cross had been freshly whitewashed, except for the wall facing the sliver of the True Cross. Here, the whitewashers spared a fifteenth-century fresco, one of the very few mediaeval paintings in any church in Ireland. It shows a Norman hunting scene, with apparently no ecclesiastical implications or symbols. Nobody knows why it's there. And it's so badly faded it soon won't be.

The highly respected broadcaster Gay Byrne was in a little trouble, but he got out of it nicely. A worried couple sent him their fifteen-year-old daughter's diary. They had read it, without permission, and were so shocked and concerned they wrote to Gay and enclosed the diary. They wanted to know if they should get psychiatric help for the gal. Gay announced all this on the radio, as I was winding my way south along the Suir as it winded *its* way south across the Tipperary Plain. "This diary is the girl's property," he said. It wasn't ethical for him to read it, it wasn't ethical for her parents to have read it, and it wasn't ethical for them to have sent it to him. He was sending it back, to the daughter, unread. He added that he realized there were two sides to the story, and he stopped short of suggesting the parents might need psychiatric help themselves. He said he was anticipating a lot of criticism for his courageous stand.

Out of the plain rose the Rock of Cashel, "like a ship at sea," to borrow a limp line from Morton, or "like a spectacular mirage of fairytale turrets, crenellations and walls rising bolt upright from the vast encircling plain," to borrow a stiff line from *Ireland: The Rough Guide*. Or, to quote from Aubrey de Vere's poem "Rock of Cashel":

There breathes from thy lone courts and voiceless aisles
A melancholy moral: such as sinks
On the worn traveller's heart, amid the piles
Of vast Persepolis on her mountain stand,
Or Thebes half buried in the desert's sand.

In A.D. 370 King Corc built a stone castle on the Rock, which had been known through the previous centuries as Fairy Ridge, and which had been created when the Devil became hungry, took a bite out of a distant mountain, and spat it at enemies he was pursuing across the plain.

Until 1110 the Rock was maintained as the seat of the kings of Munster. It was the subject of a novel by Sir Walter Scott. But its swirling, dizzying, largely unwritten history goes back to long before the Celtic invasions, and one glance of it as it rises above the plain is enough to inspire a visitor to consider, if only for a moment, the possibility of dropping everything and devoting the rest of one's life to Cashelmania.

The Rock of Cashel is Ireland's foremost tourist destination, and huge buses are constantly disgorging gangs of camera-wielding holidayers, most of whom it would appear are poorly prepared for their visit and who tend to betray their confusion in the face of these piles of stone by making hilarious jokes in loud voices.

To keep things simple, it's best to visualize the three main structures on the Rock: the splendid and perfectly preserved ninety-two-foot round tower, erected in the ninth or tenth century; the stone-roofed Romanesque Cormac's Chapel, which was consecrated in 1134 (though apparently built two hundred years earlier) and which is in a wonderful state of preservation; and the roofless ruins of the massive Saint Patrick's Cathedral, which abuts and towers above the much-smaller Cormac's Chapel and which was built immediately after the consecration of Cormac's Chapel by Dónal Mór O'Brien, the same Munster king who built Holy Cross.

There are two horrendous villains connected with the relatively recent history of the Rock. The first is Murrough O'Brien, the Earl of Inchiquin, a murderous Cromwellian also known as "Murrough of the Burnings," who, on September 13, 1647, laid siege to the town of Cashel below and slaughtered the garrison. When the population of the town scampered up the Rock and took refuge in the cathedral, Inchiquin had piles of turf placed against the walls and set on fire. Three thousand helpless, unarmed citizens were killed, many roasted alive. When Inchiquin was asked to spare the lives of the children, he refused. His famous and bloodchilling reply was: "Nits will be lice."

When Murrough died and was buried in the family plot in Saint Mary's Cathedral, Limerick, the townspeople stormed the cathedral and tossed his body into the River Shannon.

The second villain, less murderous but equally detestable in a way, was Archbishop Price, an eighteenth-century Protestant who liked to drive in state to church on Sundays but was unable to because of the steepness of the rock. In 1749 he had the lead and wooden beams stripped from Saint Patrick's Cathedral and used to enlarge a more convenient church in the town below.

Saint Patrick's as we see it today is just as he left it, in ruins.

Saint Patrick baptized King Aengus on the Rock of Cashel in 448. Patrick's visit was commemorated by the carving and erection of the seven-foot Saint Patrick's Cross, a high cross of unusual design, which has unfortunately suffered a lot of damage. It sits on a granite pedestal, about four feet high, that was used as a coronation stone for the kings of Munster for centuries.

Legend claims that anyone suffering from a toothache would be cured by placing their head at the southeast corner of the stone. My toothache was killing me and so, after making sure I had the right corner, I placed my head in the recommended spot. It might have been the power of the stone, it might have been the power of my suggestibility, but the toothache disappeared.

After gazing in awe at the transept over the north door of Cormac's Chapel, showing a centaur firing an arrow into an oversized mythological lion with a sleepy look on its face, I turned to the row of stone heads surmounting the altar, partially obscured by a quiet and dedicated television crew working high up on a series of scaffolds.

It was hard to imagine that these stone heads did not represent real people. The faces exhibited a whole range of emotions, becoming less tortured in appearance and more blissful the closer they were to the altar, so that the real and the mythological seemed fused. At some angles, the heads looked Mayan, or Incan, and at other angles Picassoesque. One of the heads, apparently representing one of the four evangelists, looked like a sad-eyed Mordecai Richler, another like a young James Cagney.

The sarcophagus of King Cormac the Magnificent, also known as Cormac Mac Art, the High King of Ireland, sat alone against a bare wall at the back of the chapel. The tomb's well-preserved motif, carved along its length in the Roman style, shows a very non-Roman greyhound all tangled up in serpents, representing time becoming tangled up in eternity, or spirit becoming trapped in matter.

And just then, fresh from their tour bus, a gang of North American tourists burst in.

"Hey, who brought the spray paint?"

"Most fun I've had on this trip was climbing up those stairs!"

"Bet it'd be hard to heat this place in the winter!"

After a few minutes they started chanting in unison: "We want lunch, we want lunch . . ."

Even on a cold, blustery March day such high-profile places as the Rock of Cashel become filled with tourists, while other less-famous places are empty. So I climbed down from the rock, hopped into my purple Satori, and sped through the town and out on the road to Cahir. I was thinking about Lourdes Brasil. She had a way with a tall tale, at least I think that's what it was. I'd mentioned that almost all the cars in Ireland had L stickers of various sizes on the back. They couldn't all be learners, could they?

She said that it was the same as Spain; it was thought that no one ever stopped learning, even learning to drive.

But why the difference in sizes?

That was so that someone who has been driving for twenty years with no serious accidents might have a small discreet L, while someone just starting out, or someone who had accidentally run over a troop of Boy Scouts, might have a huge L covering the entire rear of the car.

I later noted that the L on my car was medium-sized, showing that I had a good driving record but was not all that familiar with driving on the left.

From the bridge over the River Suir at Cahir one could see a fellow fishing for trout, just as in Morton's day. But there were no boys hauling boats across the river on ropes, as he describes. Instead, about ten well-equipped kayakers were furiously paddling as close as they could get up to the little falls, then letting go into the rapids. And from the river came a ghastly smell that I'm sure wasn't there in Morton's day.

A small young Irish woman was my impromptu guide to Cahir Castle, which was pleasantly situated on the left bank of the Suir (pronounced "Shoor"), and which, in September 1647, had been captured by the aforementioned infamous Lord Inchiquin, who then killed its occupants and destroyed the crops before heading up to the big barbecue at the Rock of Cashel.

"Cahir Castle was considered one of the best-fortified castles in Ireland at the time," said my guide. She pointed to the deadly looking portcullis, which could be dropped onto invaders. "It's one of the few still intact," she said. "It still works, after seven centuries. The mechanism operating it is on the upper floor, inside the ceiling. You're welcome to take a look at it."

Like the better class of guides, she would get a bit embarrassed if she couldn't answer a question. And she would say: "I can find out for you." Her name was Nora Creena.

She mentioned that the Irish language boasted many beautiful words, such as *tráthnóna* (evening), *uaigneas* (loneliness), and little one-syllable words such as *grá* (love) and *póg* (kiss). She said it was curious to observe that, although Ireland is considered a rather backward place in the field of women's equality, in the Gaeltacht, the purely Irish-speaking areas, a woman does not take her husband's name when she marries but retains her own.

She said that even though her parents didn't speak Irish, she spoke it better than she spoke English.

"Nor did my grandparents speak it," she said. "I started in secondary school, I suppose, and then I went to live in the Gaeltacht. I just went down for summer holidays every year, and then when I went to college I studied it full time."

Even though it was still off-season and I was the only visitor, she unlocked the door to the little museum and treated me to a special slide show of antiquities of the area. I felt like Morton at his zoo breakfast. There were high crosses, ogham stones, and so on, wonderful stone circles and standing stones, and castles here and there, and Romanesque churches. And she pointed out the white "*harling*" that still covered part of the outer walls of Cahir Castle.

"It was like weatherproofing. They plastered it all over the outside of the walls to cut down on the moisture inside. It's like stucco. And sometimes they even whitewashed the harling for some reason. But now it's pretty well all crumbled away."

There was an elderly man who had lived in Cahir all his life and loved to be called on to give tours.

"His name is Tim Looney. He doesn't get many calls for his services. I'm sure he'd be delighted to hear from you."

I called him, and he said he could see me at three the following afternoon. So I headed south for a quick Morton-inspired visit to Mount Melleray.

THE MONKS OF MOUNT MELLERAY

I was about to come across three elderly Trappist monks who knew about Morton, including an old-timer who had actually met him when he stopped off at their abbey at Mount Melleray sixty-odd years earlier. The abbey sits east of Lismore in the beautiful Blackwater Valley (the one in County Waterford, not the one in County Meath), with the Knockmealdown Mountains looming to the north and forming the boundary between counties Waterford and Tipperary. Of Mount Melleray Morton wrote particularly well, with atmosphere, history, and respect for the monks and their vow of silence. This is the section of the book where he confesses (to the reader, not to the priest) that he had brought along on the tour his silk pyjamas of red, violet, and black, which he had bought in Paris three weeks earlier.

First, with the sun going down, I stopped off at the Mount Melleray Grotto, where the Virgin Mary appeared in 1985 to three twelve-year-old boys. She told them she had a simple message she wanted them to deliver to the world: "Peace and prayer and tell the people the water is blessed."

Wooden steps led deep into the grotto. There on a long wooden porch around a small building the devout drank spring water from chipped enamel cups, then knelt and prayed amid a profusion of flowers and stared out at the dark mossy cliff face, studded irregularly with numerous bright, white, life-size figures of the Virgin Mary. The spirit of the place was serene and otherworldly. There was nothing grotesque about this grotto.

At the abbey, Brother Damien took my coat as I came in out of the dark night, sat me down at a large table in a large empty room, and brought out a large stainless-steel pot of tea. He made himself busy over by the stove and then, without asking if I was hungry, came back with toast, jam, and scrambled eggs. Then he stood over me and smiled as I ate.

Brother Damien said he had been at the abbey fifty years. He introduced me to the "guestmaster," Father Patrick, who said he had been there a mere forty years, but he knew that Morton had stayed in Room 5. I asked if that room was available. He said he would put me in Room 19, which offered a glorious view over the valley.

Father Patrick seemed a little weary with the responsibility of being guestmaster, but Brother Damien was a merry old soul.

"Morton converted," said Brother Damien, with a big happy smile.

"Really? I didn't know about that. I'd never have thought it."

"Oh, he did, he truly did. He wrote a book called In the Steps of the Master."

"Really?"

"Oh yes, and another called In the Steps of Saint Paul."

"Well, I'll be!"

"Morton wrote a lot of travel books," said Father Patrick. "One on Italy for sure."

I confessed that I felt Morton seemed to take a condescending attitude towards the Irish.

Father Patrick considered my remark a bit naïve.

"Well, he was English, you see. We Irish expect that sort of thing."

No anger or resentment. Not even much in the way of sadness. His remark was merely a quiet observation of the way things are.

I was being served, as all visitors were served, as if I were Christ. They would have washed my feet if I'd asked them, or if they thought I wouldn't have been embarrassed. In the words of G. K. Chesterton in his book *The Everlasting Man,* "The monastery would often not only take in the stranger but almost canonize him." The notion that a traveller at the door might be an angel in disguise, if not Christ himself, was still alive here.

Their only request was that I be up in time for lauds at eight. But the place seemed to energize me, and I was up in time for matins at seven, followed by mass at seven forty-five, and I took communion along with a librarian from Dublin who had brought his pushbike on the train to Mallow, then pedalled the forty miles to the monastery in the cold rain. He said he'd been having "relationship problems. That's why I'm here. And I feel a little better already. Listening to the birds as I cycled along was also good."

"And listening to the rain?"

"That too, though the rain might have been less cold."

He was a short, pudgy fellow with short legs, a long, thin, sharp nose that stuck way out, and a serious, mournful face that was yet capable of bursting into a big grin at any hint of irony. I liked him a lot.

When Morton visited in the late twenties, the monks maintained a strict vow of silence. And they raised or grew all their own food. But things had changed. Following breakfast I stuck my head in the kitchen to thank the staff and ask them if they still baked their own bread.

"We do, but that's about all we do any more. We roll our own butter but we don't make it. We're getting old I suppose."

I overheard Father Patrick asking a visitor to leave. The visitor was Seamus Dollard. He had been having problems with his family. He was in the lighting business. His partner had absconded with seventy-five thousand pounds two years ago and Seamus was still recovering from the shock. He said he had gone to England for four months, and when he returned his wife didn't want anything to do with him. He admitted that he found life more peaceful when he was away. His sons, however, still wanted him. In fact, it was a call from one of his sons that had disturbed Father Patrick and made him decide that Seamus should leave. He wouldn't tell me how long he'd been there.

"I don't want to be where I'm not wanted to be," said Seamus as the two of us strolled through the grounds. He wanted to stay longer, but not if they wanted him to leave.

To get his mind off his troubles, I started asking some tourist questions of great common interest. Did he know of anyone who still kept pigs in the kitchen? He brightened immediately.

"As late as 1972 I knew people who kept pigs indoors. When I was growing up in the fifties, my parents used to take me on holidays in the country, and they wouldn't allow me to take my shoes, because the kids I'd be playing with didn't have any."

"That was very thoughtful. They must have been fine people."

"That they were."

He said he felt an urge lately toward getting straight with God.

"The Women's Lib organization is just terrible," he said. "We live in horrible times. Ireland is the land of limbo. I need to know the basics. What is the will of God? What is the meaning of the Trinity? And what about the Blessed Virgin? I was out the other night walking around in the moonlight and I decided to have a talk about these things with Brother Damien. He told me the moon wouldn't help me, but the Blessed Virgin Mary would never let me down."

As beautiful as the various services were I couldn't help feeling a heavy emphasis on the feudal aspects of Christianity. The Lord is very much a feudal lord: Oh grant us your grace and we will work very hard for your glory. And so on. This was wonderful stuff in the fourteenth century, but the human race no longer has a feudal psychology.

The problem with such criticism however, is its superficiality, for there was, behind the feudal imagery, something timelessly real for the human spirit. In fact, I soon felt a strong sense of grace myself. It was everywhere. My little self blanked out and a larger self took over for several hours. What did they mean by God's will? I never knew. And now here I was, feeling it.

To Seamus I did not mention this. He was looking for something grander, a sense of grace that involved national issues, even global. He was a potential Oliver Cromwell, someone who could hammer Ireland back into a previous century and keep it there. If people had to die in the process, that was the will of God.

Seamus did get his reprieve, and he decided to stay on a couple of days longer, even though his son was calling for him. He insisted on spreading out my map of Ireland and very kindly spent an hour telling me which restaurants on the west coast I shouldn't miss, and which roads I should take for the best scenery.

I finally took my leave, since I had to get back to Cahir for my appointment with Mr. Looney. But first I was treated to a little meal. At the table were an Irish woman, a handsome young priest, and a stone-deaf old friar. The priest was kind and patient with the woman, who was fawning all over him. She was gung-ho on religion and confessed that she had been able to get to only three high masses last week.

We were each given two beefsteaks, peas, boiled potatoes, and a piece of pie cemented in a pool of yellow custard. And gallons of tea. Each potato had to be stuck with a fork and held upright in the left hand to be peeled with a knife held in the right. That's the way the Irish do it, and they ought to know.

The woman had started writing poems. She said she didn't know anything about writing poems, had never read poetry, but every time she knelt to pray lately, lines of poetry entered her head and she simply had no choice but to write them down. Last Easter weekend she wrote eight complete poems. She would often write four at a sitting and then nothing for a week. She was telling all this to the young priest.

Even though the priest offered her no encouragement, she brought out a stack of her handwritten poems, plunked them down next to his plate, and asked him to read them.

He gave the others a subtle little look that said, "Sorry, my friends, I don't have a choice," and buried himself in the poems. When I left, he was still reading dutifully and without a smidgen of pleasure.

So the Trappists were no longer vegetarian, no longer did they maintain their vow of silence, and no longer did they farm. All they did was bake bread, roll their own butter, and observe the ancient canonical hours. But they were still kind, generous, and capable of inspiring the sagging spirits of the troubled who sought them out.

There was an old-timer, about ninety, who had been around when Morton came through. This fellow had stories to tell about him, Father Patrick told me so, but every time I tried to approach him he seemed too busy to interrupt. He was a tall old man with a lot of energy. He was serving the Lord by washing up our dishes. From the dining room I watched him through an open door working merrily away in the kitchen. Maybe I'd pop in again in a week or two, I thought. But it was not to be.

MR. LOONEY

He was known around town as Timmy, the town being Cahir, where he had spent his entire life. But he was a man who deserved great respect, and in his demeanour and manner of speech he demanded great respect, and so I called him Mr. Looney. He was also known as Old Looney because he was an octogenarian widower living in a small house with sagging bookshelves on a side street off the old town square. From the age of sixteen he had dedicated himself to studying the history of Ireland, a fervent amateur with no time for the academies. He spoke slowly, evenly, deliberately, and soberly. He never smiled.

"It is not generally known that this is the most historic part of Ireland."

"You mean County Tipperary?"

"I do."

"Why would it be more historic than the other parts?"

"There are many reasons for that. Even the Celts when they came in here to Ireland it was here that they stayed. Just outside the town of Cahir was one of their main bases. That's going back, for they arrived in Ireland in 504 B.C. There were eighteen kings of Munster who resided just outside of town. And then later they moved to Cashel."

"Is it known where they are buried?"

"It is not."

"No idea at all?"

"Well, I think I know. But it hasn't been excavated yet."

Mr. Looney's main theme was the poverty of knowledge on the subject of the history of Ireland. Very little was officially known because very little had been excavated. For every Newgrange that had been discovered, excavated, studied, written about, renovated, popularized, and put on the tourist maps, there were thousands more that were known only to lonely amateurs like Mr. Looney, who had been exploring the countryside with a passionate eye for six decades.

From his inspired guesses about the nature and meaning of many of the unexcavated mounds of various sizes and shapes that he was familiar with, he wove theories that were potentially disturbing, even revolutionary, and conjectures that were sometimes a bit confusing.

I had driven north from Mount Melleray, back over the Knockmealdown Mountains, along winding roads offering heavenly views of the Tipperary plain bathed in bright cold sunshine, past dead sheep that had been hit by cars, and down to Cahir. Pity the season wasn't a month or so more advanced and that the beautiful rhododendrons, everywhere in bud, weren't in full blossom.

Mr. Looney invited me in. He was dressed in a black pin-striped suit, black shoes, burgundy wool cardigan with matching tie and socks, and a white shirt. He didn't waste time getting down to business.

"The main monument of Ireland is Newgrange. If you were at Newgrange and if you went to the trouble of walking around the mound, you'd find it's exactly three hundred paces. And it's about thirty feet high. Now I'm working on a mound here —"

He was referring to the burial place of the kings of Munster in a field somewhere just outside of Cahir.

"I have it located. I've had it divined – I don't know if that's a new word for you —"

"No, it's not. You're talking about dowsing."

"I am. Excavation without going underground."

"Well put."

"The place I'm working now is exactly six hundred paces to walk around it."

"Double the circumference."

"It is."

"And how tall is the mound?"

"It'd be about fifty or sixty feet."

"Twice as high."

"It is."

"Have you spoken to anyone in charge of excavations about this?"

"I have not. The trouble here is this. Now I've made a number of finds. I've walked the fields and I'm always on the lookout for something. Mounds and that. I reported an important find here in 1961 and they came along and they declared it a national monument – the mound and twenty acres surrounding it. And they haven't come back."

"And what was that find?"

"It was a court cairn. A mound that's more or less pear-shaped. And there's a souterrain passage in that for burial."

"How far back would that go?"

"That would have been built in 4000 B.C."

"And it still hasn't been excavated?"

"It has not; they never came back. Now that's the trouble in Ireland. You report something and that's it, that finishes it. I have found sites around here that they don't know anything about. They haven't money. That's the problem. They'll take the place over all right, but they haven't the money, they haven't the knowledge, and they haven't the people."

At first, when Mr. Looney said the word Tipperary, I thought he was saying "the prairie," because he pronounced it something like that. Tipperary *is* a relatively flat, prairie-like county, bordered by mountains. But the word Tipperary is said to come from the Irish *tiobraid Árann*, meaning "the well of Arann." Mr. Looney tended to pronounce *th* as if it were *t* (and sometimes *d*) and *t* as if it were *th*. He also tended to roll his *r*'s and his *l*'s and to insert an *r* or an *l* where it wasn't required. Water, for instance, was invariably "wortle." And he claimed to be able to tell by accent which county someone came from.

Morton wouldn't knowingly have had much to do with Mr. Looney, and Mr. Looney could not remember having heard anything about Morton or his books, but I have an uncanny feeling – close to certainty – that their paths did cross at one time. And in such a way that it did no less than seal Mr. Looney's fate. I had asked Mr. Looney how he became interested in studying the history of his region.

It was sixty-five years earlier. Coincidentally, Morton would have been on his whirlwind tour of Ireland – including a brief stop in Cahir. Mr. Looney was sixteen and working as a clerk in an office in town.

"The windows were open and the old characters of the town would sit outside the window on long benches. And I would hear some very interesting stories being told."

One day a very distinguished English visitor stopped and asked one of the old gentlemen for the directions to Cahir Abbey.

"Never heard of it," the old man said.

"Sure now, I thought there was an abbey in this town."

"Oh no, there's nothing like that here."

By this time the young eavesdropper was becoming a little angry. He went out, but the visitor had gone on his way. He approached the old man and asked him where he lived.

"On Abbey Street."

"Abbey Street. I thought so. And when you open the door in the morning, what's the first thing you see?"

"Oh my God. The Abbey! I never thought of that."

Mr. Looney went back in and went back to work, but he couldn't stop thinking about the incident.

"Later that day, on thinking this thing over, I decided that no man, no matter where he came from or who he was, would come into my district and ask me a question I couldn't answer. And that's how I started to get interested in my parish and the history of it and the history of the whole locality, not only of Cahir and South Tipperary, but of the whole south of Ireland – south of a line running from Dublin to Galway, which is roughly half of Ireland. I've travelled it all and I know the history and background of all those parts. The unfortunate thing is that very few people ever ask me anything about it."

I didn't ask Mr. Looney anything more about the English visitor. Even if I'd had a picture of Morton to show him, I probably wouldn't have. How reliable would his memory have been after a glimpse of someone more than sixty years ago? Besides, he apparently heard Morton's voice but didn't see his face. As far as I was concerned, the visitor could have been none other than Morton. I was in search of Morton, and I had discovered him, if only in the resounding impact he had unknowingly made on the life of one individual human being.

Morton's visit to Cahir was brief. But it was a lovely day, the sort of day when old men like to sit out on benches and chat, and he liked the town immensely. He found it "bright, clean, hopeful, vaguely busy . . . peaceful and drenched in the sanity of the eighteenth century." He mentions the castle, the bridge, the river, "the square as wide as a parade ground, and the warm afternoon sunlight."

But he doesn't mention the abbey.

Perhaps because a certain old codger, sitting in the warm afternoon sunlight, had told him it didn't exist.

"The Peloponnesians were the first here," Mr. Looney was saying. "They came from Greece. We did a lot of trade with Greece and with the Middle East in pre-Christian times. There was a big trade with the Mediterranean."

"What about the Celts?"

"The Celtic people originated on the Tibetan–Indian border and they moved from there to Ireland along the southern part of the Mediterranean and into Spain. Milesius, the king of Spain, sent his three sons in here to conquer Ireland. They arrived here in 504 B.C."

On the wall of Mr. Looney's house was a painting showing a dolmen, a smaller version of the one at Browne's Hill. Mr. Looney said he had discovered the dolmen on a wooded slope just out of town, and the painter, a local crony, had painted it for him.

"It's a huge capstone," he said.

You couldn't get a sense of size from the painting. But the capstone looked as if it were just sitting on top of the ground.

"Is it still supported?"

"It is, actually. But poorly. It was interfered with in some way. But it's a very good example of a capstone. Perfect, in fact."

"And you haven't reported it."

"I have not."

He started talking about beehive huts, which he pronounced "hoods" and described as "old drystone buildings of the early Christian period – little huts for living in, monastic cells. There are a lot of them around here but I haven't divulged the location of any. You can put in a very interesting day around here, I tell you."

Sitting on Mr. Looney's desk was a stack of old leatherbound books that looked as if they had been borrowed from the county registry as part of whatever project he was working on. I picked one up and flipped it open. It showed a town that had a population of two thousand in 1821.

"The population of that town today is five hundred," he said.

He offered to take me out to Athassel Abbey on the River Suir. We hopped into his little red Zazen.

"See that church?"

We were buzzing along the Waterford Road, heading east out of Cahir. The church was in ruins and covered with vegetation.

"That's the old parish church. There's a wall down the middle of it like, and it's known as a screen wall. And that screen wall, it divided the Catholic and the Protestant services. The two were held together then. You can see there were two belfries on it."

"Are there a lot of them like that around?"

"You'll have a job finding a second one of them, I tell you. I came across another one of them down outside Killarney. As for this one, the last service held there was Protestant – in 1795. A Catholic service would have been held just before then."

We passed a gloomy-looking crossroads, a T-junction actually, one of those landscapes that make you think inexplicably of death and sorrow, a *crux commissa* or Saint Anthony's Cross, and Mr. Looney said three men had been hanged there a hundred years ago or so.

"And just about four years ago the bloody fellow who didn't know any better took down the posts they were hanged on."

We had pulled over to drink in the gloom.

"He was bulldozing the field. And it's a tradition, even now with the posts removed, that the people will never walk past here. They always went out of their way to avoid walking past here."

"What were the men hanged for?"

"Land agitation."

"Oh dear."

"There was a lot of that in those days."

"So the people around here must have sympathized with them."

"Well, everyone did. Because, see, like if you go back to, say, even up to 1912 or 1913 you'd have a big job going around this, the most prosperous part of Ireland, finding a man with a ten-pound note of his own. There was no money. Even people working, the wages was practically nil. It was a battle of survival. I have copies of the actual paysheets; the wages was one shilling and sixpence per day. Nine shillings a week. And if you were able to supply a cair and box with yourself you got one pound a week."

"A cair and box?"

"By that is meant a horse and cart for drawing stones and that."

Mr. Looney said 160 men were hired in those days to work on the railway in Cahir.

"And that was the wages they were getting. They had to walk in the nine miles from Clogheen and be in by eight o'clock in the morning. And they walked home at six in the evening. And then be in again the following morning. And they fought at one another to get the job. If a fellow fell out, there were dozens waiting to take his place."

We parked the car by a stone wall a mile from the village of Golden and walked three hundred yards across a spacious green field down to the River Suir, where the ruins of Athassel Abbey sat quietly in the warm sunlight like a lucid dream.

"This abbey was ruined during the Reformation," said Mr. Looney. "The tourists don't come here, even in the summer."

"How far are we from the Rock of Cashel?"

"About seven miles."

"That may be why. There's no shortage of tourists there, even this early in the spring."

Mr. Looney had been a teetotaller and non-smoker all his life, and in spite of his years he scampered up the crumbling stairs of Athassel, leaving me to eat his dust as I stood in the church choir staring at the tomb of a thirteenth-century Norman knight. When I caught up with him, he was breathing quietly and gazing silently out a small window over the mythic countryside. He was about five-eight, and had a sort of Richard Nixon–Barry Fitzgerald look, but without the quivering jowls.

He didn't say anything, but I later realized that the spot at which he'd been gazing had been the site of an ancient town which had disappeared in the fourteenth century and of which no trace remained. "Disappeared" is a euphemism. Brian O'Brien burnt the town to the ground in 1329.

"Powerful weather," said Mr. Looney.

"A brief respite from the cold rain."

"Summer will be a while yet."

Over his bald head he had a few strands of feathery white hair, which were brushed back and which would puff up in a breeze so that they looked like the lonesome arches of a ruined cathedral, like Saint Patrick's on the Rock of Cashel.

"The Normans would come up the Suir in flat-bottomed boats," he said. "They even had their own bakery. But there was a lot of trouble with drink and with women here."

He said Athassel Abbey was also known as Saint Edmond's Priory.

"The terrible thing was, their libraries were destroyed. From all their manuscripts there are just a few scraps remaining at Cahir Abbey. I've had a terrible problem trying to find anything written about Athassel Saint Edmond's."

He said that pigs had been brought into the ruined abbey on three different occasions by three different individuals over the years, and in each case they didn't thrive. It might have had something to do with the consecrated ground.

"Would this be pretty consistent throughout Ireland?"

"It would not. These places aren't usually interfered with in that way."

As we got back in the car, a young man on foot, and with a large backpack with a Stars and Stripes sewn on, was coming along the road. He scarcely glanced at us, and we didn't say anything. He climbed the stone wall and made his way down to the abbey alone.

I hadn't knowingly met any Tinkers yet, but had heard a lot of different shades of opinion about them, and was about to hear many more. Also, they had been the focus of a recent spate of unpleasant stories in the country weeklies and small-town dailies, in a mean and amateurish journalistic style that was shockingly one-sided.

"The Tinkers were dispossessed during Cromwellian times and never got resettled," said Mr. Looney.

"This has the ring of truth."

"The Tinkers are the travelling people. They maintain the old Irish customs. The thing is slowly breaking down, but, when they marry, the bride and groom never meet until the wedding day. And the children are looked after first. Not one adult will eat a bite until all the children are fed."

"But they are not liked, the Tinkers."

"The farmers like these people. They are strictly honest. They live by very strict pre-Norman codes."

I was very impressed with Mr. Looney's take on the Tinkers. He thought of them as a somewhat distinct race with ancient values that the rest of us had forgotten. Most others saw them as layabouts, thieves, and vagabonds.

I had no idea where we were by this time – some farmer's lane. A group of smiling gap-toothed rustics gathered around the Zazen and said, "Hello, Timmy, how're ye bein'?"

They waved us on. We drove slowly past the farm buildings and up a slight hill to an uncultivated area. Slightly below the top of the hill was an ancient, roofless stone chapel, very small, about thirty by fifteen feet. Mr. Looney said it was built in the seventh century. A window over the high altar seemed to be lined up with the spot where the sun would be rising at the spring solstice, which was close at hand.

Below the chapel was a small group of stone crosses. Mr. Looney called them high crosses, but they didn't seem tall enough to be called high. On one had been carved six lines of ancient Gaelic.

"No one has succeeded in deciphering it yet," said Mr. Looney.

He said there were no figures of Christ on the crosses, or even in the churches, until the twelfth century.

"See this stone?" he said. A metal bracket had been secured over it so it couldn't be removed. "Saint Bechaum came to this chapel and asked for butter. He was refused, so the butter turned to stone."

"And this is it, Mr. Looney?"

"It is."

Further down, there was a small *clochán*, a stone beehive hut with an extremely narrow opening, again in the direction of the rising sun. The capstone that might have been on top – or more likely a wood-and-straw roof – had been long missing.

On the floor inside was a large flat rock with two round basins carved into it so smoothly it might have been natural. Mr. Looney said it was a *balaun* stone, that would have been used for baptizing the pagans.

"And in pre-Christian times they were used for grinding corn, is that right?"

"There's another one in Cahir Abbey," he said.

"Saint Bechaum travelled most of Ireland," said Mr. Looney, referring to his favourite saint. "He was an itinerant preacher. He was well-known in Rome, involved in changing the dates for Easter. No one knows where he's buried, but I've found traces of him all over Ireland."

I marvelled at the large number of Irish saints. Morton's book says there had been a veritable army of them.

"And of all the saints we have – hundred and hundreds of them – only three are registered in Rome," said Mr. Looney. "Even Saint Patrick is not registered in Rome. I guess he didn't pay his fee."

We both felt we'd done enough for the day but agreed to meet again tomorrow. As we slowly walked back to the car, it occurred to me that the area under cultivation had perhaps at one time been the site of an expansive village of stone huts. What we had seen had been merely an untouched remnant of a vast clearing of the huts over the centuries. Mr. Looney enthusiastically agreed.

Emboldened, I asked about the Blarney Stone.

"Would it really cause me to become eloquent? If there's the slightest chance —"

"The Blarney Stone? That's only folk stuff. That's just a gimmick."

"Well, what about the Little People?"

"That's different," he said.

His face softened, and he began to tell a story I was to hear many times on my travels, a story that was part of an extensive living mythology, one that the academics and professional historians were beginning to find in the main correct.

"Now before the Celtic people came here, there was a tribe of people occupying Ireland. They were called the Tuatha Dé Danann. They were small people. Like in early Christian times a tall Irishman would be five feet six inches. But these were small people."

"Smaller than five-six, Mr. Looney?"

"Much smaller. And the Celts were bigger people and they were all blond. The Tuatha Dé Danann built those forts you see. And when they were under pressure from the Celts, they'd disappear. And that's how this thing came about with the Little People and all disappearing into the earth. They used to go down into their souterrains, their underground chambers and passageways. They just disappeared into nowhere. That's how the thing about the Little People came about."

"When did they become extinct?"

"The Celts finally defeated them and slaughtered them all. That's the way it was in those days – even up to Cromwell's time. Massacres. Ach, but the history of Ireland has never been written."

THE WELL OF JESUS

Dotty Doyle was tough, charming, funny, knowing, and all-in-all wonderful. She was highly impressed that I had hooked up with Mr. Looney and wanted to know how I'd managed to do so. Apparently he was well-loved in town, respected for his passion and knowledge, but it was a running joke that the tourists never had time for him.

"I asked at Cahir Castle if there was anyone local who offered tours. They said the only one was Timmy Looney."

"Well, you hit on the right man," she said. "No doubt about it."

I was registering at Dotty's bed-and-breakfast, housed in an old castle in the vicinity of Cahir. North Americans made a point of staying there before their assault on the Rock of Cashel.

"It's hard to keep up with him, especially when climbing those winding staircases in the old ruins," I said.

"The trouble with him," said Dotty, "is to retain it all in your mind. It's an impossibility. You should be writing it all down."

Dotty had a large collection of Gideon Bibles presented to her by her North American guests over the years. She showed me one. It was a little New Testament, and on the flyleaf, in a tight little hand, it said:

Presented to Mrs. Doyle
1 John 3:8
Thank you for the pleasant
hospitality
June 1990

Under the inscription was pasted a Stars and Stripes sticker and below that were the words: "Righteousness exalteth a nation."

"Coals to Newcastle," I said. Dotty smiled.

"But there's one family of American tourists I like," she said. "They're staying here tonight. When we asked him where he was from he seemed to say Ohio. But he said it wrong. The accent was on the wrong syllable or one of those things. Then he pointed to his right cheek and jaw and he said, 'I've been sick.' He was groping for words. He turned to his son and said, 'Tell them what's the matter with me.' The son said, 'He's had two major strokes.'"

Turned out they weren't from Ohio at all, but from Lowell, Massachusetts.

"The man's wife spoke very lovingly about Ireland," said Dotty. "Her son and daughter, the daughter's boyfriend – they're all very nice people. The daughter's studying at Trinity. Old Looney, he was here and he was trying to make a big play for taking them to the Rock of Cashel as a guide, but they weren't buying. Not enough time for his kind of detail."

"I think there's a tendency for tourists to want to be able to say they saw things rather than really see them," I opined philosophically.

"Just to go for the sake of going and not know where they've really been," she retorted amiably.

"Just to say we've been there," I declared succinctly.

"Nuts when you think of it." She spun a circle around her ear.

At breakfast the stroke victim and his family did seem to be very nice people. I couldn't keep my eyes off them. I kept smiling at them, and they kept smiling back.

Two other Americans were there: a man and a woman, who between them had broken three bones in three separate accidents just before coming to Ireland. The man had broken his leg, and just after having had it put in a cast he fell and broke his wrist. And as his wife was taking him to the hospital for the second time, she fell and broke her ankle. Dotty kept handing them fresh bowls of cornflakes.

Then there was the clothing salesman from Dublin, quietly telling Dotty a long story about how his brother had been cheated out of his inheritance, a Queen Anne clock that had been solemnly promised to him by his aunt when she died. Dotty in turn was telling him how Lord Cardigan's First Cavalry was billeted in this very castle before they went off to be slaughtered in the Charge of the Light Brigade.

Dotty turned to say something and mentioned in passing she'd been to mass that morning. It seemed to be a big thing in Ireland, how often you went to mass, as if it were a competition.

"Oh, if I could go every day I would."

"Soft wortle," said Mr. Looney. "It never goes dry."

We were standing by the *Tobar Íosa*, the Well of Jesus. The branches of the trees all about had white rags tied to them. There was a chill in the air, and it was also going up my spine.

"Isn't this an unusual name for an Irish well?"

"It is. They're usually given a saint's name. But the fact of the matter is that these wells are pre-Christian, and were taken over when Christianity came in. Wells in those days were very important" – pronounced "impowertant" – "and up to 1886 this well, together with the one at Cahir Abbey and another at the south side of the river, was supplying the town of Cahir. There was no piped wortle in town. As the result of an outbreak of cholera it was that the piped wortle came to be presented to the town by Lady Margaret Charters. And the wortle came to be piped down the mountain to the town at her own expense and given free."

The water kept bubbling up. I asked about the rags.

"The rags, they're a symbol of Druidism. The people come here for cures, and as a result of their visit they tie these rags on in remembrance of their coming here and for favours granted. The wortle's noted for people suffering from headaches or eye trouble. They wash their face in the wortle and then there's certain rounds to be done here which have gone out at this point in time. They're no longer done here."

"Certain rounds?"

"By the rounds is meant you would walk the streams – a continuation of Druidism into Christianity."

"The people didn't consider it pagan?"

"Not now they don't, but those rags, they're the symbol of paganism, because in a Christian church you don't recognize that kind of thing. But it's still in the people."

"They must have been strong to have survived, these beliefs."

"It would have been passed down through the generations, parent to child."

"But fading more and more with each generation?"

"And whatever we know about what the pagan religion was like, it's only a small part of what it must have been."

"When it was at its peak?"

"These wells now, they are known as rag-wells."

I was devilishly curious about Mr. Looney's religious beliefs. "Would you be a believer, Mr. Looney?" I said.

"Well, I believe in this. The Druids were very learned people. You could not be made a Druid on your own. You could only be made a Druid by a Druid, because the Druids had a system of retention, and you had to master it first. And you had to prove you had mastered it —"

"That would be retention as in memory."

"It would. Now if I was a Druid and you wanted to be a Druid you'd have to come" – pronounced "comb" – "with me and you'd have to retain all the ancient fables and sagas. And if you weren't able to retain them you could never be a Druid. So there was nothing written, you see. It was all passed on. That's the way they worked. And then when Christianity came to Ireland there was a kind of compromise religion. They didn't just come in and take the place over, overnight, as you've been led to believe, like. See?"

I asked for more details about the compromise religion, but Mr. Looney had his own way of answering questions.

"And they done fierce destructions here, because they destroyed all the symbols and all the places of the Druids."

"What sort of places did they destroy?"

"All of them, but places like wells remained because they had to remain, on account of the wortle. The holly tree here" – he pointed to an ancient tree – "is considered part of the well, because the patron day here is Christmas Eve. This is the Well of Jesus, you see, and Christmas is the time. These stones here have been here since pre-Christian times. You can tell these are old stones because there's no mortar" – pronounced "martyr" – "of any description in them. It's what they call drystone building."

In a large dirty glass case behind the well was a ceramic statue of a sorrowful Jesus.

We stopped off at Cahir Abbey on the way back to Mr. Looney's place.

"There's the *balaun* stone right behind you," he said. "Like at Saint Bechaum's."

"It's like a baptismal font."

"Well, they would be in a sense."

There was a gravestone inscribed to Richard Scanlon "who departed this life 1805 age 104 years."

"His relatives are still in town," said Mr. Looney.

"And are they still long-lived people?"

"They are, actually, yes!" He almost smiled.

In his living room Mr. Looney set up his screen and projector and began treating me to a slide show.

"Here's a stone I found," he said. "It indicates that the Roman Catholic religion was not the first into Ireland, the first Christian religion that is. This is a Coptic stone, a Greek Orthodox stone." It showed a cross with four arms of equal length and a cross bar on the end of each of the arms.

"So the Celts still kept up their contacts with Greece, you figure?"

"Ach, they did! There's no doubt about that! Here's evidence that the Coptic religion came first and it came in through the Mediterranean. No doubt about that, because even in pre-Christian times we were in communication with that area. I found that cross in a very ancient site, going back to the very earliest days of Christianity. It was just standing there. Only about two feet at the outside" – he meant two feet sticking up out of the earth – "in what eventually became a graveyard. Limestone. I brought out the markings with grass."

We slipped forward about two millennia and began talking about the gallowglasses and kerns mentioned in *Macbeth* and *Richard II*.

"The gallowglasses were mercenaries. They sold their swords to the highest bidder. For example, the Keatings were Welsh gallowglasses who had a castle near Cahir with immense stone dovecotes."

He flashed a shot of the dovecotes on the screen. There seemed to be thousands of them. It was very moving. They looked like the pigeonholes in a small post office, except they were made of stone, built to last for ever.

"The fact that these dovecotes were built out of stone shows the importance of pigeons to them in those days, both for communication and for food."

I called in again to say goodbye to Dotty Doyle and to compare notes on Mr. Looney. I seemed to catch her in a fit of poetic mania. "The mountain and town and village and byroad and highroad," she was saying, seemingly to herself. "Cork, Waterford, Tipperary . . . It is the Golden Vale after all. Who called it that, many years ago? Someone did anyway."

"Ahem."

"Oh, hello."

"Hello, Dotty. I took a ton of notes today."

"You'd have to," she exclaimed, "because there'd be no way in the world that you'd put half of it in your mind, not at all, not at all, believe you me. Indeed!"

She wanted me to meet a certain local teacher. "She's one of the primary teachers in the primary school here, and she is young and very bright, and interested in these things. She trained in England. She's just different. She teaches fifth class, and she got to meet Old Looney and she got him on a few occasions into her classroom, for an hour say. She organized it all herself."

"Mr. Looney must have been very pleased about that."

"Well, yes." She gave me a look. "And he had so much to offer her little kids, because he brought in his slide collection and he started from the simple things up. The kids in town didn't realize where they lived and all they had around them. For a fellow, as I say, who never passed out of primary school, he's just terrific."

I mentioned it seemed strange that I was apparently the first person sent from the castle to see Mr. Looney.

"Well, you asked in a certain way, you see. And they couldn't think of anybody else, you see. They knew who you wanted in a sense. And you probably met Nora Creena there. And Timmy goes in and out of the castle a good bit. I feel sad that I can't do anything for him. But people haven't the time."

I mentioned that he had asked if I wouldn't mind going to the castle and telling them I enjoyed the trip. And he didn't have to ask me, I would have anyway. In fact, I had a feeling we'd be meeting again under different circumstances.

"Well, God knows," she said, sternly. "If you have five minutes to spare you just do that. You know it's frightful now he's down to this age now, he's going off shall we say, he's going down the other way, a lot. Even I am. But I really should have tried and organized something for him. But you couldn't move the people. You just couldn't."

Our eyes met for a moment. Her voice dropped. "The people have not the time to save the Lord," she said.

I gave her a little farewell hug. "That's the best saying I've heard in a long time," I said.

CORKTOWN INTERLUDE

After popping in to Cahir Castle to thank Nora Creena profusely for giving me Mr. Looney's number, I drove down to Lismore and straight west to Cork City, where I intended to spend the night. But every time I tried to get closer to downtown Cork, I ended up way out in the country. Finally, after much difficulty, including losing several games of chicken with oncoming lorries on narrow highways and occasionally having to stop and try to focus the headlights on a road-sign at a dark intersection, I arrived at a very nice bed-and-breakfast, high on a remote, dark windswept hill overlooking the Ballyhamane River just as it begins to widen into Kinsale Harbour.

A very large and friendly Englishwoman had been running the place for the past twenty years. She'd been washing the cellar floor or cleaning out the attic or something, because she was very sloppy and dirty and the place was neat and clean, a masterpiece of renovation, truly splendid in every way. She said the house was seventy years old, but when I suggested there must always have been some kind of dwelling on such a lovely hill her voice dropped and she said she wasn't so sure, and I had the feeling she didn't want to talk about it.

In Ireland it's not considered polite to ask someone if they are hungry. You just look at them, and if they look hungry you feed them. When I took off my hat and coat my generous hostess made me a thick ham sandwich and a pot of tea and included two small chocolate bars, by chance my favourite, Whispas, which were all the rage in Ireland.

This is a strange little story, seemingly a bit personal, but when I mentioned it to Lourdes Brasil later, she said she thought everybody had experiences like that, where you think you're going to die from too much laughter, pleasure, beauty, or whatever: In the morning I was psychologically incapable of opening the curtains. The sun was coming through, the birds were singing, and I knew it would be a wonderful, glorious wide-angle view, but it was as if the view would somehow cause me irreparable damage. It would render me incapable of ever leaving Ireland. Worse, it would cause my heart to go out of control, and I would die from too much happiness.

In the Cork paper the day before, a man had died of excitement while landing a big trout. As he lay dying, his friend took his line and landed the trout himself. There was a picture of the friend, looking sad, but holding up a beautiful trout.

Finally I screwed up my courage and slowly opened the curtains. Was this all I was worried about? The scene was nice, but dull: a tidal river way down below, sparkling in the sun, a castle directly on the river bank a mile or so downstream, and some farmhouses and large green patches of land under cultivation on the slope of the hill rising on the other side of the river.

There were also cattle small as aphids standing on the hillside eating their grass a mile or two straight across. The river was broad, deep, and powerful at this point, and the farmer came out with a tractor the size of an ant to cut hay or plough his field.

But as I watched, the scene gradually became rather enchanting, with birds flying hither and yon, the tide coming in and creating

constant changes in the silver, violet, turquoise, grey, and white surface of the water far below. The cattle were moving so slowly as they
grazed. They were so far away I had to get out my field glasses to count
them reliably. There were nine-and-fifty.

"It's such an ideal spot you have here," I said, at breakfast.

"Yes, that's right," said the proprietress.

I lit into the wild mushrooms and marmalade.

"Very handsome castle over there."

"Yes, it's lovely. It's a very old one."

"Been in it?"

"Yes, yes. I've been over there. It's on the farmer's land. It was used
for smuggling, and that was years and years ago, because it's so near the
estuary, and it's very deep, the water. Very peaceful. It has a history to
it, Kinsale. Have you been here before?" She gave me a few historical
highlights: Kinsale was an English town, closed to the Irish for almost
three hundred years, starting just after the English inflicted a disas-
trous (and unexpected) defeat on a powerful Irish army in 1601, with
a Spanish fleet standing helplessly in the bay.

"What were the Spanish doing there?"

"They were supposed to join forces with the Irish to kick the
English right out of the country."

Morton talks about this, and states that "one of Ireland's most
notorious traitors, Brian MacMahon, sold the plan of campaign to the
English for a bottle of whisky!"

I asked if she'd heard on the radio that people were worried about
hordes of African immigrants invading Ireland. Immigration was
the subject of the phone-in show, and it had drawn calls from fear-
mongers.

"Well, that's just the Irish. You'll find the ones that have travelled
are all right, but the ones who haven't, well they're afraid of change.
They all like the Americans anyway. They don't like the English
much, but they love the Americans."

The French couple across the table were very much in love. When they caught me glancing at them, I blushed and said, "Les champignons sont très bon pour le petit déjeuner, n'est-ce pas?" They looked at each other and started giggling, at my accent presumably.

A scene like that from the window brings back a flood of storybook enchantment from childhood. Just being in Ireland is a little like that. But there was nothing enchanting about the Irish drivers. They're friendly, they only want to tailgate. And when you pull over to let them pass, they don't want to pass. And when they eventually do pass, they do it so intimately, taking up half of your lane. Fortunately, I had the phone-in show to listen to as I drove along.

Some coldhearted pranksters had been cutting the heads off newborn foals and placing them on suburban lawns in the middle of the night – just grabbing a newborn foal before it's on its feet and cutting off its head in full view of the mother. This was the other phone-in topic. People were calling in and making sick jokes about it, some of them were. "I spit on you people, I spit on you," said the announcer, a new one, who couldn't tell an urban legend when he heard one. It must have been Gay Byrne's day off.

So the new guy changed the subject and offered a little prize to whomever could phone in with the year George Washington became president of the United States. He finally gave the prize to the closest guess: 1342.

The people of Cork still fish off the low-slung, slender bridges over the River Lee as it bends its way through town, and they eat their catch, too. I wandered around the crowded streets and kept seeing people who reminded me of people I knew in Canada. There's Annie, except twenty years younger. Or there's what Stan would look like without his beard.

A woman outside the post office was saying to a man: "You don't know a horse's head from its bottom." They must have been listening to the phone-in show.

An old man with a deceptively kind face, who was running a little men's-wear store, gave me directions to the tourist office. He took me by the arm, ushered me out into the rain, and said, "It's either the third block on the right and then on the left or the second on the left and then on the right." And then he gave me a little push and said, "Sorry I can't help you any more." He must go bonkers when the tourist season starts.

In the tourist office, I mentioned how glad I was to find one open, most being closed this time of year.

"Ach, it's all money, ye know," said the woman waiting on me.

"Ireland's a poor country. Its time hasn't come yet."

"If it ever will."

I bought a book of six walking tours and took every one, in the rain, alone, and following the maps carefully. I went into a discount clothing store and got a new motoring cap for two pounds, the old one having been lost at Dublin Zoo. The old one had been Harris tweed, the new one a much-more-appropriate Donegal tweed, lighter and more waterproof. To be truthful, it's imitation Donegal tweed, a polyester blend made in Castlebar, way up in County Mayo.

The massive Butter Exchange had been built to last, with four Greek columns at the portico and beautifully laid Cork limestone blocks. But it's no longer used for storing butter; it's now the Cork County Craft Centre. In a narrow street in a rundown area I came upon a splendid, round Georgian-style building and asked two women in aprons and pincurls who were standing on the corner chatting away what it was.

"It's the Irish National Ballet," they said. "It's the home of the ballet. They rehearse and things like that, and they perform there. It's their home."

"Do you ever attend the performances?"

"Have done," said one.

"You have?" said the other.

"Sure."

"When?"

"Well, not for a while to be true to you."

As I walked away, they were saying, "Why did you embarrass me like that in front of that nice American man?"

"You know I hate it when you lie like that, bare-faced like. You've never been to no friggin' ballet."

"But to embarrass me like that in front of an American man."

In a mood for listening to people talk, I walked into a pub and, lo and behold, the bartender was a big talker, a man with the tongue of a poet. It occurred to me, being proud of my new hat – a more sensible and sleeker hat than those which were designed for the export market and cost five times as much – that in wearing such a cap I was saying I like it here.

The bartender did glance at my hat, not with the excessive display of admiration I was hoping for, but certainly with a small flash of approval. He was in his early thirties, a short, stocky fellow who probably played a lot of football. He was very upbeat and had no problems being Irish. His mind was far from the Troubles, yet he was troubled. A bright, complex, sensitive man and his name was Myles Coogan.

"Ach, it's an incredible old country, indeed, Ireland," he said as he set down my pint. "Every country in the world, for instance Canada, is full of Irish people. They have ancestors buried in Ireland, like. You take Australia, exiled convicts, you know how that worked. Take the Americans, all over America they have the third-, fourth-, fifth-generation Irish. It's amazing. It's something very peculiar to the Irish race of people."

"Have you been abroad?"

"Oh yes, quite a few times. And when we Irish go away, we become very conscious of our own country, Ireland, back home."

"Like James Joyce." My interjections were designed to show I was listening with a bit of IQ.

"Yes indeed." His eyes were starting to go a little manic as he shifted into high. "And not only about the heritage, like conscious of that, you know – of what we left behind. But it transposes itself into work as well, you see now? I know from my time in the States and my time travelling around in other countries how incredibly well the Irish get along away from home."

"With each other you mean?"

"Well, maybe that too. But no, I was meaning to say the Irish when they go abroad they prosper, they truly do. People who do little or nothing back at home, they go to America and work their butt off. And some, many in fact, become very influential, be it in politics or be it in business."

"What do you think it is?"

"It's something quite unique, it is. When I was in the States I had three jobs per day, or I mean to say all at the same time. So I could have enough money to put myself through college. Over here I own this business —"

"The pub."

"You got it. And I'm a qualified engineer. An awful lot of people in this country don't like working, but when they go abroad they, as I say, they work their butt off."

"The fabled dreaminess or spirituality of Ireland makes them feel like sitting around loafing all the time?"

"Well, if that's true they get a rude awakening when they go to America. But maybe it's that when you're in Ireland you always feel that your friends and your family will look after you. It's an ancient tradition. And when you're in America you're on your own, and you wake up in a hurry and start working hard. That's just a thought, I don't know."

"A good thought. Might have thought it myself but you beat me to it. And as soon as you get in America you know all the money you make goes to yourself and not to support the unemployed members of your family, and you forget about the burden of Irish history and the burden of being Irish and it liberates your energies."

"Well, I don't know about all that. But America has always been looked upon as the Land of Opportunity. I've been in the States six times in total. I've often regretted the day I came back."

"Why did you?"

"I get homesick over there, and when I come back home I soon get sick of home."

"Well put."

"Thank you."

"You're describing a common ailment."

"I know. You know, you're right. History is debilitating. It's good to be free of it."

"To wake up from the nightmare of it."

"And the only way is to leave home."

"You mean go to America."

"Whatever."

Just then a big chunk of the ceiling fell down and landed right on the bar. The bartender pushed the mess aside and kept on talking. "What I want to tell you is that we have a class system in this country. I've really thought about this. In America you're really respected for the work you do. Now, whether you realize it or not – I mean it's not obvious to outsiders and it's not obvious to a lot of people inside the country either – but it exists. The class system, I mean."

"Buncha bloody snobs."

"Right. You've got it."

"Same as everywhere."

He didn't like it when I said that. Ireland was special.

"Maybe same like everywhere, to a certain extent, but you know, like, say you grew up on a farm here. Or say you went into the building trades. Now, irrespective of how successful you may become in your life, to a certain degree you're frowned upon."

"To a certain degree."

"Yes, by people who have gone to college. Like, by the white-collar workers. In the States, it's different. It's not the colour of your collar, it's the colour of your cash."

"Again, sir, well put."

"Thank you. These things just pop out."

"Never said that before?"

"Not that I remember."

"Heard it before?"

"Definitely not. I always strive for originality in my utterances."

"Well here, let me write it down. What was it again?"

I went to the toilet, and when I got back he was saying, "It's what you have in your pockets that counts. That's how I usually say it, I guess. You must have inspired me to new heights of poetic fervour."

"Grandeur."

"That's a good word."

"I'm your muse."

"I thought you looked familiar."

I suggested that the class system in the States is something that you don't notice right away, you have to live it out. Just as the various class snobberies in Ireland weren't all that obvious to me yet. "It's not that I disagree with you about Ireland, but is it all that unique?"

He thought it was, and he was convinced there was no class system in the States. He went on about garbagemen being respected over there but looked down upon in Ireland, and about degrees, and plasterers and bricklayers, corporate salaries relative to the cost of living, exchange rates . . .

"I was working for a consulting engineer firm on a pipeline contract. For the first six months I didn't have a day off. In the States there's a real incentive to really work. You get recognized for the work you do. The harder you work the more you make."

"Got it."

"Supplementing your income with an extra job, do you know what we call that in Cork?"

"What?"

"We call it foxing. Doing foxes. I don't know what you call it in Canada."

"Moonlighting."

"Moonlighting. Here it's called foxing. In Dublin, it's called nixing. Part-time work. You go into a place like and you say: 'You have any old foxes going?' I used to do an awful lot of foxing to supplement my income."

"What do they call it in Belfast?"

"Oh Lord, I wouldn't know."

"Probably moonlighting."

"Moonlighting, now. Isn't that what they called selling beer in the days when it was illegal?"

"Prohibition, that was. No, they called that, uh, oh Jesus . . ."

"Moonshining," yelled out a drinker sitting by himself at the other end of the bar. I hadn't noticed him, but he'd apparently been following the conversation.

"No, not moonshining," I said. "That's what they called operating an illegal still. Bootlegging, that's the word. That's what they called selling booze illegally. Making it, moonshining. Selling it, bootlegging. What did they call it here?"

"Can't think now. Eh, you know we have poteen here."

My eyes went wide as saucers.

"Here? At the pub?"

"Well no, but here in Ireland."

"Oh." My eyes went back to normal. "I've read about it, but I haven't had a taste yet."

"It's rare weird stuff. Its quality varies from where it's been brewed."

"It's still illegal, of course."

"Oh yeah. It clears out the system. The West of Ireland is renowned for it. The hills of Kerry. The hills of Connemara. Up in

Galway. So if you get a chance to get some. I don't know if you're going over to the West of Ireland . . ."

He showed me the improvements he'd done to the pub, including opening up a new back room with an imitation Victorian fireplace, all done up as if it and the entire room had been perfectly maintained and in constant use since the days of Dickens.

And as I was leaving he warned me about the bed-and-breakfast two-price scam.

"It's depending on your accent. It's disgusting. It happens and it's not right."

EVERYDAY LIFE IN
RATH LUIRC

The first pub I tried in Rath Luirc, there was a huge crush of people. An onstage crooner, swaying and dipping with a hand-held mike, was singing an off-key *a cappella* version of "Battle Hymn of the Republic." The second pub was quieter, so I booked into one of the rooms on the second floor, went down to the kitchen and gave Lourdes Brasil a call to make arrangements to meet back in Dublin, then went out front to the pub for a pint.

Rath Luirc (a.k.a. Charleville) was a small town with a big-town feel. It was on the County Limerick/County Cork border, on a line that ran straight south from Limerick City to Cork City. It was in an area of creameries, abattoirs, and cheese factories.

At the next barstool was a man who had spent his entire forty-seven years in Rath Luirc. Tyrone McGuckian was a rather effeminate-looking fellow, slight of build, very well-groomed, with rosy cheeks, a long pointy nose, long hair gelled straight back, and a lovely knitted sweater over a white shirt and carefully knotted tie. I thought he might be the church organist, but no, this leprechaun was spending his life working in the Golden Vale cheese factory.

I told him about my Irish friend Bill Hogan, whom I was hoping to visit in his little two-man cheese factory in Skibbereen, and who was so serious a cheesemaker that he was forever travelling the world checking out various aspects of the trade. He was busy trying to revive mediaeval cheesemaking techniques.

Tyrone didn't seem all that keen on the story. He apparently took a more humdrum attitude toward his job.

Meanwhile, the bartender seemed to have developed a concern for my welfare. She had overheard my phone conversation with Lourdes. She also knew I was thinking of going back to the noisy pub at midnight because some Irish singers were going to come on and there was going to be dancing.

"If you have to meet her tomorrow, you'd better not go dancing tonight."

I agreed with this sagacious and well-intentioned piece of advice, even though I wasn't actually planning to dance, just to watch and listen. It was nice that she cared.

"It's probably cottage cheese he makes," said Mr. McGuckian.

It wasn't cottage cheese my friend Bill Hogan made, but it was a cottage industry, so I didn't argue.

"I thought all you cheese fellows would know each other."

"No, not necessarily."

"What kind of cheese do you make?"

"Processed cheese. We bring it in from Europe and melt it down."

Out of the blue he started rattling off all the countries of Europe and their capitals, then all the provinces of Canada and states of the United States.

"Is this your favourite pub?"

"One of them," he said. "One of the four."

"How many are there in town?"

"Four."

Maybe he didn't have a very responsible job at the cheese factory, and he might have felt a little miffed by my references to Bill Hogan travelling the world. So he put on his hat and said he had to get home to his wife and kids.

"How many kids?"

"Six."

"Good heavens! How many wives?"

"Just the one."

He somehow didn't have the air of a family man, and I told him so. He took his hat off again and began reciting his old school lessons about Irish history. He said he was joking about the wife and kids. He was single. He said he lived alone in a little house in town, and grew a few carrots, tomatoes, and dahlias in the garden out back.

"The Normans invaded England in 1066," he said. "I can't figure out how Ireland, being only a stone's throw from England, it took them a hundred years to come here."

"They'd heard what fierce warriors you guys were."

"Were is right. And it's a mystery too about the Romans. They conquered Britain, but never tried over here."

"The Romans were a gutless bunch."

I asked him who his favourite historical figure was.

"Wolfe Tone and Robert Emmet. We talk about them all the time."

"Now they were gutsy guys."

"Oh, for dead sure."

We talked about the tit-for-tat killings. A Derry Loyalist had been killed the night before, shot right in front of his wife.

"That sort of thing doesn't exactly have very wide support on either side, does it?"

"It doesn't."

"And you personally don't approve of it?"

"No. Too cold-blooded."

"Do you know anyone who does approve of this sort of thing?"

"Personally? Oh yes, I do. A few. Definitely."

He offered me a King Edward cigar and apologized that it wasn't a Havana. He wanted to know if this was my first trip to Ireland and if I was playing the lotteries. All of a sudden I noticed a half-comatose Scotsman at the end of the bar. He'd apparently been there all along, quietly dozing. He woke up and said, slurringly, "This is the quietest pub I ever seen in my life. Och, I'm leaving."

He got up and stumbled. I helped him to the door. But before we got there, the door was opened from outside and a crowd of happy revellers burst in, most of them in their sixties and seventies. The Scotsman decided to stumble back to the bar, asked for another drink, and was politely refused service.

"How come all these people just came in at once?" I said to Mr. McGuckian. "Is the bingo over?"

"No, they always come in this time of night."

The bartender knew exactly what everyone drank and started pouring without being asked. Later she said to me, "This Scotsman, I never seen the like of it. He's on his holidays. He has two weeks. He decides to come to Ireland, and he's been in this pub every night for the past ten days. Just comes in, has about three pints, and becomes completely incoherent, then passes out."

I was feeling a little woozy myself, and I couldn't understand what the older people were talking about so happily, so I went up to bed.

"God bless you," a little old lady drinking Guinness called out as I stumbled towards the stairs. "Sleep tight and don't let the bugs bite."

"Bugs?" I looked startled. Several people started laughing.

"It's just a saying, dear," she said.

After I got to my room, I thought about it for a minute in a boozy fog, then sneaked out, jumped out the window onto the back shed like a rebellious suburban teenager so the meddlesome bartender wouldn't scold me, then hopped down to the ground and ran off to the dance.

The featured singer, Susan McCann, well known in Irish music circles, was supposed to be on at midnight. But already it was well after midnight, and Susan hadn't appeared yet. In fact the place was deserted, except for the crooner who had been crooning "Battle Hymn of the Republic" with mike in hand.

The crooner turned out to be the manager, or the bouncer, or both, and, in the most obnoxious manner, he demanded immediate payment of five pounds. I asked him if he had ever heard the AngloCanadian term "go fuck yourself."

"Why you —"

He made a lunge for me and, in self-defence, I gave him a whack on the back of the neck. Back in my room, after climbing back up on the shed, then back through the window, it was so cold by now I had to leave my cap on as I crawled under the covers. The papers had been reporting widespread crop damage.

I slept so soundly my hat didn't fall off once all night. At any rate it was on my head when I woke up, looked at my watch, and remembered that this was the day I was to pick up Lourdes Brasil. I was apprehensive, but it had been a lonely two weeks (sort of) and she was so friendly (or seemed to be). She'd been very excited, on the phone, about getting out of Dublin. She was the sort of clear-eyed and intelligent woman whose instincts are (almost) impossible to distrust.

Lying there, I began to wonder about the sheets, and considered asking if they got washed ever. They didn't smell all that clean. In the bathroom there were piles of old hair and dirt in the bathtub, and old towels, mouldy bathing goggles and caps, worn-out toothbrushes, and assorted verminous stains in every corner. I bundled everything up and threw it in the garbage, including the horrible rubber bathtub mat, the little suction cups of which were caked with matted hair and general filth.

By the time I had the place cleaned up, there wasn't enough hot water for a warm shower, so I took a cold one.

At breakfast a tall, handsome, prosperous-looking gentleman about forty, dressed in a black pin-striped suit, black oxfords, beige tie, and blindingly white shirt, wanted me to know he was no local yokel. I was thinking he was probably a senator.

"I've travelled all over Ireland and I've even been to America," he said. "To Albany, New York, to be precise." He'd also taken a side trip to Niagara Falls and managed to spend an hour on the Canadian side – just to say he'd been there. He said he preferred Canada to the United States because Canada had more flowers. "People care about flowers in Canada," he said. "It's much more beautiful. For me, Canada is the land of flowers."

He proudly announced that he had the Ireland-wide franchise for Kirby Products, and was incredulous that I didn't know Kirby Products from Popsicle sticks. It was quite shocking, since Kirby Products were manufactured in Cleveland. And certain of the parts were made across the lake in Ontario, right where I lived. Besides, Kirby Products had been selling well all over North America since 1916. Where had I been?

"A Kirby is sort of an all-purpose . . . well, it just takes care of the house, if you know what I mean." He wasn't sure how to describe it, because he'd never met anyone before who needed a description. Apparently it was some kind of an elaborate vacuum cleaner, but he didn't pin it down to that. I told him I led a Bohemian, nomadic lifestyle and wasn't very domestic. I wouldn't know a vacuum cleaner from a snowblower.

This man was very impetuous. He had finished his breakfast, and even though I was still in the middle of mine, he insisted that I immediately leave the table, go up to my room, rummage in my luggage, and bring down my maps of Ireland. He wanted to scribble things on the maps, notes for my travels, things I should be sure not to miss, wonderful places to have delicious seafood pancakes.

He had to leave right away, but he would do me this favour, since I was obviously a very sad case, never having heard of Kirby Products – or seafood pancakes for that matter – and practically being from America myself, where all these things got invented by gangs of expatriate Irishmen. He forced me to solemnly promise, with hand on heart, to take the cable car at Dursey Island.

Since he had to leave right away, I abandoned my eggs and sprinted up to get the maps. While up there, I made a quick check of the bathroom, and someone had put the rubber mat back in the tub, without cleaning it, and the tub was all full of matted hair again. Perhaps I wasn't the only one not to have heard of Kirby Products.

Everywhere I went, people wanted to scribble on my maps, and it was hard to say no. They were just trying to be kind. The Kirby Products fellow thought I should leave immediately for County Donegal, then work my way south along the West Coast. This seemed irrational. I said wouldn't it be better to go up the coast and leave Donegal for last – in the Morton manner?

"No," he said, with the impeccable logic of the born poet. "If you do that you'll never leave Kerry, it's so beautiful."

An hour or so later, on the Limerick bypass, a tall man standing beside a parked van flagged me down, walked up to me, and said, "You've a fair idea of Limerick, have you?" He wanted to get to Naas. He looked a little haggard and hung over, as I'm sure I did as well.

"I know it's around here somewhere," he said, "but I can't find a sign saying Naas for the life of me."

I warned him that I was only a tourist but I was pretty darned sure Naas wasn't around here, that you had to go all the way across the country to Dublin and then hang a right.

"Dublin! Oh God, what an ass I am. Of course, Naas is just outside of Dublin, I knew that just as sure as I'm standing here, I've always known that, even when I was a little gaffer I bloody well knew that. But for some bloody damned-fool reason I was thinking it was just outside of Limerick. I've driven hours and hours out of my way now. I'll never get there in time now. I'll have to phone them and tell them I'll be there tomorrow."

I felt so sorry for the man. What a tragedy for him! I told him that was the toughest story I'd heard since that girl in the Dublin paper whose hair gel exploded when she lit a cigarette and she lost all her hair including eyebrows and suffered terrible burns to her face.

He looked at me strangely. He said he remembered that story and thought there was something fishy about it. There were no follow-up stories on her condition, for one thing.

"I think she was protecting someone, I do," he said, with a solemn air. He leaned toward me so close I could tell he hadn't brushed his teeth in weeks. "It wasn't gel at all. I think she was protecting her husband. He was a sadistic brute, I'll bet, and they had a fight and he held her head over the stove."

"You mean over the gas stove with the jets going?"

"Exactly."

"You don't mean it."

"Ach, I do. I definitely do."

"Whew. You seem to know what you're talking about."

"I know what goes on behind closed doors in this country."

"Why would that be?"

"Well, my friend. You see, I should be but I'm not wearing my clerical collar right now. But I'm a priest, and people tell me things. And sometimes I feel as if I'm about to explode."

"People tell me things too, father."

A roaring fire was warming the Four Seasons Cabaret. Two fellows were playing Irish eightball, using solid, unnumbered yellow and red balls. I looked out the window. Whatever the weather had been like when I pulled in, it was different already. In fact it had started to snow a bit. In March in Ireland you get four seasons every day.

Out front, two fellows appeared out of the blue and started building a stone wall. It was lovely to see such things still going on. But they were putting on too much mortar, and too thick, and they weren't bothering to consider the shape of the stones. In a hundred years the mortar would crumble and the wall would fall apart.

I'd been told Michael Quinlan the schoolteacher was the one who knew everything there was to know about Lough Gur. Unfortunately, he was often too busy to offer tours, but he could pass you on to someone who could offer you one.

We chatted on the phone for a while, and I said I'd call him again when I was back in the area. I didn't have much time before picking up Lourdes. People through the centuries have enthused ecstatically about the beauty of this wonderful lake, a short hop south of Limerick, and the antiquities surrounding it. Particularly impressive was the Lios, a stone circle billed as the largest in Ireland. It's forty-five feet in diameter, and the stones are placed contiguously – shoulder to shoulder – all the way around. The largest stone is a thickset brute eight feet tall. Shards uncovered within the circle suggest that at one time pottery was ceremoniously shattered at the site.

"What's this called?" I said to the tall, handsome, shy, young fellow behind the counter, obviously a devoted family man and all-around nice guy. I had picked up from the counter a partially deflated football of bread and raisins.

The fellow blushed and blurted out, "S-s-s-spotted Dick." Of course. That was it. I knew it had an unusual name.

"We've got a pub in Toronto by that name. The Spotted Dick."

"Run by an Irishman, no doubt."

"I'm not sure. Probably Irish, or some Englishman who wants people to think he's Irish."

"Not too many Englishmen like that around, as far as I know."

"Oh, we get a lot of unusual Englishmen in Canada. But anyway, how come it's called Spotted Dick?"

I ripped off an end and started chewing on it after having placed a pound note on the counter. The fellow looked as if he'd never seen anyone eating a Spotted Dick without butter and jam, and without cutting off a neat piece with a good, sharp, wet serrated knife. The man's an animal, he seemed to be thinking. But he recovered his poise and became perfectly eloquent.

"One day back around 1641 or 2 a woman somewhere, probably in Tralee or maybe Rath Luirc or some place like that, made a raisin loaf, but she made it unusually long and thin, for no particular reason, just absentmindedly, or by mistake, just as chance would have it. And when her husband got home he said it looked like a Spotted Dick, so she burst into tears, you know the way women are. She sobbed for hours, and when she recovered she told her friends about it and, you guessed it, soon everybody was laughing and calling it Spotted Dick."

"Even her?"

"I would imagine so, even her."

"And it just sorta grew from there?"

"Well, yes, so to speak. It just sorta grew from there. Though its official name is still Raisin Bread."

I later remembered that Spotted Dick was something different in England, a kind of suet pudding with raisins. Same idea though.

Lough Gur was surrounded by farmland and tiny villages, with little patches of ground set aside for the standing stones, wedge-shaped graves, magnificent stone circles, and other awesome souvenirs of great antiquity. Signs everywhere said "Land Poisoned," which helped to create an atmosphere of unfriendliness.

One wedge-shaped grave consisted of four capstones surmounting a series of small standing stones, in a little hillside copse of trees, offering a pleasant view of the lake. Pleasant? All views of this lake are heavenly. To live quietly at the side of such a lake for the rest of one's life. Ah! What a blissful thought!

The grave had been known for centuries as the Giant's Grave. But when the bramble was chopped away and the grave excavated in 1988 it was found to contain the remains of eight adults and four children, circa 2000 B.C.

What a heavenly spot, though. In Ireland, as elsewhere, the megalithic monuments are always found in places of ideal natural beauty.

DROOPING
RHODODENDRONS

Lourdes was dressed adorably in a brown leather bomber jacket and black leather skin-tight trousers. On her head was a bright yellow Hamilton Tiger-Cat painter's cap, which startled me, since Hamilton was my home town – a coincidence to be sure. She had one small brown corduroy shoulder bag. She was eager to see the country and had the knack of travelling light.

Lourdes was full of questions as we drove north from Dublin into the fabled Boyne Valley. As we were browsing in Shortall's Souvenirs and Fancy Goods, in the town of Slane, she wanted to know what this saying meant: "As the twig is bent so grows the tree." As I tried to explain, a large lorry went hurtling down the main street of town with two wide-eyed little boys sitting up high in the passenger seat.

An abandoned petrol station had "Brits Out" scrawled on the flaking wall.

In Ireland a lot of fellows on the down and out, people who hadn't worked for decades and had no money, still wore suits. Old beat-up suits to be sure, but nevertheless suits.

"Once their Sunday best, now their best, period," said Lourdes.

On the Irish style of driving, she noted that the pace of Ireland is slow but the pace of driving is breakneck.

"The Irish drive like this to show that they are sophisticated," she said, "that they're not tourists, they have lots of things to do in a hurry, and they have been to maybe even America."

Already I was pleased to have her along. I couldn't stop smiling and turning to look at her admiringly. I mentioned that in North America the pace is fast, but it's considered cool to drive slowly. In Canada, at least, the women tend to drive like madmen and the men drive like little old ladies.

"In Spain also, but here driving fast means being sophisticated. Hey, look how fast I'm driving, this means I'm no fool. I'm a man of action. I've got places to go and things to do."

Lourdes liked the accident markers. A black spot the size of a pie plate on a white square meant there'd been a serious accident there. We had taken a wrong turn and found ourselves on the N1, one of the few highways in Ireland illuminated at night. The lights were red and yellow – just like the balls in Irish eightball – and were arranged randomly. There was a yellow, another yellow, a red, another red, a yellow, a burnt-out, another burnt-out, a red, a burnt-out . . .

There were signs saying "Cyclists Give Way to Buses."

"Let's hope so," said Lourdes.

"Your English has improved tremendously in a mere two weeks!"

"Let's hope so, again. I've been working very very hard on it."

We took a room near Drogheda, above a pub called the Poitín Still (*poitín* a variant spelling for poteen). On the wall was a reproduction of a religious painting, called *Mary, Queen of the Universe*, showing Mary surrounded by angels, with a crescent moon in the sky.

From a fresh pair of green boxer shorts I removed the "Now Perfect Fit" sticker, a black oval with white lettering. There was a perfect spot for it on the painting. I pressed it on neatly and smoothed it out with care, so that it resembled another angel. It would be years, if ever, before anyone noticed it.

In the morning we visited Duleek Abbey, built in 1186 on the site of a fifth-century church. Lourdes excitedly got out my field glasses. It was a handsome building in a poor state of repair. Even the eighteenth-century church next to it was an awful mess. You could see where there had been a round tower, about eighty-five feet high, then a square tower next to it had been built which incorporated the round tower, and then the round tower had been dismantled, leaving its image on the side of the square tower. Maybe the round tower just started falling apart from pressure from the square tower, and the locals started picking up the stones and carting them away for fence building and what not, and eventually nothing was left.

There was even a trace of what had apparently been a passageway between the square tower and the round tower.

"I've never seen anything like it before," said Lourdes. "It's like the round tower was removed on purpose."

The Boyne Valley was streaked with orange light. By the time we got to Newgrange, a hailstorm had broken out. We sought refuge in a little tea shop. The gates to Newgrange were inexplicably closed. A dowager with hair drawn back in a tight bun stood on the other side of the gate smirking at us.

"Closing a little early, are we?"

"No, we definitely are not. The last tour of the morning is finished," she sing-songed menacingly, her teeth flashing like little Saxon knives.

"Take good care of the tombs now."

"Don't you worry about that."

In the tiny tea shop as we sat drinking tea, Lourdes admitted I'd embarrassed her a bit with my attitude towards the old broad.

"In Spain there's a saying, you're not supposed to be ironic with people you don't know."

I agreed, and suggested even worse sometimes is saying something innocently and have it be taken ironically. I took her gentle criticism as a sign of friendship. She felt comfortable with me.

The tea shop was behind a small, old-fashioned rural general store. To go to the washroom you went through a large room at the back, which was apparently the meeting hall for, among other things, the Irish Country Women's Association.

On the wall were framed prayers and stirring nationalistic poems. One started off with the lines: "Dear land of ours / so rare and wild."

A fellow of about eighteen had an old battered motorcycle helmet on a table covered with newspapers and was painting it white. I asked him about the massive indentations on the helmet and expressed the hope that the guy whose head it had been on hadn't been killed. He didn't want to say, but it became apparent he'd found it at the dump, or paid fifty pence for it at the pub. He was doing a good job of disguising it with paint, though it would have been better if he'd tried to sand it down a bit first.

"I probably shouldn't be doing this. But it's just for me scooter."

A very large, happy lady in her late forties brought in some ham sandwiches on white and a pot of tea. There were stacks of wonderful loaves of fresh country brown bread around, and Irish soda bread as well. But after all we were tourists, so we would like our bread white. The sandwiches were cut into neat triangles and laid on a lace doily, with English mustard. She hadn't cut the crusts off.

On the wall in the tearoom were two identical decorated plates, each showing the same image of John Fitzgerald Kennedy looking thoughtful and Jackie Kennedy looking supportive. There was also a kind of birchbark painting in a terrible state of repair, apparently showing some rural scene, possibly Canadian.

There was a reproduction of a lesser-known version of the *Last Supper*, from the cathedral of Oostende. And a reproduction of a saint with his dog: the saint looking up at the six-starred halo around his head, and his halo-less dog looking up at it, too.

There was a photo of a little smiling boy, prematurely aged, wearing a black armband and short pants. Another little boy with a suit and some kind of red ribbon on his lapel had obviously won something and was pleased.

I took Lourdes's hand in mine briefly (and hopefully) as we stood reading "True Friendship," a framed poem:

> *True friendship doesn't fade away*
> *As rainbows in the sky*
> *But stays secure whate'er the task*
> *Grows strong as time goes by.*
> *Hold out your hand, a smile create*
> *And then you'll surely see*
> *Your hand is clasped, your smile returned*
> *For that's how friendship be.*

At the bottom of the poem someone had delicately painted a picture of a nest with three newly laid robin's eggs in it and surrounded by flowers. There was also a picture of Oliver Plunkett with an elaborate legend that read, in part:

> Blessed Oliver Plunkett, the Primate of All Ireland. Canonized Saint Oliver Plunkett on 12 October 1975. Beheaded 1681 at Tyburn London for the faith. Beatified 23rd May 1920. . . . Begging you to add your powerful intercession to our humble prayers.

On the far wall was a humble imitation-marble fireplace, three feet high and three feet wide, with a load of firewood and rolled-up papers ready to be lit. On the mantel a framed colour photo showed an elderly Irish couple sitting on a little sofa.

"Would you be wanting me to light the fire?" said the proprietress.

She said she had a brother-in-law in Carrick-on-Shannon who was always writing her and saying how it was always warm down there. In fact she had been down, and it was warm all right.

We complimented her on the thick slabs of tomato in the ham sandwiches.

"They come all the way from the Canary Islands, and they are very expensive, those tomatoes."

"How expensive?"

"A pound a pound."

We all smiled. I grabbed my copy of *Ireland: The Rough Guide* and gave her the Irish for Carrick-on-Shannon: *Cora Droma Riasc*, the Weir of the Marshy Ridge.

A sad look came to her face.

"Ah, that's lovely, that is," she said. "We've lost our Irish, and that's the tragedy of it."

She left the room. I must have done a good job in the pronunciation department.

The sun came out as we were eating and the storm abated, but by the time we had paid up and were getting back in the car it had become overcast again and the wind and rain were picking up. A few early-blooming red rhododendrons around the side of the building were looking a little droopy. In the midst of a freezing horizontal sleet storm we climbed a few hills and felt droopy ourselves, in spite of the tea and ham sandwiches sloshing in our tummies. We climbed a few fences and snooped around some off-limits excavations.

Newgrange was on a long slope sweeping north from the river. Knowth was to the northwest of Newgrange, further from the river. And Dowth was to the northeast and further still from the river. These megalithic tombs, the largest to be unearthed so far in Europe, formed a large triangle, each point of which was aligned with the rising sun at the spring equinox.

Knowth, which has been dated to 3700 B.C., and which contains a tunnel one hundred feet long aligned with the rising sun, was completely closed up, pending the completion of excavations and

eventual restructuring, as had been done at Newgrange. The exca-
vators were apparently finding a lot of stuff they had never dreamed
of, but it was hard to get any information. It was turning out to be a
lot richer than Newgrange, because it had apparently never been
plundered.

There was an observation tower for people to watch the work in
progress, but there was no work in progress, and you couldn't see much
except the mound all covered with tarpaulins, old truck tires lying
around, and overturned wheelbarrows. They were going to resume
excavations when the weather improved.

Dowth was closed, too, but there were no excavations going on. So
we climbed over the locked iron gate and walked around. We didn't
feel right about climbing to the top of the mound. The entrances to
the underground chambers were barred with locked gates.

The entire Boyne Valley was one frigid storm after another, with
the hail piling up on the ground in drifts like snow. So we decided to
set off for the West, to Galway, where better weather had been
reported. I also wanted to get back on Morton's route. We planned to
return to this area later, and to visit the nearby Hill of Tara, the
ancient capital of Ireland, when the weather improved. With a car
you were never far from any place in Ireland.

As we drove along, we would run into nice weather and decide to
stop to look at some old church or something, and the storm would
strike again, with gale-force winds and poor visibility.

I couldn't stand it any longer; I asked Lourdes where she got the
Hamilton Tiger-Cat painter's cap. She said a guest at the hotel had
left it behind, and she'd appropriated it. I told her it was a coincidence
of high order that she should be wearing it, since my home town was
Hamilton.

TROUBLE IN TINKERTOWN

Lourdes had a strong Spanish accent, but had also been developing an idiomatic Irish way of putting things. "They dress well, the Irish," she observed. "They have very nice suits." She'd been flipping through my heavily marked copy of Morton on the way across the country, and, after reading his rhapsodic descriptions of Galway, she found the place a bit disappointing.

"Galway's not as beautiful as Morton claims," she said.

She said she had read Morton's book on Spain, and it wasn't to her taste. She figured the art of being a tourist was to dress and act in such a way that no one would immediately peg you as a tourist. If you looked like a tourist, she declared, people would shy away from you. Tourists made people nervous. You have to look a bit mysterious and intriguing if you want to meet the natives. Tourists are so boring. They buzz into town and immediately want to see what you've never bothered going to see all the years you've lived there. Tourists are stupid, because they have the effrontery to make the locals feel stupid.

Tourists tend to look as if they're holding their breath all the time. And they tend to have what the Irish call "Saxon smiles" on their faces – the forced smile as deadly weapon.

"Look, everybody hates tourists," she said. "That's the bottom line. They're a nuisance, they have prejudices, they don't do their homework, they don't read up on the place. And they ask stupid questions, and when you start to answer them they don't listen, they fade out."

"Glad we're not like that."

Galway was a mini-version of Cork, vaguely Italian in look, with lots of fine stone walls, iron gates, courtyards, old pubs, bridges, seafood places, hotels, sea air. Mrs. Quilty of the Mullet Bottom Hotel, when we booked in, saw a sympathetic look in my eye or Lourdes's eye and started complaining that she wouldn't wish this job on anyone, the hours were too long. She was an attractive woman, pushing forty, with a look of comically ironic acceptance of her own ambivalence. She kept chuckling merrily as she spoke of her misery.

She was interested in Lourdes and me, what we were up to, and a little unsure of her own role in life, halfway between independence and subservience. We didn't notice at first that she was pregnant.

"Long hours, but a lot of fun, right?"

She looked as if she were having fun, at least at that moment.

"Well," she said, "you certainly meet unusual and interesting people from all over the world."

"Nice people?"

"Not necessarily."

She said she liked people, fortunately, since she was stuck in this job, and she particularly liked people who liked people, and she had us slotted in that category. She gave us a large room with a large fireplace and a large bathroom en suite, all very inexpensive. A series of oversized windows all around offered panoramic views of the town and out over Galway Bay to the Aran Islands – delicate light-filled watercolour strokes on the horizon – where the playwright John Millington Synge went, at the turn of the century, to study Irish.

Synge observed in his book *The Aran Islands* that most of the people who came to the islands came to "study Irish, so that the Aran islanders have been led to conclude that linguistic studies, particularly Gaelic studies, are the chief occupation of the outside world." In fact he quotes an islander as saying, "Believe me, there are few rich men now in the world who are not studying the Gaelic."

But since I was following Morton rather than Synge, my desire to get to the Aran Islands was not great. Morton had not gone there, and there was enough rain and rock and mud on the mainland to suit me.

This was a lovely old hotel, with dining rooms, assembly halls, weirdly interconnecting corridors, strangely varied views from every window, surprising pieces of antique furniture here and there, patches of interesting wallpaper, plastering, and shelving, wonderful old prints on the walls. The by-now-long-dead tradesmen who did the plastering and carpentry had been skilled in the old school.

Some nineteenth-century prints showed the Claddagh of Galway, about which I'd been reading – make that misreading, as I was soon to find out – in Morton, but which was apparently no more.

"The Claddagh, now that is where the Tinkers live, is it not?" I asked Mrs. Quilty's husband, Mr. Quilty, who had heard some laughter, popped his head in, then taken over from his wife.

"Oh, no!" He looked stricken. He couldn't believe his ears. He had a serious look on his face – one of those Irish faces not meant to look serious – as if it was a pity that I had been so misled. He'd be telling this story for the rest of his life. Gad, the things tourists say. He wished he knew the name of the villainous blackguard who had so scandalously fed me such vile misinformation.

"No? But it used to be?"

"Oh, no!" He put his hands over his ears, closed his eyes, and held his breath for several agonizing seconds. Then he calmed down and spoke slowly and softly, as if to a child. "They were old Galway, those people of the Claddagh. Real old Galway people. They were fishermen, mostly. They were never – Tinkers. The Tinkers were itinerant. The Claddagh were a poorer class of people but they were never itinerant. They were mainly fishing people but never ever itinerants."

"They're highly regarded though, the Tinkers, right?"

He paused, shot a look at my eye to see if I was mad, then figured I was just misinformed. He seemed to be saying to himself there were two kinds of tourist: the uninformed and the misinformed.

"Well, they're trying to settle them now, they are, settle them down permanent-like. But it'll take years. One girl has qualified as a teacher now. Some of them go to school. Some of them are educated."

"And they speak the Irish?"

"No. Some of them might, who go to school."

"How about the Claddagh people, do they speak the Irish?"

"They did years ago, but not too much now."

He said that a hundred years ago his great-grandfather didn't have the English, and the old guy's son, Mr. Quilty's grandfather, didn't have the Irish. That's how quickly things changed in the history of this country, full as it has been of dramatic turnabouts and tragedies. And yet they somehow understood each other perfectly. This sort of thing was common in Ireland in the nineteenth century.

And he spoke, as many others had, of how the priests beat him as a kid for making mistakes in Irish lessons, and he stopped learning it as soon as he could because of the bad taste the beatings gave him.

"And nobody looks down on the Claddagh people?"

"Oh God, no!"

"And nobody looks down on the Tinkers either?"

"Eh, not really. But they don't like them moving in beside them, either, you see."

"Why not?"

"They break in and they do damage. And they collect rubbish and dirt. And you know, they're untidy."

"Some people have been telling me that the Tinkers are very well thought of because they have a strict pre-Norman moral code and they never steal things, and —"

"Oh, but they do steal things! And at the moment now they're – a lot of them, that is – they're actually attacking old people living on their own and taking their furniture and that."

"No."

"Yes. Some of them are all right, but some of them are drinkers."

"It's poverty that drives them to it I bet."

"Oh no it's not. Because the government look after them so well. They all get the dole and they get all free medical aid. It's just the breed."

"Ah. People sort of think of them as if they were Gypsies?"

"Yes. They are really Gypsies. They don't brush their teeth, ever. And they let their animals roam."

"They do? I hadn't heard that."

"Oh yes, they do."

"What kind of animals? Old horses and ponies and donkeys?"

"Yes, some of them. And dogs."

The strain of talking about Tinkers seemed to be getting on Mr. Quilty's nerves, so I changed the subject by asking about an interesting-looking old painted board, sitting behind the front desk, with little numbered squares, one for each room.

He sighed with relief. "It's a relic from years ago," he said. "It doesn't work now. But we keep it there because it looks so nice. Actually you see them in hotels all over the Republic, you do. But they are now only decorative."

"They'd just be thrown out in Canada, because over there we don't have the same strong, instinctive feeling for the past."

"Now that's a pity."

"How would it have worked?"

"Well, you see, you would ring the buzzer in your room, and a little ball would fall into the square with your room number on it – and bingo!"

Mrs. Quilty came back in with a tall young boy and introduced him as their son Desmond. He was fifteen.

"Are you planning on taking up the hotel business, Desmond?"

He stammered shyly.

"No," said his mother. "We're just waiting for a rich American to buy . . . this hotel."

"Oh, I thought you were going to say to buy Desmond."

Desmond looked startled.

"Oh no, we'd never sell him."

"Does he have any career ambitions?"

"He loves . . . art and all that kind of stuff."

"Oh, he's the artistic type!"

"He's very good at still lifes."

"Well, I'll be darned. Are you going to go to art school, Desmond?"

"I hope to."

Galway is one of those cities that take on a different character at night. The narrow streets of Galway become charming and alluring after the sun sinks into the Atlantic behind Galway Bay. There are lots of interesting things to look at by the dim light from a distant streetlamp. The streets are under-illuminated, and the pub life is extraordinarily vibrant. Lourdes came for a walk with me. We stood in the middle of the bridge as the River Corrib in spring runoff roared down to Galway Bay. H. V. Morton was luckier. When he leaned over the same bridge, the salmon were running. I seem to remember him getting smacked in the face with one. And of course he managed to hang on to it, though not without immense difficulty, and he wound up giving it to a poor family to take home for dinner. What a guy, eh?

"The parapet of Galway Bridge is worn smooth as glass by the arms of those who lean over it when the salmon come up from salt water," Morton wrote. He added, oddly, "This is one of the sights of Ireland."

At McDonagh's, where we had fresh salmon, we ordered a pint of Guinness each, and the waitress said we'd have to go across the street to the pub to buy them and bring them back, owing to licensing regulations. The restaurant was only licensed to serve wine, but you could drink anything you brought in.

I went over to a crowded pub, the Quais, and brought two pints back to the restaurant. They were marked on the bottom, so at the end of the night they'd be sorted out and returned to the pub.

When we went back to the hotel, Mrs. Quilty was complaining of an ear blockage. Had she tried washing it out with a syringe?

"No, I have to do something about it soon, that's for sure."

"It's very unpleasant," said Lourdes.

"Oh it is. I've had it three weeks now, and I been coming and going."

"Is it from a cold?"

"No it is not."

"Is it infected?"

"No, it's not. Well, I am pregnant. And I guess the whole system breaks down. I was in hospital for a week with a hiatus hernia and also an ulcer."

"Did they fix you up?"

"No, they did not. They cannot. Not yet anyhow. It'll probably right itself afterwards."

"How far are you?"

"Six months. I have a seventeen-year-old and a fifteen-year-old, a ten and a seven. So this was a big surprise."

"Maybe this will be the one that will be a special comfort to you in your old age."

"By golly, I hope so. There's not much comfort now."

One in four elderly people were living in terror and afraid to open their doors at night, according to the front-page story in the Galway morning paper. Tinker trouble. But this smear campaign was balanced by a two-page photo story inside featuring Tinker women complaining of prejudice.

The elderly residents (non-Tinkers) were living in terror of itinerants (Tinkers, also known as Travellers, or sometimes Lazy Travellers, or Gypsies). A local boy had been savagely attacked by a dog (owned by Tinkers) and had to receive medical attention. Residents in the area of Clogheen had been plagued by an itinerant encampment since October and had demanded the removal of the itinerant families from the side of the road. The five itinerant families had harassed and intimidated the elderly. The children were afraid to pass Cappagh Cross because of the dangerous dogs and horses. Farmers were pestered by roaming goats, horses, and fowl.

This made me want to head back to Cahir and chat some more with Mr. Looney. What was going on here? How could I reconcile Mr. Looney's comments with all these news reports?

Oh yes, and public roads were used as toilets, and these people kept fowl which were used for cockfighting and vicious dogs which were used for dogfighting, both alleged to be an important part of Tinker cultural life.

The first of a series of scandals that would later force well-loved long-time prime minister Charles Haughey to resign hadn't broken yet. Haughey was still very popular. He was always delivering long Churchillian speeches on the radio. He was all set to become the first Irish prime minister to go to Belfast. What did Mrs. Quilty think of Haughey going to Belfast? When she talked politics, all her aches and pains seemed to disappear and she'd start breathing fire. But she was having problems finishing her thoughts. They sort of trailed off as new ones bubbled up to the surface of the simmering stew of her mind.

"Well, it's hard to keep a good man down. They can't stop him from going to the North if he wants to go in his capacity as . . ."

"He's a good man, wouldn't you say?"

"Ah, I like him a lot, I do, I do. But you know what? At the end of the day, honest to God, Haughey is a wealthy man. He doesn't have to give a damn about what's going on in Ireland. The money he's getting, oh it's terrific, but believe you me it's only chicken feed for him, that money. But I tell you, by God, if everyone had the courage that Haughey has . . ."

"A rare commodity, courage."

"These days for sure, and there's another side to it. When they're going around campaigning, he's not a muck-thrower, he never throws the muck if he ever dreams of it. I can't understand it."

"Would he be your favourite politician?"

"Good God, yes! The rest of these guys are university professors, and in the universities they should have stayed, because that's what they are, university professors, they should have stayed there . . ."

"What do you think of this Ian Paisley telling Haughey not to come to Belfast?"

"Oh, Paisley's cracked. He's crazy. Paisley wants nobody there. When you are what you are in a place like that, you want nobody to come in to destroy it . . ."

"He feels a bit insecure?"

"Oh, believe it. But he has a place in Canada, did you know that?"

"I did not know that."

"Well, know it from now."

"Hm!"

"You seek out your own information over there. He has a place in Canada, and if the going ever gets rough here, zip he's gone. He's surrounded night and day by bodyguards, and the police are all around his place morning, noon, and night. That must be why he hasn't been knocked off long ago. There wouldn't be too many sorry, unfortunately, I'm sorry to say."

Lourdes piped up. "He wants to keep the bad old days, with everybody fighting. He doesn't want people to get along."

"That's *right!*" exclaimed Mrs. Quilty as a particularly lengthy flame ejected from her mouth. "And he had to go to America to get his degree. He couldn't get it at home. Doctor Paisley. Phhwt!" She spit on the rug. It sizzled.

"Anybody can get a degree in America," said Lourdes.

"Yes, if you pay for it, you know. In the front door and out the back door or whatever, in the back door and out the front. That's the thing about Paisley. But Paisley is crazy, you see. I think he's a great husband and father, but he roars his head off, you see. The Reverend Doctor Mister, I don't know what."

I mentioned that I'd heard something about the Catholics in the North supporting Ian Paisley and how could that be? Mrs. Quilty's eyes told me she'd heard me, but it took her a while to get back to that.

"In Paisley's collection in church dare you to put a fifty-pence coin in the plate and make noise. Oh, no! A silent collection, if you please. Make it all notes. But I was told it must be five years ago maybe longer that he had a place in Canada and if it ever got too rough, whiz he was gone. A plane out overnight from Belfast. I am sure of that, you know."

"What makes you so sure?" said Lourdes.

"We have our sources."

Lourdes mentioned something about the former European parliamentary president being the first person to put Paisley in his place.

"Right you are," said Mrs. Quilty. "He started shouting and boiling over in Brussels. She had him out. 'Outside, get him out, get him out of here,' she said."

Mrs. Quilty was swinging her arms with extreme vigour and with a constant volley of sparks shooting several inches out from her mouth. A glittering display of pyrotechnics, it was all the more delightful for being so unexpected.

"And out," she wailed. "He was thrown out." Her voice dropped conspiratorially. "Major and all them hate him, Thatcher hated him like the blazes, don't talk about the Queen and all those, they have to put up with him, you know."

"Would you say he has some kind of irrational hatred of . . ."

"Oh Lord, yes," she cried, inflamed with passion. "He takes care of the poor Catholics on the side in his riding and that's how he gets their vote. I'm told this for a *fact* . . ."

"You mean he slips them the odd ten-pound note when they look as if they could use it."

"Yes, or a load of groceries – with his name on it."

"Well, there you go."

Lourdes was a big supporter of close European union.

"I think the way for countries to get along is to trade," she opined.

But Mrs. Quilty didn't respond. She was still swooning over her memories of Haughey's gentlemanly, courageous, even heroic, campaigning in the face of all that mudslinging.

"It's truly a terrible way to be, going around campaigning for an election and all the time mud-throwing at the other guy. But Haughey has never done anything like that, I've watched him. Years ago he was supposed to have been in the business of bringing arms into Ireland, but it was never proved against him."

Was she in favour of the extradition treaty, which was the big issue at the moment? Whether suspected terrorists could be nabbed at home in Ireland and forced to stand trial in Britain.

"I'm neither for nor against it."

"How could that be?"

"The very word IRA." Her voice dropped wistfully. "It meant such a different thing in Ireland at one time. When you think about it now, it makes you weep. All those people who gave their lives for us. Where would we be now? What would we have? We'd have nothing. We'd be downtrodden as we always were. And I think these people who call themselves the Provisional IRA are not an Irish organization. They're based in Ireland, a lot of them, but —"

The thought was snapped off by the sudden appearance of Mr. Quilty, who must have assumed nothing of importance was being said, since it was merely his wife who was doing the talking. Why, she must be boring us silly. He'd fix that. He immediately butted in and started telling us that his grandfather bought the hotel for twelve hundred pounds seventy years ago.

Mrs. Quilty checked to see what I thought of this boorish interruption, and I gave her a look of sympathy and at the same time pretended I was dozing off. Mr. Quilty, noting a certain lack of response to the news of his grandfather's interesting purchase, told us that there was only one other family in all of Ireland named Quilty.

"It's not Irish is it?"

I had thought it was a name brilliantly invented by Vladimir Nabokov, just taking the *g* and turning it into a *q* to represent the lecherous, envious, and loathsomely encroaching quilty-guilty pedophile playwright in *Lolita*.

"Oh, but it is. The other chap, he runs a little school for girls down in County Cork somewhere. Elocution, deportment, shorthand, typing, all that sort of thing. Skibbereen, I think it is. They go for that sort of thing down there."

"More so than up here, would you say?"

"Oh, nothing like that up here."

"Why would that be?"

"There's just not the interest these days. Years ago there was a school like that up here, but interest faded. And that fellow and I, we get each other's bills."

"So in Skibbereen, County Cork, there's a fellow named Quilty running a school for —"

"Yes, it's a little school for girls. He ran one for some time in Galway, but it didn't work out. He couldn't attract the students somehow."

Mr. Quilty took me down a long sloping corridor to show me a grand photo of Galway, an aerial view, circa 1940. I said he must know everybody in town pretty well, his father having bought the hotel seventy years ago and all.

"My grandfather, it was."

"Sorry."

"I know all the old fogies anyway. The old town was very small."

We stopped at the large framed picture, on the landing of a back staircase.

"My old man was the mayor then," he said.

Morton – who did a bit of photography on the side with his early Leica – had raved about the picturesque Claddagh: "Nothing is more picturesque in the British Isles than this astonishing fishing village of neat, whitewashed, thatched cottages planted at haphazard angles with no regular roads running to them."

"Where would the Claddagh be here?" I asked Mr. Quilty.

He pointed it out, but said it had been in a state of ruin and uninhabited by the time the fifties rolled around. Now there's nothing left of it. In the photo – taken a mere decade after Morton's visit – you could see the thatched roofs were falling apart. Now it's all identical brick rowhouses.

The Claddagh had originally been a settlement of Irish families which had sprung up outside the old walls of Galway, at a time when the town of Galway itself was restricted to Anglo-Norman families, fourteen of them to be exact, known as the Tribes. I began to realize how diplomatically Mr. Quilty had dealt with me last night when it somehow had got into my mind that the Claddagh was where the Tinkers lived.

Lourdes told Mr. Quilty that it was cold and frightening crossing the bridge last night, with the water screaming by so high and rushing in the spring runoff.

"It gets higher," he said. "The eyes get all plugged with water."

Lourdes looked confused. "The eyes get plugged with water?"

"Yes, them, the eyes of the bridge." He pointed to the old photo and showed us where the eyes were.

Young Desmond Quilty slouched by wearing an Australian sweatshirt with "Down Under" (upside down) on it. It was a gift from his grandparents who were world travellers.

"Yes," said Mr. Quilty. "They go everywhere. They belong to the Scholars' Club. It's a tourist organization. They take trips all around the world."

We got talking some more about the Claddagh. In the picture on the landing, in spite of the roofs badly needing thatching, each little house had its own long patch of garden stretching out behind it, and under active cultivation.

"Ach, but not now," said Mr. Quilty. "Everybody's too lazy to have a garden. They just buy what they need."

Good heavens! Those Trappists from Mount Melleray are setting a bad example for the entire country.

"When are you going to run for mayor like your grandfather?"

"Father."

"Sorry. Father."

"I'm not. No bloody way. No politics for me."

The population of Galway was seventy-five thousand and growing. People came in for jobs in the computer factories. But for every five who moved into town only one got a job and the other four stayed and went on the dole. People who came here from other places just didn't want to leave, he said.

"And a lot of tourists in the summer?"

"Yes. It's a nice town. A lovely town, really. No tough police force, no one-way streets, no major crime, really. Best city in the country, really. Not a bad place to live."

He agreed with Morton's figures on the population of Galway: forty thousand in 1910, but by 1930 it was down to fourteen thousand. And during all this time his father was the mayor.

"He was alarmed by the decrease. He ranted and raved about it. He'd be glad to know it's up to seventy-five thousand now."

"Well, goodbye Mr. Guilty," said Lourdes. It was time to move on. He looked at me and smiled, then looked back at the beauteous Lourdes.

"Not Guilty, dear, it's Quilty. Guilty is something else entirely."

"Mr. Quilty."

"And it's Ken, not Mr. Quilty. Mr. Quilty was my father."

"Okay, Mr. Ken," said Lourdes. "Good luck with the baby!"

"It's not me that's having it, it's the wife. Haw haw haw!"

Mrs. Quilty followed us to the door. "I just wanted you to know not all of us are so prejudiced against the Travellers. I like the Travellers. I think the settled people are jealous of the Travellers. They grumble and complain about the Travellers, and they say things like, 'Those cursed Tinkers have the devil on their side.' But it's just jealousy, you know. Because there's a bit of the Traveller in everyone."

THE POET'S CORNER

Lourdes was a joy. With her along, we were given greater attention, my mind was working faster, decision-making time was down to practically nothing, and I had someone to laugh at my jokes full time. The whole situation was much better than I imagined it would be. Her presence even had a beneficial impact on my way of looking at things.

We were driving along the south shore of Galway Bay, west through the famous Burren area of County Clare, stopping occasionally to drink in the out-of-time stillness and enchantment which is always on tap – though you have to give the lever a pull. We stopped to take pictures of megalithic burial grounds up the side of a hill, on top of which was a cairn and a stone fort. My leg was not feeling up to the climb. The subtle hand of the ancients was everywhere.

I'd been telling Lourdes how Mr. Looney figured the Germans like Ireland so much because of their Wagnerian notions of racial purity. After all, Ireland is still 99 per cent Irish, except for the Brits, who don't seem all that noticeable in the Republic, and who seem to be liked, paradoxically, although there are Brits who claim they're not. We also talked about the problem of Yeats, in the last few years of his life, becoming soft on Hitler. Lourdes began asking questions about Mr. Looney. Her interest in him became overwhelming. She dropped hints about wanting to meet him. I had more questions for him anyway, and he would be pleased to meet Lourdes.

We stopped at the Cliffs of Moher, overlooking the Atlantic. The tourist office was open, and to get to it from the parking lot we had to run a scraggly gauntlet of people selling cassette tapes of Irish music, even though it was only March. We bought some maps, changed some traveller's cheques, agreed we hadn't come to Ireland to look at cliffs, and were soon back on the road heading for Kilkee, an upscale resort town on the small peninsula on the north side of the mouth of the Shannon.

Kilkee (also known as Cill Choi) was full of alluring old hotels and imposing mansions – but it was so early in the season the only sign of life was the waves crashing in on the rocks protecting the wonderful, welcoming arms of the steep-cliffed harbour.

We found a pub in Kilkee, away from the resort area. The men's toilet had a sign saying "Please Use Ladies' Toilet for a Few Days Due to Repairs" and the ladies' said "Please Use Men's Toilet for a Few Days Due to Repairs." The fellows at the bar were talking about music and telling corny old jokes, such as the one about the guy who goes into a bar in Colorado and says, "What kind of music do you have here?" Bartender says, "Both kinds, country *and* western."

Another guy yelled out, "Both kinds, rock *and* roll."

On the wall was a poster featuring Fats Domino, who'd been packing them in at a concert in Dublin.

We wanted to take a little ferry across the Tarbert Race to Kerry. The sign read: "Ferry to Kerry. Seven miles during daylight hours."

"How far at night?" said Lourdes.

Someone had scrawled on the side of a wall, "For abortion information call 666." Lourdes got out a little notebook and wrote down the number, with a devilish look on her face.

We were half an hour too late for the last ferry, which had left at seven. At the Old Ground Hotel in Ennis, County Clare, we took a room, and repaired to the Poet's Corner Bar, the walls of which were covered with pictures of all the old writers.

This was a great old hotel: they had the de Valera Suite, the Parnell Suite, the O'Connell Suite, the O'Regan Suite, the McNamara Suite, and the Bridal Suite. We settled for the Anonymity Suite. The bar was crowded, and the bartender accidentally poured an entire glass of beer all over the woman who happened to be sitting on the bar stool to my left. The woman suffered in stoic silence, but Lourdes, on my right, let out a scream.

"Don't blame me," said the bartender. "I'm English. I'm not responsible."

I helped the woman over her shock. She was a kind, gentle lady, about forty, with a large nose and receding chin. I whipped out my Leica and took a snap of her in profile for my collection of photos of people with handsome honkers. Lourdes, with a seemingly innocent look on her face, stood wiping the woman's breasts and thighs tenderly with a bar rag, very tenderly indeed, and the woman started crooning about Ennis and all the wonderful things there are to see and do – for instance, the statue of Saint Francis (with stigmata) standing in the Ennis Friary, and, for instance, Milliven's, a fine restaurant where you only go for a special treat, certainly not every day. "It's a bit classy," she said, as Lourdes hopped back on her bar stool.

"I don't have classy clothes with me."

"Oh, anything'll do really."

She added that she had never been outside of Ireland – but there was only one place she wanted to see. "It's my lifetime ambition to go to Italy." She'd had enough to drink to admit the reason she hadn't gone yet was because her husband wasn't interested in going and refused to allow her to go alone. With all the pictures of poets staring at us from the wall, I told her I thought Chaucer was dead on six hundred years ago when he said love will not be constrained by mastery. She laughed bitterly and stared into my eyes.

When we mentioned we'd just driven through the Burren, she said that, when Cromwell came to Ireland to *chastise* the Irish (nervous laughter), "he was up in the Burren area at a certain point, and he took a look around and said there's not enough water here to drown a man, not enough earth to bury him, and not enough wood to hang him." Her eyes went all misty.

We took our brandies over to the comfortable old armchairs by the roaring fire in the lobby. There was a lovely marble fireplace, surrounded by a polished brass fender with cupids, and on the walls several large old oils, portraits of locals long dead. There was a self-portrait of a woman in her twenties, in a classic pose, at the easel. She apparently lived for sixty more years, well into her eighties, painting every day. People seemed to have vivid memories of her, though she'd been dead a hundred years.

A fellow who claimed to live in the hotel came by, and, introducing himself as Paul Boylan, started telling us a long, dull story about how the hotel got its name. I had the feeling he was an impostor of some sort, that he was not the manager. Lourdes later said she felt the same.

"The Old Ground Hotel was built as a private residence in the early part of the eighteenth century . . ." He went on and on. When he finally detected our lack of enthusiasm, he began telling us about the most recent bomb scare.

"We were away at where the wife's from, now – in Mayo. We were there one night only, and we got a phone call to say there was a bomb scare here. That was the time of all that high action in the North. The kids were pretty small at the time but we had a bunch of blocklayers having a meeting here and we knew a lot of them and of course we jumped in the car and it took an hour and a half to come back but sure the blocklayers had taken the kids out of the cots and taken them away and everything. They were simply wonderful about it all."

"Did you know who the scare was from?"

"I presume it was the IRA or whatever it was. Some sort of dissatisfied group. There are all sorts of them out for revenge or whatever, and they don't want to be known. Hah heh heh."

"Why would they single out this place?"

"Oh, just public places in general. No reason really. They know there's a big meeting going on, so they make a phone call and then they come by to watch the people clearing out. And then they, I mean we, we do a lot of international business, you know. Business people from all over really. We're only fifteen miles from Shannon Airport."

"How easy would it be for us to get to talk to a guy in the IRA? Would that be hard to arrange?"

"Not really. You probably know about this Gibraltar shooting and stuff now. That girl who was shot up there, her brother comes in here quite a bit. Now obviously I'm non-political and non-sectarian, but obviously he's pretty hot, because his only sister was blown up by the English. Now the English, I don't give a tupper's damn for all that, because when the Irish need work they go over to England for sure. They don't complain about British money, they complain about the problems in the North and freedom and all that, and to me that's history, forget about it, it's gone, let's get on with tomorrow."

"If you ask me, more of that sort of positive thinking is needed."

"Oh, obviously. But I mean this woman's brother, he comes in and he wants to tell the town his troubles. He's on the telly every day."

"Giving the IRA point of view on things?"

"Well no, not openly. He would be very cautious the way he would word things. But he does protest about his sister getting shot, and she was a recognized member of the IRA so it was disclosed after the shooting obviously. The last place she gave a public speech was here. I didn't find out till her brother told me after she was shot, that she had spoken at a meeting here. I didn't even know about it. People come here all the time to hold meetings, and I don't always know what the meeting is about. Her brother came in one day, and he said, 'It's hard to believe this is the last place Mariead Farrell made a speech . . .'"

"Mariead Farrell. I remember that case." I'd seen a film on her, *Death of a Terrorist*, which featured an interview with her just before she and two male companions were shot dead by the British on the suspicion that they were going to blow up a marching band at Gibraltar. The film showed home movies of her growing up in Belfast.

I told Mr. Boylan I figured she was unjustly shot for sure, based on my viewing of that film, and that for sure she was in the IRA for purely idealistic reasons, having witnessed great suffering under the British occupation. Inspired by Martin Luther King and the American civil-rights movement of the sixties, she thought of herself as a freedom fighter. She said things like, "Your mind's your strongest weapon. They can't destroy your mind." And she loved real life: disco dancing, platform shoes, makeup, earrings, lipstick, fancy dresses, the latest hair styles. And she knew that the Falls Road area had been a swamp settled by Catholics who were not allowed to live within the Belfast city limits, just like the Claddagh and Galway – and, more recently, like Johannesburg. I told him I thought she didn't deserve to be shot just on suspicion.

Mr. Boylan smiled knowingly. It wasn't cool to argue with tourists, especially if you were in the hotel business. "The police force in this country," he testified, "they know every single person. Everyone! They know what you're doing, where you're going, they know all that. It's a real cat-and-mouse job. The mouse runs in and the cat runs in after him and the mouse runs out again."

Like many Irish, North and South, Mr. Boylan seemed to think the IRA were a bunch of desperately impoverished, unskilled, uneducated, illiterate contract killers with bogus, self-serving, insincere political ideals – if that – but who were being paid by the agents of international arms manufacturers and got to ride around in nice cars and have dangerous fun. But Mariead Farrell certainly didn't fit that picture, and neither did her brother as it turned out.

"It's all personal gain, really, behind the thing," said Mr. Boylan. "They're not just doing it because they feel deeply about it, they're doing it because it's a living. And obviously a good living. There are people paying people to shoot other people, and that's what it's all about. You can call it any words you like, but everybody knows . . ."

And what about the sincerity of all those prisoners who starved themselves to death?

He mumbled something I couldn't understand. The phrases "romantic nonsense" and "self-delusion" were semi-audible.

Had he ever heard of the IRA being involved in Mafia-style extortion?

"I hear they're involved in that. But here? No. Touch wood now. We're lucky in this town. This is a brilliant town really."

He seemed to believe that sort of extortion took place in the North.

"Protection money. This kind of stuff. So I believe, now. I have a sister married in the North; her husband, he worked in a meat factory up there. And she said it was miserable. In the factory you had to go and park your car here in a special place away from the others because you couldn't be parking beside somebody else, because if his car would be blown up and so on, yours would be ruined too."

"And Mariead Farrell's brother, what does he do for a living?"

"I don't know, but I have a feeling he works at the university."

"Oh? I thought you'd say he was unemployed."

"No, he's too businesslike to be that kind. He comes to have meetings with the university crowd. The sort of people who shout about socialism and all that. I don't know whether they're in laboratories or whether they're lecturing or professors or whatever the hell they are. Don't ask me."

In the morning Lourdes said that while I was away from the bar last night, she'd asked the woman who wanted to go to Italy how she and her husband had met.

"Do you often ask such questions?"

"I'm always interested in how married couples have met. The stories are always interesting."

"So how did they meet?"

"They were in an amateur play together. He had the role of a blind violinist with a cup on the corner and she had the role of a flirtatious floozie who makes friends with him. And then she seduces him and marries him for his money."

"Money? A blind violinist with a cup?"

"Yes, er, he had a large secret bank account. And she said it was a very strange beginning, because she is always being haunted by the mysterious connection between their roles in that play and their roles in married life."

"What form does this mysterious connection take?"

"She didn't want to get into the details."

We strolled through the hotel and looked at the pictures on the walls. Why was fox hunting the subject of so many paintings? In one watercolour, a woman driving a one-pony cart had stopped to let the hounds and horses go by. A print showed O'Connell in the House of Commons, and a reproduction of a painting by Arthur J. Elsley, 1898, showed a fox hunt with a viewpoint from the interior of a little cottage. The frantic fox had sought refuge by running into the cottage through the open door, and all the hounds were following, with chickens scampering out of the way. And through the window you could see hunters on horseback about to charge through the door as well. The family of eight little kids were frantically overturning furniture and running out of the way. The old grandmother was just horrified. But one rotten little boy in the background had an evil little smile on his face, he looked quite happy about it all.

And what did this little family have hanging on the wall in their cottage? Why, a map of Europe! I took it to be a subtle political cartoon from before the Famine. Those who would understand it today would be few.

THE DARKER SIDE OF DINGLE

At the Craggaunowen Project a few miles east of Ennis, after a walk through the woods, we came to the castle museum, which had a small number of wonderful displays including, over the fireplace, the head and rack of a long-extinct giant Irish elk – at least that's what the attendant said it was. If it indeed was, it must have been fourteen thousand years old, for the remains of the Irish elk have been found only in what is known as Zone II mud – indicating they died out in the late-glacial period. About two hundred of them have been found.

The Tim Severin version of the boat Saint Brendan used in his legendary transatlantic explorations was on display in a glass house. The voyage was chronicled in Severin's book *The Brendan Voyage*. Also on display was a ring fort with a souterrain, and replicas of old thatch-roofed conical huts looking like traditional African dwellings, which made one think of a possible ancient link between Africa and Ireland. After all, there are flowers in the Burren that are not known elsewhere outside Africa.

"Is there still a lot of lace made in Ireland?" Lourdes asked the lady bartender in a pub on the outskirts of Limerick.

"No, not a lot. It takes too long. Too hard on the eyes. You have to have a lot of time and patience."

Lourdes, who had a powerful Spanish *señorita* look about her – in fact you might guess that she was a flamenco dancer – sipped her brandy thoughtfully, her nostrils quivering, then looked up and said, "If you didn't hear us speaking and you just saw us, would you think we might be Irish?"

"No."

"We couldn't pass for Irish?"

"Not at all! He could maybe, but not you."

The look of disappointment on Lourdes's face was registered by the bartender.

"Well," she said, "with television you see all these Russians and all that and . . . we all look alike, really."

"You could pass for Canadian," I whispered.

Lourdes rolled her eyes, then noticed that my feelings were hurt, so she ran her hand surreptitiously along my thigh. The bartender went on to say she had worked here twenty-four years. It had always been a neighbourhood pub but, since it happened to be on the main road, it therefore did double duty as a good pub for travellers as well. "No stranger is a stranger," she said.

We picked up a paper and read about some nuns who had sold their convent in Germany and bought a villa in the South of France, and a Mercedes Benz. One, who was smoking a cigar, was quoted as saying, "Why should we have to be sixteenth-century people in order to be spiritual?"

A car with a bumpersticker reading "Narrow Minded & Proud of It" kept passing us and slowing down. We kept noticing stone circles off to the side of the road and tall, slender, graceful ogham stones, and Lourdes at one point cried out: "Oh, they're just so natural. Isn't it wonderful! They've been sitting there for so long and nobody's moved them."

"Or scarcely noticed them," I added, thinking again of Morton.

Elizabeth and Laurie O'Leary ran a bed-and-breakfast at Inch above the seven-mile-long sandbar known as the Inch Peninsula, which protects Castlemaine Harbour from the cruel-but-glorious storms of Dingle Bay, and where the Siobhan McKenna version of *The Playboy of the Western World* was filmed – *Ryan's Daughter* as well.

It was an old, melancholy, immensely solid greystone house sitting high on a cliff and gazing southwest across Dingle Bay and toward the vast grey Atlantic. A gloomy film could be filmed in that house. It was a serious house. Ingmar Bergman would have loved it. It had the look of a house that didn't mind getting rained on every day.

The road that goes all around the Dingle Peninsula was a rugged piece of work, as were the stone fences that go way up the sides of every hill in Ireland.

"Starving men built those roads and those stone fences," said Elizabeth O'Leary. She was a serious person, as solemn as her house, a sober poet with a strong interest in the darker side of life. "These were relief projects during the Famine. And as for that friary in Ennis, the one where the statue of Saint Francis is, they had to stop construction of that for several years on account of the Black Death."

You meet this woman and within minutes she's on about the Potato Famine and the Black Death – with even more to come. She was English and had married an Irishman. She was doing a lot of historical research, apparently on an amateur basis only, and probably so that she would be able to defend the honour of the English race when called upon – or when she found herself confronted with overt anti-English sentiment. Her intellectual pursuits were the equivalent of someone who, finding himself living in a rough neighbourhood, decides to take up aikido. She was building a case for her people. Right now it was the Famine that was occupying all her attention. She was particularly interested in countering the widely held opinion that the Famine was all the fault of the English.

"The North had its linen industry; the southeast counties, Wicklow and Wexford and part of Waterford, they grew wheat. The problem was in most places they grew potatoes and nothing but potatoes."

"You can feed a family on potatoes?"

"Yes, on potatoes, and that's what fed the family. Indeed, you can. Get all the vitamins and nutrients you need. And it's a fairly easy way of feeding, you don't need a lot of land. An acre, a half an acre, or whatever, will grow enough potatoes for a family. And they'd live literally on potatoes, and occasionally a glass of milk or something."

"And fish, of course."

"No, sir! No fish. They didn't know how to fish. I mean, people in England couldn't understand: well, why on earth don't they go out and fish?"

"And so why didn't they?"

"A good question. The answer in this area was that there were no trees to build the curraghs, the boats to fish in. They had all these beautiful natural harbours, but no tradition of fishing at all. So the English would say, oh they're terribly lazy. All these fish waiting to be caught, why on earth don't they go out and catch them? The English tried to help at first, but like Ethiopia – look, we've given all this food and money, why are they still starving sort of thing?"

"But, but . . ."

I was later to read about the Great Famine in James Charles Roy's *The Road Wet, The Wind Close*, in which he refers to the "massive starvation on the one hand and a multitude of fish on the other" and states that "one still hears the slur now and then that the peasants were too lazy to fish." The problem was not laziness, according to Roy, nor was it the lack of curraghs, but that the curraghs were too frail and too low in the water to allow the use of nets: "The great runs of fish are all in deep water, several miles offshore, where nets are mandatory. Tricky weather and rough Atlantic waters sealed off the venture to any but the foolhardy, and so the people starved amidst the plenty."

Elizabeth ignored my buts. "They sent them an awful lot of corn," she said, "Indian corn it was, maize, without realizing there were no mills in Ireland. And you couldn't cook it; you didn't have an oven. Potatoes they cooked on an open fire in a pot. And nobody could bake bread or knew what to do with corn when they had it. See, unless you're on the ground and can see the problems. Like Nescafé sending milk powder to Africa not knowing the children couldn't digest it. Or maybe they knew and pretended they didn't."

Lourdes started sputtering, but gave up.

"And there was also difficulty in communication. Trains were just starting up, but basically everything was done on horseback. No cars and trains to go and find out what was going on."

She had a shelf full of old books dealing with the Famine and about committees in England set up to do something about it.

"There seemed to be no comprehension of what was going on then. Total incomprehension. But they were trying their best, according to their lights."

I said I'd always heard the English landlords gouged the Irish tenants so much there was nothing left for them but potatoes.

"That's just a story. I've found no evidence for it at all."

"But it's well-known that the English have never been overly imbued with sympathy for the Irish."

"No, that's definitely not true. They were. Believe me. They thought they were being philanthropic. They were trying their best. I've been doing all this research, and it's just amazing how hard they tried to help."

Besides the Black Death and the Potato Famine she was engrossed in the subject of the treatment of insanity in nineteenth-century Ireland. She had several volumes on nineteenth-century Irish lunatic asylums, written by the English inspectors who travelled around making sure the mentally ill were being well cared for.

"The inspector of lunatics, as they called them, had to visit two of these institutions every six months," she said. "They would note exactly what the inmates were wearing, the bedding was weighed, they kept books on bedwetting. It was a black mark against you if you wet your bed. And when they started this in the 1860s, conditions were fairly bad."

"I bet they were."

"But they had two fairly enlightened inspectors. They found out who could play musical instruments, and they set up bands so they could have dances for the inmates. They'd take them to the towns on weekends, so people would get used to seeing them, they wouldn't be afraid of them. Get them used to handling money, so they could get back to their old life eventually. They bought pictures to hang on the wall."

"Foxhunting scenes?" said Lourdes.

"Probably. And the superiors, they argued that the inmates came from poor homes, they didn't have pictures on the wall at home, and so they had no need for them here."

"That's not fair."

"But this is part of the treatment, the inspectors would say. To make their surroundings pleasant. Considering this was Victorian times and considering it was Ireland, these attitudes were very enlightened. Ireland might as well have been Fiji as far as the English were concerned. I was very surprised. They wanted to install central heating in all these places. It surprised me how philanthropic they were. One doesn't think of Victorians that way, not until one does a bit of serious historical research."

We sipped our tea. The conversation might seem to have been a bit one-sided, but I'd been caught off-guard. Furthermore, I didn't go to Ireland to have the Irish listen to me, I went to listen to them. And I'd been lucky. One fascinating person after another for our delight. This one was delightfully gloomy, and her husband was about to prove to be equally so.

Elizabeth turned to the Troubles. Ridiculous, she said. It would be suicide for the South to annex the North. "A few years ago they had this study of the consequences of taking on the North, how much it would cost them. It would have doubled their national debt each year just to take the North on. Children's allowances, social benefits – everything is about twice as high in the North as in the South."

"Who did the study?" said Lourdes.

"Everybody had a say. Even the bishops agreed that, yes, they'd have to change the constitution, they wouldn't be able to ban divorce and abortion and all the other things that we ban now. Big change in lifestyle. General opinion was hands off. Because it was going to make just too big a change to the South. Only in the last eight years has contraception been legalized."

"It's legal now?" said Lourdes.

"Yes. Well, you can't buy it over the counter, mind. You can only get it if you're married. You get it through your doctor. A chemist in Dublin got taken to court for selling condoms over the counter."

Mrs. O'Leary offered an interesting story about some friends in nearby Tralee who were having some trouble with their marriage.

"They stuck it out, though, and they're fine now. They could have gone to England to get a divorce, but they didn't. And this is why: you see, his dad died. He left the farm, most of it, to his son. Except for a long strip right along the road, which he left to his daughter-in-law. And the fields are all behind the strip. And the son would have no access to the fields without the strip. That's how careful they are. Solomon-like, they are."

"That's how much the Irish hate the idea of divorce," said Lourdes.

"That's right. The idea and the fact of it both."

Lourdes told Elizabeth we'd seen some darling donkeys just before pulling in.

"Oh yes, they're lovely," said Elizabeth. "The donkeys are still used for haulage and so on. And many of them are like pets. We took some children for a ride on a donkey, and we were followed by this other donkey who was very interested in the first donkey. Apparently it was a wild donkey, didn't belong to anyone, just came out of the woods or something."

"Maybe it was a Tinker's donkey," said Lourdes. "They let their animals roam, I hear."

"Maybe. But it kept getting into things, kept hiding behind hedges and jumping out and braying at everybody and rolling over in the road and scratching its back."

"There's a guy like that in my neighbourhood in Toronto," I said.

"Donkeys are terrific," said Lourdes.

"They're very noisy," said Elizabeth. "You can hear them half a mile away."

"An ass's roar away," I remembered.

Elizabeth hadn't heard that one.

At breakfast Elizabeth's husband, Laurie, who had been almost completely silent last night, though he'd been listening intently, began arguing about the environment. He said he was glad he had seen the world when it was still beautiful. He'd been born in 1934.

"It's touch and go," I offered.

"No," he said, "the world's finished. I'm calling for a total ban on the cutting of trees. Anyone who cuts down even one tree should be thrown in jail."

Lourdes said something about there being hardly any trees in Ireland left to cut down, even though Laurie seemed to be speaking with a global passion rather than a national one.

"No," he said, "the trees of Ireland, they were cut down by the English over the centuries for their ships and their toothpicks and whatnot, and the destruction also helped militarily, for it helped flush out the rebel soldiers of the forest, who had been troublesome."

"Just like Vietnam," offered Lourdes.

Elizabeth looked a little steamed.

"Lo, you know damned well there were hardly any trees in Ireland when the English arrived in the thirteenth century," she declared witheringly.

"Lo?" I said.

"They call me that because of my initials," he said. "L. O."

He added that he had a friend called Woof, because his name was Ken Hall.

In preparation for our trip around the Dingle Peninsula, I bought a thick green rubber raincoat with hood and matching draw-string trousers in a pub in Dingletown for nine pounds. They only had one set, and it fit me. So Lourdes was out of luck, but she had her bomber jacket and leather trousers to keep her dry and warm.

Dingle was a town of many bookstores, but business wasn't good in any of them. The tiny public library on top of the hill, however, was full of avid readers, with many favouring the Irish-language publications. This again was the Gaeltacht.

We were browsing in one bookstore, in which, to go to the washroom, one had to travel through a veritable Cretan maze. The experience brought on one of my manic spells. I told a seemingly humourless bookstore clerk that my brown cow had died.

"Eh?" he said. "What's that again?"

"My brown cow has died."

"I'm very sorry to hear that, but I don't think there's anything I can do about it at this stage."

I explained that this was a widely understood code phrase in the twenties, a code used by H. V. Morton during his travels in Ireland whenever he fancied a taste of the illegal poteen. Codes like this have a very short shelf life, of course, since they are ineffective when not understood and equally ineffective when too widely understood.

No codes were needed for poteen on the Aran Islands when Synge was there around 1900. I took a copy of Synge's *The Aran Islands* from the shelf, flipped it open to page 34, and read aloud to the clerk:

> One cannot think of these people drinking wine on the summit
> of this crumbling precipice, but their grey poteen, which brings
> a shock of joy to the blood, seems predestined to keep sanity in
> men who live forgotten in these worlds of mist.

"We don't have any of that here," said the clerk.

It must have been something in the well water – wormwood, perhaps. This bookstore clerk made Elizabeth and Laurie seem like Lucy and Desi. I wish I could have offered him a "shock of joy to the blood."

The Dingle Peninsula is the extreme west end of Europe, "the outskirts of Europe" as the Irish call it, with unearthly mountains like great sailboats tilting seawards as they rise out of the Dingle Plain, and with a village here, a village there, perched on the side of a mountain like a nest in a tree, to borrow an image from Heinrich Heine. Canadians seldom travel just to see the scenery, but when beautiful scenery shows up, it should be enjoyed, for it's good for the soul.

The Blasket Islands, which haunt the western tip of Dingle, are no longer inhabited, but they possess a rich literary tradition. Unfortunately, it is not much known outside of Ireland. Lourdes had bought a copy of Tomás Ó Crohan's *The Islandman*, an essay on mournfulness in the guise of a novel narrated by an old man who had lived on the Blaskets all his life. He was blessed with a strong memory of childhood events and a strong sense of the richness of that life, now gone forever. The last residents left the Blaskets in 1953.

We stopped at the lookout point at Slea Head and looked out with great respect at Great Blasket Island, also at Beginish and Inishtooskert and Inishnabro and Inishvickillane and the lighthouse on Tearaght. Their closeness in our field glasses added to the sense of desolation and sadness. We stopped at a lot of places around the peninsula, including the Dún Beag (or Dunbeg) promontory fort, which has been slowly falling into the Atlantic since the time of Christ. I took some pictures of Lourdes with just her head sticking out of a long narrow souterrain and a donkey looking as if he wanted to bite off her nose. We also paid fifty pence to a ten-year-old boy who guided us up a little hill to view a set of early Christian *clocháns* – stone beehive huts. The boy climbed all over them. We were so nervous about him falling and breaking his head that we got out of there fast.

Across misty green fields studded with ancient high crosses –
including a stone pillar still adorned with the familiar swirling
Celtic La Tène decorations a thousand winters hadn't obliterated
completely – we came across the famous Gallarus Oratory, a ninth-
century church in the form of a simple stone nave – and nothing else –
about fifteen feet high which stood alone in a meadow. With walls
three feet thick, the strange-looking little pre-Romanesque church,
like something from another planet, remained exactly as it had been
built a thousand years ago, without a stone out of place and still water-
tight, in spite of the fact that it was built without mortar. It looked like
the hull of a boat turned upside down, its interior measuring ten by fifteen feet, and with a lintel stone sitting over its single entranceway.

It was around these parts in 1580 that the English – with the partic-
ipation of the poet Edmund Spenser of *Faerie Queene* fame – massa-
cred a large group of "rebels," including women and children.

It was strange being in Kilmalkedar, the ecclesiastical centre of the
Dingle Peninsula, with its buildings associated with Saint Brendan,
including the ruins of a seventh-century monastery, and with its
twelfth-century Romanesque church filled with ogham stones.
Strange, because we found ourselves in a dark, unfriendly pub, watching the Academy Awards from California. The Irish movie *My Left
Foot* received the best-actor and best-supporting-actress awards. The
two of us were the only ones watching. We felt out of place, and
seemed to be under suspicion for taking an interest in such things. But
all this gloom was just a coincidence. No one can tell me the residents
of the Dingle Peninsula have a monopoly on melancholy.

Much friendlier, but still odd, was the Armada Restaurant in a
nearby town, the name of which I've forgotten. There were two small
upstairs bars separated by a staircase: one decorated with movie posters, the other with theatre posters. The bartender was a tall, blonde
woman who wouldn't have looked out of place on a poster, and who
paid too much attention to me for Lourdes's taste (though not for
mine). The blonde, whose name turned out to be Eileen Kernaghan,

said they'd done that two years ago, put the theatre posters in one bar and the movie posters in the other.

"And, my good man," she whispered in my ear as she smoothed the collar of my shirt, "you are the first person to have noticed it."

"You're kidding!"

"I am telling the truth, so help me God."

We beamed at each other, while Lourdes muttered away in Spanish under her breath.

Eileen's husband was a smiling, red-faced fellow named Louis Kernaghan. He zoomed in on us and made it clear, in a jovial, good-natured, and most friendly manner, that he was the boss, and his wife, as intelligent and beautiful and sexy and flirtatious as any fool could see she was, merely took orders like any other wife.

"The wife's from Northern Ireland, I'm a Dubliner," he said.

He was sitting at the table with us as we nibbled on an interesting taste combo: Guinness, fresh-caught salmon, and dry soda bread. He'd worked in England and Italy as a young man. He didn't like Italy. Too much pasta.

"Dublin, now there's a tough town," said Louis. "North of the Liffey there are more car break-ins than cars." Lourdes looked confused. She thought it might have been an idiom. I told her it was a joke. "No joke," said Louis.

Louis called the cook out to meet us, and we complimented her profusely. Her name was Frannie Dwyer, and she kept saying, "You must visit my country before you go, you must, you must." It was a most impressive and persuasive display. Her country was County Donegal, where she had been born nineteen years ago. She felt homesick. She uttered the most melancholy moan imaginable when I told her H. V. Morton had referred to Donegal as "the most enchanting place on earth."

I complained about how Canadians get mistaken for Americans wherever they go, and immediately regretted having done so. Louis Kernaghan laughed and accused me of not having enough problems, which of course sobered me up considerably. "The Canadians aren't alone," he said. "Wherever the Irish go, they're mistaken for English, Belgians for French, Kiwis for Aussies."

"And the Spanish for Chinese," said Lourdes, causing me to laugh and forget to be embarrassed.

We repaired to the more spacious pub downstairs, where the delicate little songstresses, Liz O'Riordan and Patricia Connery, were singing and playing the kind of Irish music that everybody loves. They had a whole raft of traditional instruments. They produced their own tapes and travelled Ireland performing in both Irish and English. Good Irish music and war memorials, those are the two things that almost invariably bring out the tears in me, so I prepared myself for a little session of crying in my Guinness.

Yet, in this pub on this night, we could scarcely hear the music. The ignorance of the drinkers – they were so rude and noisy – was scandalous. But Liz and Patricia continued performing with great dignity, as if they had the perfectly attentive audience they so richly deserved:

> *The taller that the pine tree grows*
> *The sweeter is its bark*
> *And the fairer that a young man speaks*
> *The falser is his heart*
> *For they'll kiss you and caress you*
> *Until they think they have you won*
> *And they'll go away and leave you*
> *For some other one.*

All this in their sweet, haunting voices, accompanied by their concertina, guitar, whistle, bodhran, and uilleann pipes, as the crowd, belching and hollering, showed them their backs. I bought a tape, fortunately, for I've been listening to their haunting version of "I Wish I Was in Carrigfergus," "The Stone Outside Dan Murphy's Door," and other songs all through the typing out of this book, and other Irish music as well – the Dubliners, the Wolfe Tones, Big Terry McAloon, Paddy Reilly, the Dublin City Ramblers, Barleycorn, Danny Doyle,

De Danann, the Black Family, the Furey Brothers and Davey Arthur, Johnny McEvoy, Any Old Time, Jolly Beggarman, Dolores Keane, the Fair Isle Folk, Fiddler's Green, Mary Bergin . . . Just typing out these names brings tears to my eyes – for instance, Dolores Keane singing, along with De Danann, their "Anthem for Ireland" to the tune of "Danny Boy": "One heart and soul, one land my love united / Where we shall live until this world be done."

But Liz and Patricia are the best.

We were heading south to Killarney, with Macgillicuddy's Reeks glistening on the horizon, great mountainous rocky desolate peaks at the beginning of the Iveragh Peninsula so greatly loved by tourist buses, which pick up crowds of tourists from Shannon Airport, take them around the 110-mile Ring of Kerry, give them an hour or two at the Rock of Cashel and an afternoon at Trinity College checking out the Book of Kells and the gift shop, then drive them up to Dublin Airport for their trip home. Now they can just read this book and give to charity the money they would have spent on the trip.

Farewell to Dingle; we certainly met some gloomy people.

"Wouldn't it have been fun tooling around Ireland like this in the twenties?"

"That's what Morton did, and we're following him," said Lourdes.

"Right, but we haven't been lucky enough to arrive in a town on fair day. Morton did, though."

"He was a lucky fellow. We've seen a lot of cattle and sheep on the road so far, but none in towns yet and certainly none in houses."

"Morton was right when he said the Irish seem to savour their words before projecting them into the air."

"Morton, I think, was a tall man, large."

"A big fat guy."

"That's what I mean."

I suggested that Elizabeth O'Leary had been giving us her speech on the Famine for her own benefit, a rehearsal of sorts. She was getting ready for the next time she got cornered by Irish people saying what did you English do to help us when we were starving to death, you bastards?

"There were many faults in her argumentativeness," said Lourdes. Her eyes bulged comically and stayed bulging for several seconds. Lourdes really knew how to bulge her eyes. This was a multi-purpose gesture, the meaning of which ranged from mock irony to the slightest hint of self-congratulation. She noted that Elizabeth had confused Nescafé with Nestlé, and that the problem was with the water used to mix the powder, not the powder itself. She also noted that one didn't need an oven to cook corn, a pot of boiling water would do just fine.

"Maybe, but I'm a guy who is more interested in what people believe pure and simple, rather than trying to figure out what's right and what's wrong with their beliefs, generally. Sometimes I feel like a folklorist at heart."

"You're not a fighter."

Was she disappointed in me for being docile during Elizabeth's lectures? Perhaps I'd enjoyed the whole experience more than she had, particularly since we were possibly talking a bit fast for her.

"Usually not," I said. "Unless it's something really serious. Then I can get into it. Not that this wasn't serious, but it wasn't serious in an immediate sense. Besides, she had all those books and all we had was crummy old Morton."

"Also we didn't feel like arguing or challenging her in any way because we were guests, right?" She seemed close to tears.

"Right, like you're not supposed to beat a man at his own pool table. Also she didn't seem to be inviting challenges."

Elizabeth had made it sound as if she blamed the people of Waterford, Wicklow, and Wexford for not helping the starving Irish in the West. They grew wheat but didn't help. Ulster was already heavily industrialized. But nobody helped. The Irish themselves ignored the plight of the starving, while the English tried desperately to help but kept being frustrated at every turn.

THE MAN WHO BELIEVED
IN FAIRIES

A cheeky jarvey in downtown Killarney, a clean and prosperous little city with very nice bookshops, pubs, restaurants, and sweet-shops, stepped in front of the car, just as a narrow, congested road was disgorging into a broad street, and forced us to stop at the exact moment we wanted to step on it. He wanted to escort us around the beauty spots in his horse and buggy.

"My name is Danny, sir. And I guarantee you'll enjoy yourself. We'll go out through the national parks, and that's when I'll take you around the lakes and through the national parks, where there's no automobiles allowed. I'll give you the history of all the mountains and the islands and all the castles that Saint Patrick visited and every-thing. Like I say, I'll take you through the national parks where you can take nice pictures and I'll take you around the lakes and all the way through the national parks where no automobiles are allowed. And I guarantee you'll enjoy yourself . . ."

An afternoon with this guy would drive us batty. I told him we were late for a business meeting in Cahirciveen, which turned out to be pure prophecy. He apologized and jumped out of the way.

The jarveys haven't changed much since Morton's day.

We were way up in Macgillicuddy's Reeks, at the highest point of Ballaghbeama Gap on our way south to Kenmare and the start of our journey around the Ring of Kerry (a.k.a. the Kerry Way). Silence prevailed, the Mortonian silence of the wind whistling through the heart, the bleating of sheep, the squawking of birds. The day was warm, with a sunny, cloudless sky, the sort of day Glenn Gould disliked and that would have provoked him to say, "Behind every silver lining is a cloud." Lourdes was complaining that she got a footstool one year as a Christmas gift from her father, when she was about eight. Geez, thanks Dad. Her mother had died the year before. Then, the year after the footstool, she got a parakeet in a cage, and she was all of a sudden very glad of the footstool, so she could reach the cage to feed the bird.

Population pressures in the past were never great enough to push people up into the inhospitable area of this high pass we were crossing in our purple Satori. No churches or megalithic tombs. If the Little People had been forced to come up here on the run from the Celts, from these heights they might have hurled down their bloodchilling curses – curses which are still in effect in the minds of many Irish, as in, "This is a cursed country."

Those were real curses.

When Morton arrived in Kenmare, he found herds of cattle in the street and a fair day in progress: "Kenmare is as typical a southern Irish country town as you will see in a day's march. It is beautifully placed beside Kenmare River."

Today there were no cows and no fair. The town seemed completely devoted to hikers. Every second store sold tents, boots, compasses, and maps. People were going hike-crazy. The Irish Army was sponsoring a 150-mile walk to raise money for cancer. Perhaps there were some hikers in Morton's day, and that inspired him to use that line about a day's march.

One thing about Kenmare that hadn't changed since Morton's day, since the days of Tutankhamen for that matter, was the lovely stone circle in the waterfront park. Fifteen stones, each one a beauty.

Tough little Dotty Doyle had told me about the Tidy Town Award, awarded annually to the tidiest town. She said it was a prize of two hundred pounds. "Sometimes it's a big trophy, a big cup or something, you know. It makes people to make an effort."

We stopped in Sneem, the recipient of last year's Tidy Town Award. *Sneem*: even the name has a certain tidiness about it. There was a piece of contemporary sculpture – a T-shaped set of stainless-steel forms representing standing stones – in the town square, and everything visible was freshly painted in a grand variety of light-hearted pastel shades. But it was all a bit too tidy, too neat, too cute, too pretty. I was gasping for a little blight.

"Maybe you don't want to admit how much you like this tidy town," said Lourdes.

"That's very shrewd of you. But untrue, so there, dear heart, and let's not argue. Maybe some ice cream would cheer us up."

"Fresh-packed?" said Lourdes.

"Of course," said I.

"Factory-packed, we have here," said the jolly, clean-shaven, red-cheeked old fellow behind the counter of the corner store. "You were looking for fresh-packed, were you? Only two places in the village where you can get them. You see the house with the blinds down? You can get them there. Or you can get them at the little shop below the bridge."

"Oh, give us a couple of factory-packed," I said, before checking with Lourdes. A look of annoyance flashed over her face.

How would you like a megalithic tomb for your front lawn? Or a ring fort in the backyard for the kids? That's what the West of Ireland is like. Why is it that kids are always building forts? Or that they are so unfriendly toward new kids in the school or neighbourhood?

If you imaginatively delete from the landscape in County Kerry all the houses that are less than sixty years old, it'd be barren. It must have been desolate when Morton came through with his happy smile and the sad news that his brown cow had died.

Staigue Fort is a huge, blind structure of indeterminate antiquity and mysterious origin, pointing straight down the valley towards the Kenmare estuary three miles to the south. The wall of this massive, egg-shaped, roofless construction is thirteen feet thick at its base and eighteen feet high. The fort is about ninety feet in diameter, and there are no windows. One small, lintelled door is the only entrance. There are two rabbit-hole entrances into souterrain crawl spaces inside the walls. Anyone over five feet tall would find it difficult to get into these cavities, which might have served as hiding places and for storage – much like the stone towers that would spring up later in the Christian era as protection from the Vikings.

It's said Staigue Fort was built by the indigenous people, defending themselves against the invading Celts, about the time of the founding of Rome. Built against the inner walls is an elaborate arrangement of well-constructed steps in X-shaped formations, leading to positions of defence atop the wall. The wall slopes inwards – what is known as a "pronounced batter" – and there is no base or foundation of any kind. These ancient people just started building a circular wall slanting inwards in a most pleasing and evocative manner, in stunning harmony with the surrounding hills and the general downslope of the valley in the direction of the sea.

Such a fort in such a valley is like a major theme in a symphony. The eye keeps going back to it. How long was it occupied and by how many different people? No one knows.

And why is it so beautiful?

The Fort Staigue Hotel is an eighteenth-century manor, with the outer walls painted pink and, on the ground floor, a small pub, where a small man who looked like Dylan Thomas with a beard was drinking a glass of Paddy's straight up. We wanted to spend the night, but first we were hungry and the kitchen was closed, so Dylan directed us to the nearest restaurant, Smuggler's, about twenty minutes to the west. We broke our promise to return, for Smuggler's wasn't to our taste, and we had to drive further before finding a place that was. After eating, we were too tired to head back, so we took a little room in Waterville.

Our hostess played a Beethoven bagatelle on the piano, as if from memory, then averred that she knew nothing about music, a ghost was guiding her hands. In the middle of the night Lourdes sat up in bed and declared there was a ghost in the room. My hair stood on end.

"Anyone we might know?"

"Yes, actually. It's Beethoven."

In the morning we were unable to get someone to take us sailing out to Skellig Michael to see the remains of the eighth-century monastic settlement on a high rock ten miles out in the Atlantic. Even though it was a lovely, calm day, everyone said the weather wasn't suitable. "No trips out there till May. There's a terrible swell out there this time of year."

I thought this was bad luck caused by our breaking our promise last night to the folks at the Fort Staigue Hotel, but Lourdes simply didn't believe them, and she started grumbling and muttering. She grumbled that it was simply off season, the boats weren't ready, and it wasn't economical to go out there with such a small party. And she muttered about how it would have been a different story if we'd started flashing hundred-pound notes.

We went into one of those little stores that sell everything, including books for tourists. We bought a book on Skellig Michael. I flipped through it appreciatively and said to the guy who ran the store, "This is every bit as good as being there. If I read this book I could pretend I'd been there." I could feel one of my manic and talkative moods coming on. Was this going to be the day I got into serious trouble?

"But you don't appear to be a pretending sort of man," he said.

"True, and thank you. You've captured my essence there. Now let me look at your store. Oh, it reminds me of the Irish shops we have in Toronto, but they're not nearly as . . . funky."

Oh oh! I shouldn't have used that word. The guy thought I was being sarcastic.

"Funky?" he said, suspiciously.

"Funky, as in they don't carry things like this and this and this . . ." Among the tourist items, identical to what could be found in Irish stores around the world, were scattered a range of more homely things for the local market, like toiletries, flypaper, and underwear.

"But," he said, "we have to earn a living here, too."

His feelings were a little hurt, and I'd been an ass. He thought "funky" was an insult. Yet I hadn't been insulted when Lourdes told me I was "pretty funky for a guy my age."

The green hills of Ireland become greener than green in the summer. Green hills are greener than blue skies are blue. All the hilltops were veiled in mist as we drove the Ring of Kerry around Ballinskelligs Bay. The mist made the flanks of the hills shine like emeralds, a green impossible to understand in the slanting bright waves of clear light.

Ballinskelligs Bay is where, according to legend, Cessair, the granddaughter of Noah, became the first human to set foot on Irish soil. An alignment of four ghostly stones, standing tall on a hill overlooking the sea, was said to have been erected, shortly after the landing, to commemorate the event.

Little schools of cyclists, abnormally delineated in islands of clarity in the sea of morning mist, would suddenly come sailing by, two abreast and dressed in bright blue track suits.

Thirty German trout fishermen had been in the restaurant last night. A large group of tall, healthy, blond, and rather dull-looking men, with pink cheeks and little or no English. They were certainly chugalugging the beer, but they were remarkably quiet, thank God. I didn't feel up to a chorus of German drinking songs.

Lourdes and I had our first little tiff. I complained to the manager, good-naturedly I thought, that here we were on the sea but we couldn't get fresh fish. The manager became defensive, prompting me to escalate things by adding that I thought the thawed-out fish with chips was a little pricey. Lourdes thought I was acting like a rude tourist, like Pepe in his own house, and she was dead right. I didn't know what to say, felt terrible, couldn't speak, tears came to my eyes.

She saw my sad look and forgave me. I apologized and ordered the most expensive bottle of wine on the list and soon all was forgotten.

Somewhere south of Portmagee I made a wrong turn and stopped to ask directions. We were in the Gaeltacht again. The woman who'd been walking the road between two villages couldn't understand my accent at first, and didn't know whether I was speaking unintelligible Irish or unintelligible English. "Do you have the English?" she said.

At Lough Currane we turned off along a donkey path and were afforded, through the field glasses, a splendid view of the small twelfth-century Romanesque church on Church Island, on which Saint Finan had built a monastery in the sixth century. A farmer dressed in kneehigh black gumboots and blue coveralls appeared on the road, so we stopped to chat and to ask if we could get a boat to go out to the island. He gave us the name of someone who might let us row out and pointed to a house on the far side of the lake.

"This is a cul de sac," he said. "You don't go flat out, now."

"This car won't go flat out," I replied.

He laughed.

"Flat out?" said Lourdes. "What is flat out?"

The farmer kept smiling. "And what part of the United States would you be from, *sor*?"

"From the Canada part."

"From Canada! Oh my God! I really thought you had a slightly different accent."

"We're smarter than Americans, too, and easier to get along with. And this lady, she's from Spain."

Lourdes smiled seductively.

"Oh, my!" said the farmer. "A Canadian gentleman and a beautiful lady from Spain both in the same car. This is my lucky day."

"She's one of those flamenco dancers."

"My oh my! Imagine! What a coincidence. My wife's a flamenco dancer, too. Why don't you park the car and come up and meet her? She'd love to meet both of you. We can get to know each other a bit. We have quite a collection of Spanish flamenco music."

Lourdes didn't look very excited at the prospect. After all, she'd really just taken a few dance lessons as a child. Nothing serious, though she certainly looked the part.

"I think this is too weird for us," I said. "We're just simple folks."

The fellow with the boat wasn't home, so we just sat there, gazing at the island through the field glasses for an hour. Built into the wall of the church, according to the *National Monuments Guide*, is an unusual stone of uncertain date, depicting a goat-legged musician playing an early stringed instrument, a kind of broad violin. The island also has traces of several older buildings and eight pillar-stones, two with old Irish inscriptions, one that has been translated as "A blessing on the soul of Anmchadh" and the other as "A blessing on the soul of Gilleinchomded O'Buicne."

Lourdes had it all figured out: the legends of the Little People were invented because the Celts felt a strong sense of guilt for having killed off the indigenous folk.

"The Little People are not dead, we never killed them off, they are just hiding from fear in their underground forts like rabbits. And they are still powerful and spiteful. That is what the legends say."

Through the window of a pub in Portmagee, on the extreme north-west tip of the Iveragh Peninsula, we could look out across Valentia Island and Dingle Bay. We could almost see the Blaskets, from a different angle this time. "There's nothing but ocean between you and Newfoundland, 1,900 miles away," reads *Ireland: The Rough Guide*, adding that Valentia Island was the starting point for the first transatlantic cable in 1857. For a few years the people around here had better communications with New York than with Dublin.

The pub was dead quiet. We asked if we could get a sandwich. The bartender disappeared and came back five minutes later, out of breath but armed with a bag of groceries.

Lourdes gave him a curious smile. "Where were you?" she said.

"Shop down the street. We were a little low on supplies."

He pulled a ham out of the bag, a jar of mustard, a loaf of bread, Canary Island tomatoes, other things.

"Could we ask how much were those tomatoes?"

"A pound a pound."

"Same as last week in the Boyne Valley!"

"Prices are pretty well the same everywhere in Ireland. Too high."

After lunch I asked him if we should go to Valentia Island.

"That you should," he said, instantly, as if he knew I was going to say that. "Knightstown is lovely."

"Too rough though, isn't it?"

"It's not rough at all. It's a very nice place."

"I mean the sea."

"Oh, the sea!" He laughed. "It's pretty calm in here, but there's some big swells out there."

"It was too rough yesterday," said Lourdes.

"Oh, it would be, yes," he said patiently. "But, you know, it's only half a mile across. And you can always drive over the bridge."

They both looked at me. I didn't realize there was a bridge.

The bartender was George Kennedy, a red-haired, rosy-cheeked fellow who was about the same age as Lourdes. We weren't the only customers. An English cyclist had been sitting quietly in the corner with his pint. But now he was talking, with a sarcastic and repetitive air: "Ireland is the only country in the world where the bartender goes next door to buy stuff for the sandwiches. I don't believe it. Ireland is the only country in the world where somebody would go to the shop to make you ham sandwiches."

"Maybe this is true, maybe not," I said softly to George. "But I want you to know we're grateful for what you did."

"Thank you."

"He's just jealous."

George laughed nervously.

"Besides, I don't think it's all that unusual. In rural parts of Canada they would do the same. Only in the big cities do they think of profits first, service to the tired and hungry traveller last." And in a whisper I added, "Besides, he's just a condescending Englishman with a typical English penchant for generalizing about everything."

George rolled his eyes and smiled.

The Englishman came over to the bar to find out what we were whispering about and to tell us a few things he thought we might not know, as people from the imperial centres are wont to do.

"You're better off in a pub," he said. "Bar food is cheaper, of course. The restaurants have the fish, but the fish is fairly dear, though."

"This is so," said George. He sensed I was getting steamed. "Especially this time of the year now. There is no catching of the fish, you know, the fishing boats are not out now." He was determined to keep the peace. "The weather has been so bad we couldn't go out, you know. The big fishing boats from Europe can come in now. They're allowed, with the Common Market and all that. The big factory ships from Europe, they're too big. The boats we have here are only small boats."

Lourdes gave me a look that said See?

"Oh, darn it," I said. "And there I was last night complaining about the fish being pricey. What an ass I am."

Lourdes looked away.

"But it's the same in Canada," I persevered. "We only have small boats, and the huge boats from the States, Japan, Russia, France, Spain, Portugal, with their driftnets and so on, all that technology, come in and our little fishing boats have to sail out and give the big ships hell with megaphones. And they retaliate with earplugs."

The Englishman paid up and left. George immediately relaxed.

"Are you from here?" I said to him.

"I'm *from* here, but not from *here*."

"How could that be?"

"I moved down the road two miles. But I've been here two years."

I looked around. "Lively in the evening?"

"We have the traditional dancing every Sunday night. And the traditional singing on Friday, Saturday, Sunday, and Monday nights."

"So there's singing *and* dancing Sunday night."

"That is so."

"Our timing has been off on this trip. The only time we heard good Irish music, the pub was so crowded with loud-mouthed louts, drunken oafs, and ignorant layabouts you could scarcely hear it."

"Really? Good Lord! Where would that have been?"

"Across the bay in Dingle."

He was shocked. A glance from Lourdes suggested it was time I shut up and let George talk.

"Now here," he said, "you'll find a more respectful crowd for all the types of Irish music. Nobody talks, everybody listens, if it's good serious Irish music and it's, like, live, not recorded. Except for fiddle music, then you can talk and holler all you want."

"And dance."

"With dance music it's all right to make a lot of noise. It's expected; it shows you like it."

"But this wasn't dance music at all! This was tender old Irish folk ballads, with traditional instruments, all sung so sweetly by two young women sopranos, they sang like angels."

"What was their names?"

"Liz O'Riordan and Patricia Connery."

"Liz and Patricia! You don't say? And they wouldn't listen to *them*?"

"That's right. You know them, do you?"

"They've played here dozens of times. And we've always had a respectful audience."

He watched me eat my sandwich. I mentioned that we hadn't heard much in the way of Irish stories. "People always say that everywhere you go in County Kerry people will tell you stories."

"You mean like about the Little People and all that?"

"Yes."

"If you were here by night now," said George, "there are three or four old men that could tell you stories, really good stories. This is the thing about *here*, you know."

"Stories?"

"Good stories!"

"And these old men. They would tell you about the old beliefs about the fairies and all that?"

"Actually there's a house near where I live, you know, three miles . . . You don't believe, I know you don't, nobody does."

Could he be just practising up for the tourist season, like sweet, dear old Kitty Ricketts? My instincts said no. He was a lovable character, rather without guile. But then again, so was Kitty Ricketts.

"Oh, I believe in haunted houses," said Lourdes. She'd just been in one the night before.

George Kennedy launched into it:

"Not at the moment, now, but it was in my father's time. It's a very long story. But I'll tell you quick. There were landlords, right? People, I can't tell you their name, the people who owned it, the people are still in the town."

"We can make up our own names. What would they be, Irish? English?" Lourdes poked me in the rib.

"Irish they were for sure. And they don't like you talking about the dead. Now, a member of the family who owned the house accused someone who worked there of raping her. Everyone knew he was innocent, you know. But he was thrown in jail. And there he died."

Lourdes let out a very impressive howl of despair.

"And then everything happened in the house. The fairies began to haunt the house. The people got sick. The grandmother who had said the fellow raped her niece, she died. The cat was seen at her wake to be running away from a mouse. The mice chased the cat all over the house, and the cups and plates went flying all around the room."

"Whew," said Lourdes, "that's unusual. What does it all mean, George?"

"I suppose it means the devil is in the house, really," he said. "The devil is loose. But even to this day, I tell you this now, I live next door to them and I'm good friends with the son. And he says he can't work on his car after midnight, because if he puts a wrench down, then goes to pick it up, it's gone."

"Working on his car after midnight?" said Lourdes.

I poked her in the rib.

"And what was it, forty years ago the guy died, the wrongfully convicted man?" I said.

"He was in jail from age twenty to age forty, in the jail in Limerick. His sentence was up, and the day before he was to be let out, he died."

"This is truly a terrible story."

"That it is. And the priest got involved; he said special rites to get the fairies all in one room, then they locked up the room and it's still locked."

"After all these years."

"After all these years."

"Big house?"

"Oh, it was a big castle of a house. Now it's all fallen down. Except for the room where the fairies were locked in."

"And that room is still locked?"

"Yes."

"And you're," I said, "a believer?"

"Oh, I'm a believer," he replied instantly. "Definitely."

"And what would happen if we were to go there and unlock the door?"

"I don't think it would be a very good thing to do."

"You wouldn't want to join me in doing so, just as an experiment?"

"I don't think so."

I looked at George, then at Lourdes. Lourdes looked at George then at me then back at George. George looked at me then at Lourdes then off in the distance, out the window and out over Valentia Island.

"I ask you, George," I said, "did you ever hear a banshee?"

"About a year ago I did, maybe more like just less than a year."

"Eleven months." My hair was standing on end.

"About that. It was springtime, just about midnight."

I wasn't sure I wanted to hear any more of this story, for fear I'd be hearing the banshees myself.

"Now George, you're not yet thirty, a fairly young, modern man, sophisticated, intelligent. You're definitely no fool. Would you say other people in your age group in this area, are they believers?"

"I wouldn't say so, I don't think they are. Some of them are. If they go through certain experiences."

"Certain experiences?" I started trembling.

"Like the hearing of the banshees. But all my friends have gone to America. America or England really. Or Australia. I don't think I'll ever leave here really. I love this place to tears."

There was a sign on the wall with a picture of a bed. The sign said, "Many are called but few get up." There is a bit of a fetish about laziness in Ireland. Laziness is akin to saintliness. People wear "Lazy Guys Club" T-shirts. Bad things don't happen to people who stay in bed. But we were still talking about the poor fellow falsely accused of rape.

"Those people were really bad."

"That they were."

"Everybody knew he was innocent. Everybody knew he was twenty years in the Limerick jail unjustly, for something he didn't do."

"Because he was poor and he was accused by the wealthy."

"Right you are!"

A tear dropped from George's left eye. Or was it the right eye? I forget now, it's been a while.

DIARMUID O'DUIBHNE AND GRÁINNE

The Little People had definitely been bugging the car when I told Danny, the cheeky jarvey in Killarney, we had to rush off to a business meeting in Cahirciveen, because now here we were in Cahirciveen (also known as Caherciveen), and actually attending a business meeting. It was no lie after all. We had been taking pictures and snooping around at Leacanabualie and Caregal, a pair of stone forts on the south shore of Dingle Bay about a half mile apart, and also at Ballycarberry Castle, a splendid sight in the mist. All three were in alignment in the soggy, cold, misty, late-afternoon countryside.

At the castle we were adopted by a pair of springer spaniels, mother and daughter, who met us at the car, guided us up to the castle, and sprang up and down the stone stairs with us. There was no one else around. These hopelessly beautiful brown-and-white animals seemed to have been trained to welcome off-season tourists. They were so intelligent and warm it was hard to part with them.

We stopped at a petrol station and gift shop and got chatting with the owner, a super salesman of great charm, a promoter of all things local, a terribly handsome man with a big square jaw and a big toothy smile. He introduced himself as Pat Golden.

After asking us where we'd been and what we'd been doing, he told us we'd be absolute idiots to miss the meeting of the Killorglin History and Folklore Society, scheduled for that evening. It was a business meeting, but there'd be a talk later we'd find fascinating.

The speaker was an archaeologist in charge of the Southwest Kerry Archaeological Survey. Her name was Ann O'Sullivan, an Irish-woman who had studied at the University of Ottawa, then returned to Ireland to run this project, which was expected to last several years.

The talk, accompanied by a slide show, lasted several hours. I wished I'd brought Mr. Looney along. Forts like Staigue Fort, said Ann O'Sullivan, were not roofed, but rather the wooden huts that were inside them, and of which time has left no trace, were roofed.

As for the *balaun* stones, they were used for grinding corn – and only later were they picked up by Christian monks to use as baptismal fonts. Water found in the cups of these stones was considered holy and capable of causing cures.

Many forts had secret escape hatches, which the archaeologists still have trouble locating.

She confirmed what we had heard about a large and strange-looking castle sitting in downtown Cahirciveen. It was built in the wrong place because of a bureaucratic error of such magnitude that people still shake their heads about it two hundred years later. The castle was to have been built on the northwest frontier in India.

Mostly there were men at the meeting, and their remarks seemed a touch condescending at times. They sounded as if they wanted to give special encouragement to Ann, as if they were simply being kind, and she, as a mere woman, was courageous to be involved in such a project, and needed all the encouragement she could get. At other times they seemed to resent that she was a woman and didn't want to consider that she might actually know more than they. Or maybe it was just because she was an academic specialist, and they were passionate purist amateurs on a more eclectic footing and with a broader grassroots perspective.

Ann seemed anxious not to displease anyone. After all, it was the Killorglin History and Folklore Society that devised the plan for the project in the first place, and was supporting it in large part.

The survey was intended to be a complete compilation of the archaeological sites of the Iveragh Peninsula. Every archaeological site on the peninsula would be visited, evaluated in various ways, photographed, classified, and so on. Tonight's talk was to be an informative run-through of all the categories of sites on the peninsula.

For instance, she went through the four categories of megalithic tombs from the early Bronze Age: court tombs, dolmens, wedge tombs, and court cairns. She described a wedge tomb as consisting of a chamber that decreases in height and width towards the rear. "And they're constructed of large unhewn stones, and there are usually two or more roofing stones, which are supported on upright slabs called ortho slabs. Originally most of these tombs would have been covered with a cairn – a huge mound of small stones – but mostly today this rarely survives, as a lot of it would have been taken away for use in building walls."

Some of the tombs were associated with mythological events, for instance the great story of Diarmuid O'Duibhne and Gráinne, the daughter of Cormac the Magnificent, the High King of Ireland. Cormac had given his daughter in marriage to Finn, the leader of the Fianna, but, at their betrothal feast, she took one look at Diarmuid and fell in love with him. The two spellbound lovers fled.

Early this century Lady Gregory wrote a play about this ancient myth of romantic love, much in the Tristan and Isolde vein, with touches of Venus (with Gráinne as the sun goddess) and Adonis (with

Diarmuid as the god of the underworld). But it's not a good play. It's reminiscent of the things poets such as Duncan Campbell Scott were writing about Canadian Indians at the same time. She has the characters coming out with lines like: "And is it not a poor thing, strong men of the sort to be mocking at a woman who has gone through sharp anguish, and the breaking of love, on this day?"

There were two Iveragh Peninsula tombs each traditionally called Diarmuid and Gráinne. Ann said they were "places the ill-fated lovers were supposed to have slept on while they were escaping around the country. And those tombs belong to the late Stone Age or the early Bronze Age, so you can give a rough date of around 2000 B.C."

The reign of Gráinne's father, Cormac, whose sarcophagus still sits in the little Romanesque chapel on the Rock of Cashel, was in the third century A.D., so the tombs that are named after Gráinne and Diarmuid were ancient even then.

Ann O'Sullivan was certainly covering the bases when she said that alignments of standing stones were thought by some to have something to do with ritualistic purposes or astrological divination, and to others they were merely cattle scratchers.

She also spoke of radical climate changes that created the peat bogs, and how with the increased cutting of peat in recent centuries the remnants of old wooden corduroy roads, stone trackways, and fences from five thousand years ago are being uncovered.

"And also found beneath the bog are areas of cultivation ridges. Because the land was so bad, the farmers had to dig ridges through the soil and then put seaweed on the ridges themselves and then put the soil above that again. That was the best way to drain the land, so they could plant their wheat and barley."

Shell middens had been dated to 3500 B.C., and various kinds of elaborate cooking sites had been located.

There are between thirty and forty thousand ring forts in Ireland. They're usually dated to the early Christian period, though it's known that many were built in the Iron Age, and it's thought that there may even be some, such as the sublime Staigue Fort, earlier than that.

Each ring fort was probably the settlement of one family, and each was a self-sufficient farm site. The enclosing wall or bank of earth would have been used to keep the cattle and sheep in at night, safe from wild animals or rustling parties.

At one point she was talking about the ancient swastika symbol, and someone in the audience made a tasteless joke about the Jews. A lot of men in the audience were subtly making interjections intended to show they knew their stuff too. No one actually contradicted anything she had to say; I don't think anyone could have, or they would have, so anxious to do so did they seem.

She also spoke of the slab shrines found at many early Christian sites. Inside would be the bones of the saint who founded the monastery or whatever. The faithful would make pilgrimages to these sites. At one end there would have been a round hole, so the pilgrims could put in their hands and touch the bones of the saint.

At the reception we were given the ubiquitous ham sandwiches on soda bread and vast quantities of tea. In Ireland you can't have too much tea. By some mystery of the Irish climate, tea doesn't have the diuretic effect it has elsewhere. Capacity for whiskey also is much greater in Ireland, for you soon discover exactly the right amount of whiskey to drink, so that it takes away the chills, lifts your spirits exactly the right amount, provides exactly the right amount of comfort, and dries your socks should they be wet (as they probably are). And it never makes you drunk.

A tall, hefty, generous sort of American man in his early sixties had recently retired from his job in some San Francisco financial institution, moved to Ireland, and taken a large but solitudinous house on the west coast. He chatted merrily, with a mug of tea in one hand and two ham sandwiches in the other. He was a happy fellow who had nothing but praise for his neighbours. He refused to let anyone make him feel self-conscious about being a foreigner, and he said he never missed a meeting of the Killorglin History and Folklore Society. I had the feeling the others could have been a bit friendlier to this relative newcomer, he was being ignored and isolated like the new kid in the class, but he didn't appear to notice anything amiss and he certainly seemed to be enjoying himself. He reminded me of H. V. Morton.

THE HAG OF BÉARA

A man was standing outside a remote farmhouse on a lonely road a few miles south of the village of Tuosist, on the Béara Peninsula, the southernmost of the major Irish peninsulas jutting out into the Atlantic. He was an Englishman, a signpainter who had sold up and moved to this quiet part of Ireland. His name was Peter Bullough, and his house was at the bottom of a sweepingly high steep hill. He pointed out an interesting stone circle three-quarters of the way up the hill. Through the field glasses we picked it up, but just barely.

Lourdes was all for climbing up to have a closer look. I felt lazy, but came along anyway, and, as often happens, the closer I got to the stones the more enthusiastic and energized I became.

There were nine stones, and the configuration had been lined up with a sharp and towering mountain peak off in the distance to the west. This would have been Knockatee Mountain, with Knockanouganish, slightly higher, to the south, but not visible from where we were because of the angle. From this point the peak of

Knockatee looked as if it would coincide with the setting point of the sun at the summer solstice.

When we returned a couple of hours later, Peter said he could see the stones from his bedroom window and often at night, when there was a good moon, he would get out his modest four-inch Schmidt-Cassegrain telescope and lie there gazing at the stones and pondering the manifold mysteries of the lives of his ancient neighbours. "It's almost completely unimaginable," he said. "Rather heartbreaking, actually."

The Béara, one peninsula south of the Iveragh, was the home of the blind Hag of Béara, who over a thousand years ago wrote her famous lamentation about the joys of youth and the miseries of old age. The poem comes down to us in numerous versions; the one chosen for modern translation by Thomas Kinsella – "The Hag of Béara" in *The New Oxford Book of Irish Verse* – seems agonizingly personal, but as one reads the voice becomes the voice of Ireland, and one becomes convinced that whoever wrote the poem fully intended that chilling duality. In this poem the political and the personal become one. And the Hag's spirit is still alive on the Béara, where one does get the sense that Ireland is miserable in its old age but was once joyous in its youth.

> *Nothing but narrow bones*
> *You will see when you look at my arms.*
> *But they did sweet business once*
> *Round the bodies of mighty kings.*

In a restaurant in Castletown Bearhaven, on the south shore of the Béara Peninsula, Lourdes had a disorienting experience. A door from the dining room led into the pub. She walked across the pub and into the toilet. There were four drinkers at the bar and one bartender. When she came out of the toilet the bar was empty, no bartender, no drinkers. Then she looked through a little opening and saw the four drinkers and the bartender in another pub. So she went back

into the washroom and left via another door and found herself outside in the cold night air. So she re-entered the washroom and finally
managed to get back into the first pub, and thence back into the dining room.

"It was like a mirror image. They were watching me all the time,
but they didn't offer to help or anything. They just watched me coldly
without smiling. I made a remark about going through the wrong door
but they didn't say a word, just kept staring."

We'd driven over the Healy Pass and then along the shore of
Bantry Bay to Castletown Bearhaven, an old port town (a.k.a.
Castletownbere) sandwiched between the Slieve Miskish Mountains
and the calm deep waters of Bear Haven, billed as the second-largest
harbour in Ireland and freckled with freighters and fishing boats. The
town was full of bored-looking sailors from Spain, Sweden, and San
Salvador. In a pub Lourdes seemed scandalized when she told me the
Spanish sailors sitting at a table behind us were blissfully chatting
away about how ugly and standoffish the Irish women were. For a
moment I thought she was going to attack them.

When we returned that evening from visiting a stone circle on a
hill overlooking Castletown Bearhaven, our bed-and-breakfast lady
recommended a local schoolteacher, Cornelius Murphy, as someone
who knew a lot about prehistoric monuments.

We went to see Cornelius the next day, and he turned out to be a
treasure – modest, unassuming, and full of fire. Also generous. He
gave us three large home-made, computer-generated maps of the
region with points of prehistoric interest numbered and keyed to a
printout listing descriptions of the spots.

He brought in the tea, sat down, and asked if we had any idea of
what the stone circles were. I told him I thought of them in part as
giant clocks, lunar or solar timepieces.

"Very likely that's true. And they're Bronze Age, they've been
gauged to that period. In other words they're somewhere in the region
of 1500 to 2000 B.C. As for the wedge tombs, they would be from the
same Bronze Age period, so they would be the older antiquities,

among the oldest in the peninsula. There's a stone circle up above Castletown Bearhaven —"

"We went to see that last night," said Lourdes.

"Oh good. Well there's a lot of research going on into this at the moment, and they've discovered that the people who erected circles such as these were a very sophisticated people. You've heard of Newgrange?"

"We were there," said Lourdes, "but we didn't get to go in. We're hoping to get back there."

"Well, in essence that's really just a larger and more-elaborate stone circle. Basically much the same as what we have right here in town. And there's normally an entrance that would have the two tallest stones normally facing in an easterly direction. On the west side there's almost always what's called a recumbent. In other words instead of being upright, which most of the stones are, one is always on its side – usually the most western. And for ages nobody knew exactly why —"

He paused and took a big gulp of tea.

"And now they know?"

"Well now they have found out that this doorway" – he was refer-ring to the portal stone at the eastern end – "forms an alignment with the recumbent stone at the back, and it forms a line in many of them on either the longest or shortest day of the year with the sun at either sunrise or sunset. This one up there above town, I went to visit it in June to see what was going to happen as the sun was going down —"

Another glug of tea went down.

"And what happened?"

"If you had seen what would be the tallest stone with the point on it – one of the portal stones, the other has fallen beside it – as the sun set on the hill behind it, it was exactly in line with the middle of the recumbent stone behind it. In other words that was the farthest north the sun was going to go."

"Shortest night of the year."

"Right. From then on the sun was going to be setting, you know, just going back again."

We pretty well knew this from books, from talking to others, and also from looking at the stones, but it was satisfying, even exciting, to hear him tell us so precisely and confirm certain things – and simply to be there listening to him speak with such devotion.

"So that was just that one there from my own observation of it. But they didn't do it, obviously, just for that alone. It would be much easier to have a stone alignment, a series of three standing stones or more, which would have indicated the same thing."

"Yes, I've thought about that a lot."

"Now there are these alignments of three stones also in the locality and again dating from the same period. As for the complex stone circles, there are various theories but everybody who's looked at this knows it was more than just for determining the solstice. But what else? It's hard to say."

He was wearing a white shirt, an old thick woollen sweater, a pair of faded and rumpled jeans. There were piles of students' papers and books all around. His wife and teenaged kids were huddled in the kitchen. Obviously our presence in this little house was inconveniencing them and it was time to go.

"Those maps will keep you going for a few hours," he said. "If you don't bring them back, I'll send the police after you." This was his way of saying we could keep them. He had lots of copies. He mentioned that, in addition to being a schoolteacher, he was president of the local historical society. And he mentioned that Ann Lynch, a well-known Irish archaeologist, had written her thesis in part on Peter Bullough's stone circle near Tuosist.

We drove around in heavy rain with the maps. For the longest time we couldn't find anything we were looking for. We kept getting lost. The roads didn't match the maps. High in the Slieve Miskish range above Castletown Bearhaven, we found a standing stone not marked on the maps. We got out of the car, hopped across a ditch, climbed a fence, and slogged across a muddy field to have a closer look.

It was strange, a flat standing stone, two arm lengths in width, with a flat, wedge-shaped bevelled top that seemed to be pointing to something. I'd never heard anyone talking about anything like this, but as I looked at this stone, I began to think that it was some kind of prehistoric road sign.

My intuition proved correct when I looked to see what it was pointing towards: a series of three small wedge tombs, about eighty yards away in another field on the far side of a stone fence. It seemed strange that I had noticed the marker rather than the tombs, since both would have been equally visible from the road.

My heart did a little *boing* as I excitedly climbed the stone fence to get to the three wedge tombs, without taking the time to explain to Lourdes what I'd discovered. I looked back. There she was, still standing by the marker stone.

On looking back, I discovered another much larger wedge tomb – a large capstone sitting on four smaller upright support stones – that had, somewhere over the centuries, become incorporated into the stone fence I had just climbed.

The marker stone, the large wedge tomb, and the set of three smaller wedge tombs were perfectly aligned. When we got back to the car we found these four tombs were marked on the map, although the prehistoric highway marker was not, and these were the tombs we happened to have been searching for, with no luck, when we found the marker. In other words, the ancient marker was a more reliable guide to the tombs than Cornelius Murphy's computer-generated map of the area. According to the map, the traditional name for the large wedge tomb, which had been incorporated into the stone fence, was King Lear, and the three smaller ones were the Three Daughters.

They were all in alignment with the stone marker. And, it seemed, with the setting point of the sun at the summer solstice.

A few miles north of Castletown Bearhaven, near Eyeries, on the north side of the peninsula, we parked and, after long walks across foggy bogs and up and down soggy hills, we confronted the Ballycro-vane ogham stone, the tallest ogham stone in Ireland, a ridiculously tall, skinny stone 5.18 metres high, taller and skinnier than any stone anywhere in the world. In his *Guide to the National Monuments in the Republic of Ireland*, Peter Harbison describes this stone as "looking almost like a modern piece of sculpture."

My left leg was throbbing, and I'd been losing energy steadily for hours in the cold rain and boggy fields. Lourdes had been constantly bounding ahead of me, then patiently waiting for me to catch up. I kept wondering what I was doing there. Why wasn't I at home reading a book in front of the fire with my kittens in my lap? It got so bad that at one point I put a little too much weight on my cane, it sank a little too deeply into the bog, and, when I tried to pull it out, it came out without its rubber tip.

But there was energy in the stones. As I got closer to the ogham stone, standing there atop the highest of the many low hills in the area, just at the point where it was marked on the map, the stone's energy took over and made me forget my pain, my weariness, and my missing rubber tip. The power of the mysteries took over and magne-tized me. Soon I was waiting for Lourdes to catch up.

The ogham inscription, hacked into the stone in the early-Christian era, already millennia after the stone had been erected, read MAQIDECCEDDAS AVI TURANIAS ("of the son of Deich descen-dant of Torainn," is Harbison's translation). The ogham script, pecu-liar to Ireland, was a fifth- and sixth-century alphabetic system for transcribing Latin with a series of notches for vowels and lines for consonants. It would appear that Latin was all the rage in Ireland at that period, though little is known as to why this should have been so.

URAGH

In the deserted hills above Eyeries on the northwest coast of the Béara Peninsula, a modest little tea shop, bookstore, and crafts studio sat by itself on the side of a hill a hundred yards straight up from the road. For four pounds I bought an antiquities map of southwestern County Cork, exclusive of the Béara. It was called "Ancient, Sacred and Historic Sites of West Cork," and it listed three hundred sites, and included forty or fifty charming little ink drawings.

Ann and Phil, who ran the shop, told us a little about Jack Roberts, the author/artist/designer/mapmaker, a transplanted Englishman of rather eccentric ways, who lived in an old stone millhouse near the town of Leap, east of Skibbereen on the south coast of County Cork. If we needed more information about any of the sites, we could give Roberts a call. They gave the impression that Roberts, like Mr. Looney, was a recluse who loved visitors but seldom got any.

They also told us about a wonderful stone circle, further up the

peninsula but hard to find and not on the Roberts map or any map.*
According to dowsers, the circle was on the spot where three major
ley-lines crossed. Our hosts had camped at the stone circle last year,
at the summer solstice. They said they fell silent as midnight
approached. Phil said he felt waves of energy all around the area,
while Ann felt a column of energy coming up out of the earth and
going straight up into the air from the tops of the stones.

This was the Uragh stone circle, a few miles east of the village of
Tuosist, but in a much more remote and heavily wooded area between
Lough Inchiquin and the Cloonee loughs.

We drove east along the south shore of the Kenmare estuary until
we returned to the village of Tuosist. I thought we might visit Uragh
first, and then revisit Peter Bullough at his place south of Tuosist to
see if he knew anything about it. Ann and Phil said they knew Peter,
and they seemed to think he had a much stronger interest in the old
stones than he had indicated to us, in general, though he was certainly interested in the one sitting on the hill above his house.

At a certain point we made a right turn and drove until we reached
what Jack Roberts would later say was a Stone Age trackway. It followed the east side of the Cloonee loughs. Soon we were in a deep,
narrow, uninhabited valley wedged in beside steep-rising mountains
on one side and the fresh mountain lakes on the other. But we kept
failing to find the stones of Uragh, and the road ultimately faded out
in the forest south of Lough Inchiquin.

Lourdes's eyes were wide and moist. A mood of silent timelessness
was everywhere. The silver surface of the lake lay only an inch lower
than the narrow lakeside stone road, and little waves lapped almost at
the car tires. Where were those damned stones? As soon as we realized
we had gone too far one way, we turned around and went back the
other way. There was no one to ask directions of. We were the only

---

* It has since appeared on Jack Roberts's more recent map, "Antiquities of
the Béara Peninsula."

people in the valley. And then, after three or four sweeps of the area, suddenly there was another prehistoric road sign.

It was suspiciously like the marker stone pointing out King Lear and the Three Daughters, but much smaller. It was a thin, wedge-shaped stone, standing about three feet high on the narrow margin between the road and the shore. The top of the stone was bevelled, with the narrow, lower end pointing down and the thicker, more-elevated end pointing out directly across the lake to a doughnut-shaped island that up to that point had somehow escaped our attention.

And in the hollow of the concave island sat what had been drawing us, a set of upright stones, so small at this distance that we would never have spotted them without the help of the little roadside marker that had been quietly standing there for thousands of years. Just as the King Lear marker had helped us when Cornelius Murphy's maps had proven unreliable, so this lakeside marker gave us a boost when Phil and Ann's directions proved a little too vague.

The stones we'd been visiting had an inhuman quality about them, as if they had been erected by beings so close to nature that their lives and modes of behaviour were, as Peter Bullough had said, impossible to imagine. After all, according to certain legends they could control the weather and levitate, like the pre-Buddhist shamans of Tibet.

But these subtle little markers added exactly the human touch that made the stones come alive for us in terms we could almost relate to. It was easier to imagine a devoted, solitary craftsman carving and erecting such a marker stone than it was to imagine whole gangs of sorcerers and shamans engaged in the huge project of erecting a stone circle.

Twenty feet along we found another small stone marker, a twin of the first, pointing out to the island at an appropriately sharper angle. Where the road left the shore of the lake, we parked the car and walked through the woods toward the point where the island almost touched the shore. We waded barefoot across a pair of fast-moving, frigid, stony-bottomed streams, and traversed a sloping meadow until we were standing at the edge of the hollow and looking down into it, the hollow at the centre of the island.

We were looking down towards the Uragh stone circle, marvelling at the stones, the sense we had that they were alive and sentient. They produced a sense of excitement in us, in some way beyond our powers of analysis but having something to do with the subtlety of their positioning, the gravity of their demeanour.

It dawned on me that we were standing in the middle of an ancient trackway, a processional route fifteen feet wide that snaked across country, jumped over to the island, and crested the hill on which we were standing. It was a road like no other road, a heavenly road, a road that ended at an altar of great luminosity. The road coasted gently down toward its destination: Uragh.

There were six stones altogether, and they were hefty, solid, indomitable stones. They were standing there like great dark-brown dreamlike ancestors, old but still strong, like a memory of a previous life that has suddenly floated ashore from the sea of forgetfulness. The first two formed a gap, an entranceway, and then the road immediately ended against a large recumbent stone, lying on its side so that it formed a kind of altar about three feet high.

Immediately behind this altar was the largest of the standing stones, a stout, thick, dark, rich-coloured stone about thirteen feet high and five or six feet in diameter. This was the end of the road. On each side of the recumbent stone was another smaller standing stone.

From our position, one would walk a hundred yards down to the monument to enter the small enclosure. From up here the main stone and the recumbent lying in front of it created a feeling of sublime religious amazement, similar to the feelings aroused at the altar of a great cathedral, but much more powerful, if only because less familiar.

These stones had obviously been standing here for eons before the arrival of the Celts, though the Celts were said to have venerated such sites. It's not known if they were built by the Tuatha Dé Danann, who live on in the stories of the underground fairy people in a mirror-image underworld, full of magic and immortality. According to the *Irish Book of Invasions*, compiled in the twelfth century, the Tuatha Dé Danann were the fifth people to invade Ireland, having defeated the mysterious and supposedly dimwitted Fir Bolg at the battle of Magh Tuireadh in County Sligo. After their defeat the Fir Bolg folk fled to the Aran Islands, where, on the island of Inishmore, they built the massive stone fort of Dún Aonghusa. The demonic Fomonians were another race said to have inhabited Ireland. These nasty folks were extortionists and tax collectors, and if you didn't pay up they cut off your nose. All we know is that the same culture that set up the Uragh stone circle also built Newgrange, Knowth, and Dowth. The Tuatha Dé Danann have my vote, for what it's worth, which is nothing really. It's amazing how little is known.

Far past the southern end of the lake could be seen a tall, thin waterfall shooting silently straight down from a mountain. We were encircled by mountains and lakes. I walked back along the trackway, turned, and re-approached Uragh, coming back over the hill and suddenly seeing the stones again sitting quietly below. Each time I looked at them, it was with a little shock. I had the feeling I was being healed of diseases I didn't know I had, or that I hadn't yet contracted. The spirit of the place was multi-layered, savage, and overwhelming. The rest of the world didn't exist.

The trackway was a broad, clearly worn path that went right up the hill and down towards the stones in what was obviously a ritualistic route. A tall, stout stone stood alone on the shore of the lake below, and, on the far shore, the two small, wedged marker stones both pointed their narrow edges in the direction of the little island and its one hill and its circle of grand stones in the hollow below.

Lourdes and I sat on the recumbent stone, looking back along the trackway. We could see that it went up another larger hill and down through a small valley on the mainland before coming up this final hill. In fact there were clear-cut gaps in the hills, stones had been removed to make the way smoother. We scarcely noticed the cold rain, though it was pouring.

Two very large stones on the mountainous ridge far above would certainly have been positioned so they could be clearly seen from this spot, as their distance from each other seemed to equal the width of the trackway. The mist, the rain, the sound of the little rivers joining one lake to the other, the vast waterfall plunging out of the mountains too far off to the south to be heard – all this conspired to induce in me a vision of Ireland four thousand years ago, a land composed of stone circles in places of unearthly beauty and all interconnected by standing stone markers, broad highways, trackways, pathways, grassy roads. "He made the world to be a grassy road / Before her wandering feet" (Yeats). "Roads so old they seem to have been made by the gods" (Chesterton).

The trackways were perhaps not as much for ritualistic purposes but so people could go on pilgrimages from site to site, meeting other wayfarers and so on. We certainly don't know much about the pre-Celtic Irish. They had ways of being human we know nothing about. And they were smart. But these stone monuments, and the trackways that connect them, formed a primary part of their culture.

Even so, this one, at the intersection of three strong ley-lines, whatever ley-lines are, must have been particularly powerful in its beauty and magnetism. But others too, in less-fortunate localities which have now been eroded by agricultural and urban development, must have been much more impressive in previous eras.

Soaking wet, cold, but happy, as if we'd accomplished exactly what we'd set out to accomplish, we drove back to Kenmare, and drank a good measure of Paddy's each in a bar on the main street, followed by salmon sandwiches.

Everyone in the place was absorbed in watching the latest episode of an Irish soap opera. When it was over, the women went to one end of the bar and the men to the other. A French couple we had noticed eating sandwiches at Phil and Ann's place near Eyeries, and who had been at the bed-and-breakfast on a hill overlooking the Ballyhamane River and eating mushrooms and marmalade for breakfast a week or so ago, were eating salmon sandwiches a few tables away. The four of us were the only ones not engrossed in the tube.

In chatting with Lourdes since leaving the Inchiquin area, I think I must have been using the word *magic* too often. Lourdes leaned closer in a comically dramatic fashion, and said solemnly, "Your book, you should make sure you don't use the word *magic* in it."

"Why not?"

"It's just not a good word to use."

"What book?"

"The book you're going to write about this."

"What makes you think I'm going to write a book?"

"Oh, well what do you call that big fat green thing you're writing always in?"

"My notebook. Just notes. Like your taking pictures."

"You don't like me taking pictures?"

"Of course I like it. I'm always encouraging you and suggesting shots, aren't I?"

"Okay."

"You don't mind me suggesting shots once in a while, do you?"

"No, it's okay. I like it."

"And why is *magic* not a good word to use?"

"Just like in Spanish, it's used too much – it's meaningless."

We headed back to Theresa Darragh's place on the Killarney Road about two miles out of Kenmare. It was the same place we had stayed two nights before when we were heading into the Béara Peninsula. Theresa said she'd had the strangest feeling she was going to see us again.

In the morning it was pouring. We didn't get going until noon. We drove north to Killarney, and the sun came out, so we celebrated by buying ice-cream cones, then the sun went behind a cloud again and it became even colder than before. We decided to head southeast along the Cork Road to Macroom, where we had coffee and whiskey in a small hotel. Then we drove aimlessly through little side roads on

our way to Bantry back on Bantry Bay. The "magic" of the stones –
and the "magic" of Lourdes's presence – seemed to have seduced me
away, at least temporarily, from my intention of following Morton's
venerable route. But Morton would not be forgotten for long.

"Art doesn't have to be difficult," Lourdes was saying.

"What do you mean?"

"It's not hard to be an artist. Just get a big stone, tip it up on its end,
and you've got art that will last seven thousand years."

"Aren't you forgetting something?"

"What am I forgetting?"

"All the work of dreaming up the original vision, then finding suitable stones, then selecting the ones that will be used, then transport-
ing them and erecting them. All the work and organization that
would go into selecting the spot and determining the design in the
first place. And the great mystery of it all. It's not easy to put that kind
of mystery into a work of art. But the most interesting works of art
have it, and accumulate it in greater measure over time . . ."

She didn't seem to be listening.

I'd heard that somewhere – County Antrim, it might have been –
there is a golf course with a stone circle in it. It is traditional that, if a
ball comes to rest within the stone circle, one must not hit it out but
pick it up and take it out and hit it from there. One day a tourist from
Arkansas scoffed at the superstition, gave the ball a good whack from
within the circle, then promptly suffered a cardiac arrest. I asked
Lourdes what she thought.

"It seems like a true story. Even if somebody just made it up, it's
true."

"Yeah, you don't mess around with those stones."

We drove high up in the hills above Kealkil, which provided us with
telephoto and wide-angle views out over the silver waters of Bantry
Bay five miles to the southwest, and, far out in Bantry Bay, Whiddy

Island, where the filmmaker Woody Allen is reported to have a summer home.

I was becoming convinced that the Tuatha Dé Danann (also known as the Tribes of the Goddess Danu) had had a tremendous spiritual affinity for beautiful scenery. This pleased me, because I am a sucker for scenery myself. Give me a camera and I come home with the most sentimental pictures of mist, flowers, trees, gravestones, fountains, and hills. But then again, the more remote and untouched the area, the more likely there will be traces of the distant past – and coincidentally the more natural beauty will surround it.

On this barren hill high above Bantry Bay we came upon seventeen small standing stones in a perfect circle about fifty feet in diameter. In the middle of the circle sat a stone cairn, only a couple of feet high but composed of hundreds of small boulders half the size of soccer balls that had been lying there undisturbed for four thousand years, too far from settlements for it to be practical for them to have been transported away and used for building materials or fences.

Close to the cairn, placed in what appeared to be random positions but obviously representing some kind of significant alignment, stood two giant stones next to each other – one eight feet tall and one eleven feet tall. The latter was originally seventeen feet, but six feet had broken off during a fall somewhere along the line. This portion had been set upright during excavations in 1930. There was also a perfect little five-stone circle, including a recumbent, sitting roughly halfway between the outer edge of the cairn and the large outer circle.

The entire effect was riveting, the assembly of stones sitting on top of a treeless hill with sun-drenched views, with mountains all around. It was of course impossible to figure out what it was all about, which contributed to the strongly emotional feeling I had, for one can't look at the good stones without such a feeling.

After much crossing of boggy farmland, stumbling over dead sheep and foxes with holes for eyes, I jumped down from a stone fence, landed square on the foot of the bad leg, and was about to let out a great scream of pain when I was rewarded with the sight of four dolmens very close together forming a square. This assembly of stones had been badly disturbed. Originally the four dolmens were probably within a stone circle.

Later we caught *The War of the Roses* in the movie theatre in Bantry. It was as bad as I thought it would be. Any movie about divorce, however, would be welcome in a country that forbids divorce. And it would be hard for a movie to compete with what we'd been looking at the past few days. We'd be hard to impress no matter what the film.

FAMOUS PLAYERS OF
BALLYDEHOB

In Ballydehob on the south coast of West Cork we went into a pub three centuries old and met Miss Thelma and Miss Velma, twin sisters in their seventies who were born in the pub and had been working there all their lives. In her left ear, Miss Thelma was wearing a blue crescent moon inlaid with tiny opals, and in her right ear an opal earring in the shape of a cat. She was swathed in purple and plaid. She ushered us to a seat. There was no room at the bar, which had been taken over by a large party of businessmen.

As we sipped our pints, we realized that four of the businessmen were Americans. One of them was of the Kennedy brood, a handsome fellow in his early thirties. Miss Thelma couldn't remember his first name. He was talking about some project they were working on. Someone was worried about protests by environmentalists.

"You have to take your hit," said Kennedy. "You can't duck it." He didn't seem overly sympathetic to environmental concerns. At one point I heard him talking about tossing a torch into a pile of ideas.

"That's one of the Kennedys," Miss Thelma kept whispering. "One of Bobby Kennedy's sons."

I was pretty sure it was Michael Kennedy. I was impressed about being in the same Irish pub as a member of the famous Kennedy clan but – alas! – Lourdes wasn't impressed at all, and she definitely was less than enchanted about me being impressed. In fact she indicated with a look or two that she was disappointed in me.

Miss Thelma showed us some old photos of kids running around with no shoes on. "Oh we were all like that as kids," she said. "We didn't get our first pair of shoes till we were eighteen."

Lourdes had a question. "Didn't your feet get cold in the winter?"

"Oh no, running around like that, the blood gets running and warms the feet."

Miss Thelma knew Bill Hogan the cheesemaker, whom I had met a few years earlier in a train station in North Wales, and with whom I'd corresponded a bit, but she hadn't seen him for a couple of weeks. "He comes in here to pick up his messages, but he lives in Skull now, I believe," she said.

Miss Thelma dressed like Madame Blavatsky with a touch of Tallulah Bankhead and she knew everyone: the Kennedys, Bill Hogan, and Marilyn Ferguson, the author of *The Aquarian Conspiracy*.

"She's been living here the last few months working on a book. Last couple of days she's been out with an archaeological party looking at stone circles."

I cringed.

She also knew Lyall Watson, the author of *Supernature*.

"He lives here. He's in England right now promoting his new book. He travels all over the world, collects all his notes and research data, then comes back to write. Always drinks here, and he always gives us a copy of his new book when he comes out with a new one, which is fairly often, since he writes a lot."

This Mr. Kennedy had a long wave of hair over his low forehead, below which bright, confident, close-set eyes had been arranged. He was wearing fawn Italian-style cords, a dark green V-neck wool sweater, and a navy blazer with two gold buttons and no crest. His sweater was sexily tucked inside his white silk boxer shorts, which were covered with large red hearts. The shorts came into view high above the belt, at least in part, whenever he reached for a peanut. He had a red face. It could have been booze or the sun, but it was more likely what Saul Bellow calls the "cynosure flush."

He and his friends – one coincidentally looked like Saul Bellow – took their Guinnesses over to Annie's for dinner. They'd been looking at her menu and making orders at the bar and, when the food was ready, Annie herself came over to get them.

The one who looked like Saul Bellow was dressed in a black suit, a pink V-neck sweater, a white shirt, and a tie, and had white hair and a florid face. He was about sixty-five, too young for Bellow. He was having an animated conversation with the two sisters who turned out to have the same last name as his stepson – Symons. So he asked Miss Thelma and Miss Velma to write a note to the stepson. "Tell them it's from his Irish cousins."

Over in another corner of the bar was a painter, quite well known apparently, though I missed her name, a beefy Irishwoman about forty, very tall and masculine in appearance. She sat astride her stool as if it were a horse, and she was showing her portfolio to a couple of potential buyers. She was also talking about John Banville's new book. Her paintings were eighteenth century in style, accurate copies of livestock in profile and so on.

I asked Miss Thelma, when Kennedy and the other Americans took their pints over to Annie's for dinner, how she got her glasses back.

"Oh, they fly back all by themselves in the morning."

"I didn't notice any wings on them," said Lourdes, a bit miffed.

"Oh, my dear, surely you know that what is essential is invisible to the naked eye," said Miss Thelma.

I couldn't help giving her an excuse-me-I-just-ate look, but she didn't notice.

"Just like in Galway," Lourdes reminded me. She meant the glasses.

Miss Thelma straightaway said, if we wanted to see the heart of Ireland, we had to visit the stone circles. She had automatically assumed we hadn't been. It was depressing. We thanked her and left, and just as we got out on the street, a woman in an old beat-up pickup truck came barrelling around the corner and smashed into a sparkling new brown Volvo that was parked there. The owner of the Volvo wasn't all that upset. He was wearing blue coveralls and rubber boots – Irish farmer costume. I told him we'd seen the accident, but he said he didn't need any witnesses, the woman had promised to pay for the damages.

The next morning, at breakfast at Mary and Brendan Coughlan's bed-and-breakfast down the street from Miss Thelma and Miss Velma's place, Mary set us straight about the glasses: "Miss Thelma has them specially marked with a red mark underneath, so they won't go in Annie's dishwasher. She herself doesn't believe in dishwashers."

Mary and Brendan were lovely little people, just a shade over five feet tall. "They're so small and cuddly," said Lourdes. They had a walled garden full of camelias, wallflowers, and red rhododendrons – all in bloom so early in April.

"You're supposed to write to the *Irish Times* when you see the first rhododendron bloom," said Mary. "But no one bothers."

"I work for a builders' provider's firm in Bantry," said Brendan. "Lots of driving, some selling, some debt collecting." In fact he was rushing off to work, but he took a moment to say hello. He also said his family name, Coughlan, was pronounced Collin in Cork City, but Cocklan in the rest of the county, and in fact the rest of the country. He preferred Cocklan. Mary preferred Collin.

When Brendan left, Mary sat down and got into serious gossip with us about the tourist business. "Now the Americans, they tend to come in April or September. It's rare to see an American in any other month. The Germans and French, though, they always show up in July and August." She said she likes the Americans and the Germans, but "the French, they're arrogant. They have to have a go at every-thing. They eat all the food and then they complain about it. Some-times they seem on the verge of eating the table legs or whatever."

On the way to Bill Hogan's we picked up a crippled girl. We were driv-ing slowly down a long slope and had a long unimpeded view of her stashing her bicycle in a garage, then limping down to the road with great apparent difficulty and sticking out her thumb. She was going to Skull (it's pronounced Skull, it's Skull on the roadsigns, but it's Schull on the maps) and told us about her baby and how difficult it was even today in Ireland to have a baby when you're not married.

Bill Hogan, like Lyall Watson, was in London on one of his many promotional trips, unfortunately. Bill and his young friend Sean Ferry lived on the second floor of an old stone cottage, the main floor being devoted to the production of two kinds of cheese. One was named Gabriel after the 408-metre-high mountain looming in the distance and the other was named Desmond after the old name for Munster. Sean insisted we take generous samples of each, and refused our money. We chatted about the cheese business for an hour, then said farewell, took our loot, and drove off back down the long muddy lane to the main road.

VISIONS OF
ANCIENT IRELAND

Jack Roberts, the reclusive mapmaker and lover of antiquities, lived in a large, cold, and poorly maintained stone millhouse a few miles east of Skibbereen on the Corktown Road. Thomas Hardy, a renovator of old country churches before he became a novelist, would have called Roberts's place "decayed," and it was decayed, possibly as much as it had been when Hardy was a lad. But it was pleasantly decayed. The house had its charm, people stopped to take pictures of it, and Roberts's solitude and freedom were admirable.

The old millhouse would have been even quieter and more private had it been situated a little further back from the traffic, but even with it smack on the road it was hard to find. First we were directed to Roberts's father's place, a cute rose-covered cottage a few miles further out, which had an unusually well-trimmed lawn, fresh curtains, and well-dusted knickknacks on the windowsill.

Roberts *père*, a man who had the air of a retired military man, very tall and with soldierly bearing, seemed a bit embarrassed to have to tell us his son was living in such a dump. Not that I would have called it a dump you understand, but one could imagine certain family pressures on Roberts *fils*, pleading with him to do something about the state of repair of his place, especially since it was right out on the road for all to look down their noses at. How would the village of Leap ever win a Tidy Town Award? The elder Roberts probably would not have had his place so immaculate if the junior Roberts had maintained his place better. That's life.

Jack Roberts, Junior, was in his mid-thirties, and like his house, also seemed not so well maintained. He had bad teeth, madcap eyes, a zany smile, and crazy hair. He offered a sort of instant intimacy. He was the sort of man you could discuss your dreams with on first meeting. Chances are he would have had the same ones somewhere along the line, but in a different order. He dressed plainly and lacked pretensions. For a man like him, life was too short to take the time to rinse out the tea cups, sweep the floor, wash the windows, repair the lock on the front door, take down last summer's flypaper, or tell people what to do. He possessed an air of danger, very attractive to women I would suspect. I could sense Lourdes's knees weaken and heart flutter when he smiled at her, as he often did.

Jack beamed when we mentioned that we had met his father. The father might have had problems with the son, but the son had no problems with the father. Jack was right proud of the old guy. "He was a lifelong atheist," he said, "but when he moved to Ireland he joined the Catholic Church."

So I told Jack my vision: how at remote and beautiful Lough Inchiquin in the cold rain I had had a sudden intuition of Ireland being, for most of its history, a country studded with stone circles at points of great natural beauty, and the circles being consolidated by an intricate network of broad interconnecting trackways. The trackways – also known as *togher*, an anglicization of the Irish *tochar* – were the only roads in a land where for millennia peace prevailed.

"You've got it, that's it, that's the whole thing." His voice dropped. "Ah, but a vision, you know, a vision – it's a dangerous thing . . ."

"So one could just travel from stone circle to stone circle . . ."

"A bit difficult today, though in places . . ."

"And meet people, exchange information, tell stories, and move on, just spend your whole life wandering along the trackways."

"Yes, you've got it all right."

"A trackways culture."

"Yes."

"Now I ask you, Jack. Who were these people? What were they like, and what the heck are ley-lines?"

"Well now, I don't necessarily believe in ley-lines. If you get a map with all the prehistoric sites marked, you can connect them in any way you like. You can draw five-pointed stars, circles, squares, straight lines, anything. I'm not debunking Watkins. He had a valid vision. But it made him into a bit of a crank, I think. See, it's very dangerous to have a vision."

Alfred Watkins was the Englishman who around 1912 became enthused with a vision that all of the sacred monuments of antiquity were built on invisible ley-lines, straight lines that transmitted energy, natural power-lines with which our remote ancestors were as familiar as we are with electrical power, and which they knew how to tap. Dowsers claim they can detect the power, and it does run in straight lines. There are many stories of people receiving electrical jolts from standing stones, and wonderful little theories of witches using the ley-line power to fly or to levitate large stones – or maybe even to control the weather.

Watkins was a legitimate character who had decent credentials. For instance, he's credited with inventing the photographic light meter, and his book, still in print, is called The Old Straight Track. His work is discussed by such contemporary writers as John Michell, author of The New View over Atlantis, and Geoffrey Ashe, author of

The Ancient Wisdom. He may have been wrong, as Jack Roberts suggested he was, but he wasn't a crackpot. Barmy maybe, but not a crackpot. Well, maybe he was a crackpot, but he was a beautiful one. Morton would never have heard of him, I suppose.

"Am I right?" I cried. "Was this a vast era of peace? Is my vision foolish or were these stone circles never used as places where humans were sacrificed?"

"You, my good man, are perfectly correct," he said. "There was a high standard of living in those days. The people had lots of leisure time. They must have, because it took a lot of time to erect a stone circle and stone circles had no defensive or military significance whatsoever. But up they went, and up they went all over the place."

He said there had been a stone circle excavated in 1957, and the cremated remains of a youth were discovered in an urn buried in a central pit. But radiocarbon tests have shown that the cremation took place around the time of Christ, an example of pre-existing neolithic monuments being adopted for ceremonial purposes by the Celtic people, for whom the stones were probably as great a mystery as they are for us.

In my mind I had been ridiculing my own naïveté, but Jack seemed to think I was right on the beam, even when I confessed that I had the feeling that the race of people who put up the stone circles must have had a highly developed sense of natural beauty.

"Ah, yes," he said. "It would seem so for sure. The older the monuments the more beautiful the setting. Your wedge tombs and your stone circles, the oldest of them are in the most beautiful settings."

"And of course the monuments are beautiful in themselves."

"Extraordinarily so. You never get tired of them."

Jack claimed the Celts never really conquered Ireland. "It's not really a Celtic country. Never was. The Celts just sort of seeped in over a millennium, starting around 1500 B.C. There weren't all that many of them, for one thing. And the Celtic culture by the time the Celts reached Ireland was fairly well dissipated. Ireland is basically a Gaelic country."

The last statement threw me. It was like saying they're not vegetables, they're carrots. I thought Gaelic was a specific Celtic language, not a separate race.

Jack was a regionalist who knew more about County Cork than he did about Ireland. He said the ancient system of trackways still runs right around the county, picking up in various places here and there, then disappearing.

"You can drive it in places, but in some places it's wrecked."

He said when he drives it from Skibbereen to Cork, he only needs to take a few detours and he makes better time than his friends who take the direct route, the one on the road map.

"They're partly ritual and partly useful, these trackways. When you try to discover the old track system, you discover all the old stone circles and standing stones. They lie directly on the trackways. The old trackways go all around the Béara Peninsula, and if you follow the old trackways you don't need my guide, my maps. Right up to this century it was used for walking. The trackways are so ancient – the fact that they interact with the stone circles proves it."

The highest concentration of stone circles in Ireland was right here in the Cork–Kerry area, said Jack, although there was a pretty good sprinkling of them in Ulster. Similar circles could be found throughout Europe, of course, but the Irish circles are distinguished by being erected for the most part in a northeast-southwest alignment. Further, the Irish variety almost invariably featured a northeast entranceway, flanked by two tall stones, and a recumbent on the southwest side. I forgot to ask him about the small stone "highway markers," and later, going through the scanty amount of literature available on the subject of stone circles, I could find no mention of them. Possibly I'm the first person ever to write about them.

There was a knock at the door, Jack opened it, and a woman stood there for a moment then threw herself into his arms. She had been in California for three years and had just appeared at Jack's door with no warning. They excused themselves and went upstairs. Half an hour went by, with Lourdes and me sitting quietly downstairs. I began to feel cold, in a sick way, though Lourdes insisted it wasn't cold at all. I went to the car and put on an extra sweater or two, then came back in, but soon began shivering again. It was more than just cold; I felt disoriented. I went out to stand in the warmth of the bright sun, and Lourdes came out to keep me company. But she insisted it was no warmer outside.

I left her standing there and got in the car and turned on the engine and then the heater. Finally, after leaving an emergency farewell note for Jack, we took off in the car, searching for a little warmth. But soon I became so chilled and so weak I couldn't drive. Lourdes took the wheel and I slouched down in the passenger seat as we drove up into the hills overlooking the Atlantic Ocean.

Next thing I knew we were in a hotel room and Lourdes was trying to take my clothes off and get me into bed. I insisted it was too cold to get undressed, so she helped me climb under the covers with all my clothes on.

It was a splendid old hotel in Skibbereen, and we spent two nights there. Lourdes was a saint. She patiently watched television and read magazines, newspapers, and a big chunk of *The Pickwick Papers*, while I would spend an hour sleeping, followed by an hour hallucinating and an hour lying there feeling terribly weak and helping Lourdes watch the CNN twenty-four-hour news channel from Atlanta, Georgia, which seems to be shown non-stop in every hotel on the planet. I'd get my strength up just enough to go down for tea with Lourdes, then I'd resume shivering and back up to the room we'd go.

Lourdes kept assuring me the problem would soon pass, and she was sure I didn't need any medical treatment. She felt helpless, I suppose, particularly when I kept complaining about how uncomfortable the bed was, but she remained calm and never sighed, groaned, muttered, grumbled, or showed any sign of irritation whatever. The bed was really okay, but I was hallucinating that it was two smaller beds pushed together and that little bands of Irish fairies kept pushing them apart, just slightly, the crack between them widening just enough to drive me bonkers.

Finally it passed. We checked out and drove down to the fishing village of Baltimore, where we met a vast number of English people who had come to Ireland in recent years for the quiet life. We were beginning to marvel at the number of English we were meeting. Arthur, a big fat man, had been running a little French-style restaurant in Baltimore for about a year. His kids were grown and he had no responsibilities – so he came to Ireland. He had lived in Canada for a while, in the early sixties, on Yonge Street in Toronto, which was so dull in those days they were forced to slip over to Buffalo, New York, for excitement every chance they got.

"I even stayed with a Doukhobor family once."

"In Buffalo, New York?"

"Guess again."

"In Castlegar, British Columbia?"

"How did you know?"

"That's where they live."

"Oh, I thought they lived all over Canada from coast to coast, but I just happened to meet up with some in Castlegar."

"What did you think of them?"

"Strange people. Hard to get to know, to really know, you know? They sure love their food. Very fattening, their food."

"Is that where you started to put on the pounds?"

"That's all muscle, my friend."

"I'm a Doukhobor myself, actually."

"You should be proud. They're wonderful people."

"That's not what you were saying a minute ago."

"I'm sorry if I offended you, sir. What's your name? Ivanoff? Bobaloff? Onandoff? Or, my favourite, Jerkoff?"

"I'm just kidding. I'm not Doukhobor. But I know tons of them."

"Why would that be?"

"I don't know what it is. I've been attracting them like flies all my life."

We stayed at a rural bed-and-breakfast in the hills above Baltimore. Again, the people who ran it were from England, from Portsmouth, just around the corner from the birthplace of Charles Dickens, who had just been discovered by Lourdes Brasil. Mrs. Flemington was alone, her husband and son were away on a business trip. She wanted to talk about her husband. She told us he was a toolmaker by trade, but ever since childhood he just wanted to be a fisherman. He loved the boats. But his parents didn't want him to fish, they insisted he learn a regular trade. So he became a toolmaker, but he hated all the grease and grime and he wasn't good at collecting bills.

"Nobody was paying him, because they knew he was a soft-hearted soul. He used to come to Ireland for fishing holidays. And with each trip he fell more and more in love with the country. It really is quite beautiful, actually, don't you think?"

"We were just saying how ugly it is around here, right Lourdes?"

The woman's face dropped.

"He's just fooling," said Lourdes. "We think it's beautiful around here."

We all started laughing.

"You're a card-carrying card, you are," said Mrs. Flemington.

Finally her husband fell so much in love with the Baltimore area on the south coast of County Cork that he found this house and pleaded with his wife to come and have a look at it. She thought it positively mad at first, as did all their friends. But she became smitten finally.

"Now I'll never go back. Thirty thousand cars a day streamed past our house in Portsmouth. Now here maybe we get one an hour if we're lucky, and this is the main road to Baltimore. It's made a big change in

our lives, that's for sure. He wakes up every morning full of energy.
So do I."

"What about anti-English feeling? Do you get any of that?"

"We were afraid of that, to be sure, as were our friends. But honestly
I can say we've never felt any Brit-bashing at all. We're just as accepted as can be."

She said her husband had the idea of renting out fishing boats to
tourists, but the insurance would have been too high. So now he takes
them out to fish. At the moment he was in Portsmouth getting ready
to bring another boat across. His son was driving the car back.

In the morning we took a boat over to Sherkin Island, where there
were dairy farms and a pub and the ruins of an old abbey which were
being excavated. On a long walk along some country lanes we ran
into a red-faced little fellow, a farmer about thirty-five years old. He
spoke in endlessly long sentences, his voice rising and soaring and
gradually going out of control and exploding into laughter. His name
was Diarmid Heamish, and he was born here on this island amid the
five-hundred-year-old drystone farm buildings. As soon as he was old
enough, he went to Corktown to get himself a wife. Then he brought
her back and they started raising kids.

"There she is now," he said.

A small woman with huge breasts and bright red hair came out of a
small stone shed, flashed a shy smile, then went back in.

A cow came down the lane and hurried around us, mooing discor-
dantly all the way, then crossed a path to the main farmhouse, and
stood outside bellowing to be let in.

On the boat coming over to Sherkin we had met a couple from
London with rings through their noses and ears as well as being on
their fingers and thumbs. They probably had them other places too,
but I was too polite to ask. Badges advertising various rock groups
were sewn on their black leather jackets. Their hair was an unnatural
shade of black.

The woman had a job as a sales clerk in a bookshop in London. But she had quit last week in order to go on this trip with her boyfriend. She entertained us with several stories revolving around the unpleasantness of the customers she would have to serve in the store, and various sarcastic remarks she made to them in return, often startling them and upsetting them terribly. They would say they'd never shop in this store again, and she would say, "Good!" Her boyfriend was a Londoner, and he had spent time in Canada. He was a musician and had played with some bands well-known in Canada, such as Cowboy Junkies, Sonic Youth, Roxy Music – or so he said.

We had chatted all the way over to Sherkin, but our new friends disappeared when Lourdes and I went into the old friary to inspect the digging going on. *Catholics*, a film based on a novel by Brian Moore, had been shot there. We climbed the tower and looked out. There were stone walls leading the eye off in all directions, down to the sea and up to the hills in the centre of the island.

Later, when we arrived at the pub, we found the black-leather couple standing at the bar drinking Guinness. They already seemed quite tipsy. The signs said the pub was called the Jolly Roger. Since it was the only pub on the island, however, it was known simply as the Pub. There were old framed etchings of shipwrecks all over the wall, and mariner's charts in frames.

The bartender was Welsh and his wife was English. Not a native among us.

Even the archaeologists at the abbey were English.

The Welsh bartender smoked his pipe and told us he was a stonecutter by trade. He had moved to Ireland because he wanted to be a writer, and he liked the idea of not having to pay income tax. But he soon gave up writing, because he found he was better at tending bar.

"We all do what we're best at, right? I'm a piss-poor stonecutter, and I soon found out I didn't have what it takes to be a writer, whatever that might be. But I'm one helluva good bartender."

He kept going on about Irish writers not having to pay income tax. This was what he came to Ireland in the first place to take advantage of, but it really bothered him now that he had given up writing. He felt it was being abused by people who made big money writing for television. He felt it should be reserved for the less-commercial fields of writing, like poetry and fiction.

"What kind of writing were you trying to do?"

"Ever heard of an old bloke called Samuel Beckett?"

THE OLD REPROBATE

It was raining in the market town of Macroom, which we had buzzed through a few days before. Lourdes was sitting on the bed mending a tear in her black silk pyjamas, taking little sips of Paddy's from my silver flask, and shedding a tear because she felt homesick for Spain. I was gazing out the window of our room overlooking the town square.

We were back on the trail of H. V. Morton, heading back up the west coast of Ireland – destination County Donegal. But driving is tiring: I wanted to spend the rest of my time in Ireland right there, at the window of our room in this lovely, warm, old comfortable hotel. It was April in Macroom, which was situated on the River Sullane which swishes down from the Derrynasaggart Mountains, sideswiping Macroom Castle, then joining forces with the River Lee for a combined assault on the low stately bridges of Cork City.

"The Irish people are very quiet," said Lourdes, through her tears, as she sewed. "Not like the Spanish. They talk quietly in pubs, and did you notice they hardly ever honk their horns?"

"You mean when they're driving?"

"No, when they're parked."

Just then a horn honked.

A disembodied spirit floated over the town square trying to imagine the intimate lives of the people below. Over to the right stood a massive gatehouse, all that remained of Macroom Castle, which had been destroyed by fire in 1922. And on the other side of the square was the old Market House, in front of which a fellow was selling fish in the cold heavy rain.

It's amazing what can be seen when one is floating thirty feet above the town square, and invisible. Some people keep returning into the scene. It's hard to take a step without having to stop and chat, unless you fend off the garrulous by sweeping by while pointing at your watch, or mouthing the words, "Late, can't talk." But you can only do that so often before people begin calling you nasty names behind your back. Travel is so superficial – spending a day in a place where people are spending their entire lives. They know everybody, but they don't necessarily like everybody. The patterns of loyalty can be complex, with the random circumstances of birth or childhood usually taking precedence over natural affection.

A man gave another man the evil eye. It was chilling. The victim was about thirty-five, a farmer, wearing his uniform of blue coveralls and black rubber boots. He had a florid face and a great shock of curly red hair. The other man, who was wearing a green hooded raincoat, glared at him as he passed, and there was so much evil in that look that the farmer froze for a moment, then shakily got into his car, got a bottle of Paddy's out of his glove compartment, took a swig, then had a terrible time trying to get out of his parking spot and into the street. He put the car into first instead of reverse and shot forward, forcing an elderly woman with dark glasses and two white canes to skip smartly out of the way.

Cars were parked haphazardly all over the place. There weren't enough police in the entire county to ticket them all, so they never got ticketed. A woman got out of her old rusted-out turquoise Issa, slipped off her comfortable shoes, and put on a pair of high heels. She was tiny, about sixty, dressed in a red sweater and an open black coat. She left her car blocking several others.

A man walked along reading his newspaper, then stopped to unlock the door of his clothing store. A drunk with long hair and beard, who looked as if he'd been sleeping under the stars all winter, stopped him and started waving his arms. The businessman stood there on the sidewalk, still reading his newspaper. After a few minutes, the drunk stopped his tirade and continued on his way, and the businessman, without having stopped reading, stepped into his store.

A self-conscious woman with a camera hopped out of the passenger side of a car stopped in the middle of the road, looked around, and seemed to be worried that someone was watching. She snapped a picture of the massive gatehouse with surrounding vegetable and fruit stalls, then looked around again, caught someone's eye, looked away, hopped nervously back in the car, and zoomed off.

Tourist in trouble! An old red Basho has my Satori blocked in. A woman sees my plight and immediately springs into action. She goes running up and down the street screaming, "Who owns this car?"

The manager of a little sweetshop comes out and hails this red-cheeked, baby-faced cop who's been ambling across the road and stopping every few steps to direct traffic in a nicely laid-back manner.

The door of the old red Basho is unlocked. The car is on its last legs. The cop creaks the door stiffly open and climbs in. He gets out his huge collection of car keys as he sits gingerly down on the seat, which has pointy springs breaking through the worn and torn upholstery.

"Oh that one I had last night, that would fit for sure," he says, having managed to nuzzle down into the seat without any serious problems, like a mama bird into the nest.

There is quite a crowd by now. An excessively polite young fellow in a business suit comes along; he has been blocked in, too. "Me next, if it's not too much trouble, for I'm a mere Irishman," he says, self-deprecatingly. He points to his van: "Cork Confidential Shredding – Security Shredding – Confidential Document Destruction – Paper Recycling – Nation-wide Service." Everyone turns to him, and the cop hops out of the old Basho. We get together and lift the van and place it down a few inches over, which allows the document destroyer to squeeze out. This gives us room to push the old Basho out of the way, which we do. Then I drive my purple Satori out, park it ostenta-tiously in the middle of the town square, and go back to the others.

"Let's push this Basho back in here. Maybe someone'll block him in to see how he likes it," says the cop, who turns out to be a real ordinary guy at heart – though of course no true Irishman would ever really trust him, being a cop, baby-faced or not, no matter how hard he worked at earning their trust, and no matter how mellow he was.

So we push the red relic back in to where the confidential van was, the friendly, happy cop flagging down traffic in both directions as we do so.

Everywhere I went in the Republic of Ireland, it was the same story: The Irish Republican Army is the equivalent of an asylum of murder-ous Don Quixotes, whom we love but do not approve of. The IRA is inspired by old stories of glory and sacrifice, but it is now out of place in the global scheme.

The situation in the North can be seen as a military occupation, as much so as the Israeli occupation of the West Bank, and the Protes-tants of the North may lord it over the Catholics in obnoxious ways with their big pompous parades and so on. They may be asking to be murdered, but why give them the pleasure of doing so? The support for Sinn Féin (Ourselves Alone) – the political arm of the IRA – is minuscule in the Republic, under 4 per cent. Most seem to feel about it as James Joyce did when he wrote *Ulysses*: "Sinn Féin. Back out you get the knife. Hidden hand. Stay in. The firing squad."

A woman who said she ran an upscale bed-and-breakfast was having a quick drink at the bar of the hotel in Macroom. She said a middle-aged couple from Derry in Northern Ireland had been travelling in the South with their elderly father, who was quite ill – on his last legs in fact. He was also quite bigoted. He said to her, "You're one of us, aren't you?" – meaning that she must be a Protestant, otherwise she wouldn't be able to run such a neat, clean, upscale B&B. Everyone knew the Catholics were lazy, dirty, disorganized, promiscuous, drunken, foolish little Papists.

"I told him no, I was a Catholic. His face dropped a mile, and he started gulping his pills. Honestly, this man was on his last legs, going to meet his Maker, you'd think he'd be a bit more tolerant. Then a priest friend of mine happened to drop in for a visit. The old man took one look at this priest and started screaming, 'Get me out of here, get me out of here.'"

We swerved and just missed a chicken on the road to Knocknakillen, or a name much like that, twenty minutes north of Macroom. At a lonely crossroads, far from the closest village, sat a handsome little five-stone circle with a huge recumbent lying flat, as if it had toppled over rather than having simply been set that way in days of yore. Behind that was another circle, which appeared to be a rough copy of Uragh, that masterpiece at Inchiquin, both in its alignment, the type of stone, the ratios and dimensions, and the relationship of the whole to the surroundings. But it was much smaller, either a copy or a prototype, and definitely without the same kind of fizz.

Sometimes these circles are in extremely remote and beautiful settings, other times in intimate relationship with a modern town. In the latter case, the stones are usually fenced off as in the town of Kenmare. Houses back on to them, as if they were not particularly admired, perhaps feared and detested ever since the demise of the culture that created them.

In most cases, though, the stones are on a hill of some sort, often a low one. But even if it is a low one, it's usually the highest point for miles around. On the odd occasion when they are not on a hill, it is for obvious aesthetic reasons, as with the Uragh stone circle in the hollow beneath a hill on the island in Lough Inchiquin. Since the lough is set deep in a steep valley, it would be too obvious to put the stones on top of the relatively tiny hill on the island. These people were great and profound masters of subtlety. More is known about the origins of the universe than about these stones, which riddle the viewer with strings of unanswerable questions.

When there are groupings of stone circles they are usually pretty well all at the same height, though often each sits on its own small hill.

Lourdes had dreamt the night before that each stone circle had once been the centre of a settlement, a village. But the archaeologists claim there's no evidence supporting a notion like that. Nothing has been dug up.

Behind the second stone circle sat a third, a smaller one which showed signs of having been put up in recent times. A baby circle of small unsettled stones that did not bear the signs of time, rather the signs of impermanence. It looked as if it had been set there as a lark one drunken night around, say, 1954.

We went along interesting narrow roads north and west, avoiding Killarney, and in a few hours arrived at Tralee, sitting at the base of the Dingle Peninsula. I asked a newsagent if he knew where I could go for a tip for my cane. But before he would tell me he needed to know the exact details of how I came to be tipless. Nothing was too trivial for his interest. I told him I lost it in a bog. "Ach," he said, "it'll be dug up a thousand years from now and put in a glass case in a museum as a priceless artifact."

"And they won't be able to figure out what it is."

"They'll figure it's some sort of fertility symbol."

I told him there had to be at least one cane tip lost in a bog some-where in Ireland every day. He agreed and said he didn't understand why all these foolish people persist in going walking in the bog with their canes.

"If they're so unsteady on their feet that they need to walk with a cane, they'd better be sticking to the public roadways."

I promised never again to walk in the bog with my cane, if only he would give me a tip as to where I could purchase a new tip.

"I've got a tip for you. Why don't you go next door to the pub, and swipe one off of the leg of a bar stool?"

I told him I'd done that in several different pubs over the past few days but couldn't find a tip that fit.

"You've got a point there," he said. "A tip's not worth spit if it don't fit."

"Is that a famous old saying?"

"My grandmother was forever saying that one, sure."

Meanwhile Lourdes had slipped quietly into the shop and was reading the classifieds in the *Tralee Advertiser*. When I was a boy soprano, I could often be found singing "The Rose of Tralee" at meet-ings of the Gaelic Society of Hamilton, Ontario, with my voice coach, old Fergus Maclise, pounding away on the piano.

"Anything there in the lost and found about a lost tip?" said the newsagent.

"No, I checked already," said Lourdes. "Nothing in items for sale either."

The fellow gave me an eye-contact smile, very chummy, which said nice Spanish girlfriend you got there, pal.

Lourdes took me to one side to show me another article about elderly people living in fear of Tinker attacks – except the word "Tinker" was never used. The paper had taken a highly scientific poll, which showed that over 70 per cent of respondents were upset by assaults on the elderly, while 60 per cent were deeply disturbed. Something to ponder. The margin of error was not given.

Appearing inside the *Tralee Advertiser* was a two-page series of first-person one-paragraph stories by female Tinkers.

Said one: "For all you know your father could have been a Tinker. They traditionally go from town to town fixing things in their caravans. They don't do much of that anymore, but they're still dumped on."

Another complained: "The settled people will not let us forget we're Tinkers."

A third noted bitterly that the taxi drivers demand four pounds fifty in advance as soon as you say you're going to the Tinker area. Tinker: "Do you not trust me?" Driver: "It's not that. I've been done a few times before." Tinker: "Looks like you class all travellers the same, which is wrong."

Another had a humiliating experience at a supermarket checkout counter: "I'd taken out the fruit and was about to take out my messages when the store detective tapped me on the shoulder and said: 'You and your kind are not being served here.' 'Why? What's the difference between me and anyone else?' 'Never mind. It doesn't matter. Get out.' I was very ashamed and embarrassed in front of everybody, so I just walked away."

Another noted that things were getting worse for the Tinkers: "My father used to do repairs for the country people. Dad used to be a tin-smith, travelling with his pony and trap. He fixed buckets and cans. The settled people in those days were lovely. They would invite you in for tea and a good old chat. But the settled people have changed. They wouldn't invite us into their homes now. It's not fair the way we are treated."

Others complained about poor medical services. One woman with pneumonia told her doctor the pills he'd given her had done no good. He took them off her and threw them in the wastepaper basket, then gave her another batch – of exactly the same pills. "My husband took them and threw them in the fire," she said.

Another complained that when they went to a dance to hear Joe Dolan, the doorman said they couldn't get in without a ticket. And to get a ticket you had to go across the road to the corner shop. "We went over. The man in the shop said the bouncer was only having us on, he didn't have any tickets. I tried to phone Joe Dolan in his dressing room to tell him what was going on but he was already on the stage. A traveller is only a traveller but I consider myself as good as that bouncer any time."

I asked the newsagent if he could tell a Traveller from a settled person if they were both dressed the same. He said he doubted it. What about a Protestant and a Catholic? He said some people claim they can tell the difference from a block away. Some people say they can even smell the difference. "Some people, they have these things down to a fine art. But not me. I don't know how they do it."

We chatted away about the racial purity of Ireland – how everywhere you go you see Irish people and nothing but. I had to admit I'd run into a surprising number of Anglo ex-pats, but no visible minorities at all, no Asians, no Africans, no Aborigines – except for one extremely unhappy looking black man, standing outside the bus terminal in Cork City, dressed in a three-piece grey suit, carrying a black briefcase, and looking terribly lost, worried, and unhappy.

"I suppose that's why we have to be prejudiced against the Tinkers," said the newsagent. "Who else do we have?"

By this time Lourdes had read all the papers and was thumbing through a little book called *How to Win the U.S. Immigration Game*.

"Oh, why didn't I think of it before?" said the newsagent. "I know where you can get a tip for your cane. There's a little shop around the corner that sells hospital supplies."

A florid, fat little man, old to be running a shop, showed us his selection of tips. I pointed to the biggest, fattest, ugliest, tightest-looking tip imaginable. He grabbed my cane.

"Help me on with this tip," he said. "There! That's not too loose, is it?"

"No, it's a lot tighter than the one I lost."

"Well, it would have to be now, wouldn't it?"

He wanted to know everything about me, where I was going and why. He wanted me to go to the car and get my maps so he could mark all the best routes northward. A framed painting of a dolmen was hanging on the wall behind the counter.

He had another tip: he told me to be sure to take the mountain route rather than the coastal route to Connemara. This was of the utmost importance. He wouldn't say why, but I think it might have been the wild herds of Connemara ponies we'd miss if we dared to disobey him and took the coastal route. Just then Lourdes strolled in, and in the friendliest manner imaginable put her arm lightly and tenderly around my waist. The old guy looked shocked.

"Why, you old reprobate," he exclaimed. "What are you doing with such a beautiful young woman?"

Cheeky old fellow. I told him she was my aunt. I smiled and thanked him for both tips.

Lourdes felt guilty that she had read all those papers and magazines without buying anything, so on the way back to the car we had to drop in to see the newsagent again. Besides, I was so proud and pleased with my new tip I simply had no choice but to show it to him.

He admired the tip, but it turned out he didn't care much for the old fellow who ran the hospital-supplies shop. He was a cheapskate.

"Ach, he's still got his communion money. He doesn't have any pockets in his pants, he doesn't spend any money. He was the governor of the hospital, and when he retired they gave him a home worth a hundred thousand pounds, no less. I think he spends a little on drink. No, he'd be too mean to drink. Actually, he has a medical problem. He has to take tablets that give him all that fat. The redness in his hands, too, it's some kind of heart disease or something like that."

I mentioned that I found him to be a kind person, basically. After all, he had me get out my maps, and suggested certain routes to take.

"Oh yes, he's nice as long as it doesn't cost him any money. In his younger days, now, he would hardly talk to you. But since he left the medical profession up there and returned to private business over here, he likes everybody now."

The newsagent was a little upset at first when I mentioned the guy had called me an old reprobate for being with such a beautiful young woman. We both looked at Lourdes. She put down her magazine, struck a sexy pose, and beamed back at us.

"That guy, he had no right to say such a thing," he said. "Think it, yes; but say it, never. I was thinking the same thing myself now, mind you; but I'd never say it. I don't know what's the matter with him. He's used to having a little power, you see, and he doesn't like it when . . ."

"When somebody else has a younger, sexier, more charming travelling companion than he has?"

"That's exactly what I was thinking."

"Don't worry about it," I said. "It was just a joke the old guy made. And it was a pretty good question actually."

"Was he smiling when he said it?"

"Yes." I lied. "And there was a merry twinkle in his eye. But you know Canadians, it's hard to insult us. His comment didn't insult me at all, and neither did your earlier insulting comment."

"My earlier insulting comment?"

"The one about people having to be weak-minded to go walking in the bog with their canes. It didn't insult me at all, being a Canadian."

"Ach, that was a joke pure and simple. And speaking of jokes, now," he said, "did you hear about the worried man from Cahir who decided to leave town? He wanted to become Cahirfree."

Lourdes was reading all the magazine articles she'd skipped the first time through. And the newsagent kept jabbering on.

"You see it doesn't make a damn difference where the hell you end up, as long as the people are nice and you're nice to the people. You never see 'Mister' on a tombstone. It's important to like your work. If you like that you can endure any place you happen to live. Difficult conditions make it more interesting, more of a challenge."

"Nobody where I come from is interested in challenges," I said. "All they want is to make money. It makes them dull. It's difficulties that make people creative, obstacles that make them interesting, setbacks and suffering that give them sparkle and fizz."

He took the bait. Being critical of the country you're from is a time-honoured device for getting people to wax critical about their own country.

"But this is the way the old system goes, if there's no incentive to work. That's what's lacking in Ireland. No incentive, no incentive whatsoever. Take the civil service. They're about one-third of the population now."

"No. That can't be true. Say it's not true, please."

"Oh, it's true all right. One-third would be a modest estimate. And they don't want to go to work until ten in the morning. They break for a coffee break and take the newspaper with them, and after they read the paper they do the crossword puzzle. And they break for a big lunch break and they finish up at four. And they haven't done nothing."

"Ah, it's sickening, it is," I said. "Just like Canada."

"You send in forms to tax your car or to get planning permission to do anything and it's, 'I haven't got time today,' they say. 'I'll do it tomorrow. I have to read the paper today because there are horses on the television.' I tell you, it's all red tape. They just literally do nothing at their end of it. They should put in a commission system. For every so much brought in, there should be ten pounds for the manager and one pound each for the staff. Something like that. Do them faster, get them out faster."

"Not a bad idea."

"I've got a lot of ideas, some even better than that. You know, I had two little tractors and I wanted to tax them. And I sent the form in the other day. I got my green form – you can't go down because of the queue from here to there, practically all the way down to the next village and back, and you waste your whole day. So you post it in, and they get it back to you the following day or two or three or four or a week. I had to get a policeman to state that these little tractors hadn't been on the road in the time I wasn't paying the tax. So I took it to a policeman friend of mine and he just stamped them – boom! No problem. I sent it off. After a week it comes back with two other forms in it to fill out and get them signed by a Garda again."

"Good heavens! This is a veritable nightmare of a country."

"Well, it has its good points too, though right on the spot like this I couldn't come up with a very long list of them to be sure. You see, there has to be incentive. The guy who doesn't work, let him die of hunger out there."

"Send them all to Sherkin Island," I offered.

"There shouldn't be queues for anything," he averred. "You shouldn't have tax investigators or tax inspectors. Tax reps – like the guys who come to (let's say for the sake of argument) the pub to collect the money for the Guinness, they come on the first day of every month. 'You owe me two thousand pounds, pay me now.' And when you pay them that's finished – boom! And then you wouldn't have any backlog. Put him on 1-per-cent commission, say. The more calls he gets through today the better. One rep for all the pubs, one rep for all the newsagents, one rep for all the clothiers, and so on. Of course there are more pubs than clothiers."

"Very good reason for that."

"Which is?"

"Well, you can wear the same clothes over and over; but you drink a pint of Guinness once and that's it, you need a new one."

"True. Bit of Irish in you, is there?"

"I didn't think so till I arrived here. But I just want to say I was lying there a minute ago what I said about Canada. There are no problems in Canada at all. You should emigrate to Canada. No problems in Canada whatsoever."

He believed me for a moment, then I smiled; and then he laughed, as the universal nature of human stupidity struck him and for a brief moment he realized it wasn't only Ireland.

"Ach, we've got a brilliant country," he exclaimed, "but we've got a screwed-up government, and we've got a screwed-up civil service."

"And a brilliant little town you've got here."

"Glad you like it."

"Any place here to get ice cream?"

THE WAY PEOPLE TALK
IN IRELAND

We took a series of narrow crooked roads back up through the counties of Limerick and Clare. It was a grey day, still wintry, but then we would round a bend and there would be brilliant green shafts of light, pink and white blossoms, early crimson rhododendrons, brilliant green hills with dreamlike little castles, and winding streams full of silent white swans and arched by crenellated bridges. The owner of the Ballymaquiff House Hotel, somewhere between Portumna and Loughrea, was bragging over breakfast that all the scriptwriting and preliminary work on the famous film *My Left Foot* had been done there. "If it weren't for the Ballymaquiff, that film would never have been put together," he said. He admitted he didn't know anything about the film at the time it was being done, "but it didn't start in Dublin and it didn't start in London and it didn't start in New York and it didn't start in Hollywood, California, *sor*, it started right here at the old Ballymaquiff House Hotel."

"You must be pleased, especially with it being so successful and winning the Oscar and all."

"Oh, indeed. Very proud. Eh? An Oscar, did you say? It didn't win an Oscar now, did it?"

"Yes, it did. Just last week."

"You mean like at the Academy Awards in Hollywood, U.S.A.?"

"I do indeed."

Like many braggarts, this fellow was also a bit of a complainer. He wanted people to know it wasn't all that easy running a hotel. Apparently, throughout the Republic of Ireland it's a bit of a running gag that people who run hotels have it pretty danged easy. This fellow's big aim in life was to set people straight.

"Somebody stayed here and got sick and was rushed off to the hospital and had a ten-pound job done. And the hospital has been sending us the bill ever since."

"What can you get for ten pounds at a hospital?"

"Oh, lots of things. An emergency appendectomy or hiatus hernia or an ingrown nose hair or chronic halitosis or something, all I know is we can't find the fellow and the hospital wants its money."

He wasn't convinced when I said I couldn't see why he would be responsible if one of his guests didn't pay a hospital bill, and it wasn't his job to try to track the scoundrel down. I mean what if ingrown nose hairs, for instance, turned out to be contagious?

"Then I'd have to sue the hospital, I guess. It would be my civic duty, if nothing else. By the way, you didn't happen to hear anything of the fine action we had last night now, did you?"

"Didn't hear a thing."

"That is surprising. It was the next room to you. About three in the morning. We had an elderly lady get sick. Old man comes down just as we were closing up the bar, and he says, 'My sister is very ill, very ill. Could you organize a doctor and a priest?' I says to him, I says,

'We'll get on it. We'll organize you the doctor. We'll organize you the priest.'"

"So you organized the doctor and the priest?"

"Well, they arrived in ten or fifteen minutes, did the doctor and the priest, and they sorted out the problem. She's fine now. And I just get back to sleep, you know, and the phone rings at four in the morning: 'Have you accommodation for three people?' I tells them, 'Try the Great Western, they have a night porter.' And then I hangs up."

"Good for you. Inconsiderate swine."

"You know, we had gangs of priests and doctors and dentists and lawyers and night clerks all running up and down the stairs last night – and it didn't even wake you up."

"We must have been tired. All this touring around Ireland just wears you out something fierce, I tell you."

"Ach, it's like running this hotel. You don't get any time off."

"At least I had a good night's sleep."

"Have any dreams?"

"No, but I had a good one about ten days ago, when I was down around Kilkenny way."

"Can you remember it in vivid detail?"

Turned out he had a diploma in dream interpretation from the Jungian Committee of the Republic of Ireland (JCROI). We exchanged names. His was Raferty.

"Like the blind poet?"

"Direct descendant. Slight change in spelling."

I told him my dream about Lourdes being the doctor and me having a severe case of apnea. It only took him a minute to interpret the dream, and he did it rather brilliantly. Soon we were back to real life.

I didn't tell Mr. Raferty about what had happened last night in the dining room. The young fellow waiting on tables told us we were in the Molly Room, which we had already noticed from the large, shiny wooden plaque over the door.

"It's named after James Joyce's wife," said the waiter, proudly.

I told him, quietly, that Molly was a character in Joyce's novel *Ulysses*, not Mr. Joyce's wife. "There is a difference, wouldn't you say?"

"I guess so."

"His wife was someone else, Nora Barnacle or something."

The waiter was genuinely anguished. And I was surprised, not being used to having people believe me immediately when I tell them they're wrong. It must have been the "American" accent; it's like a badge of authority in certain parts of Ireland.

"I've been telling people ever since I started working here two years ago that Molly was Joyce's wife, but nobody ever told me before it wasn't so."

"I'm sorry, I shouldn't have said anything."

"Don't be sorry. Now I won't be making a fool of meself anymore. Nora Barnacle, was it? Almost sounds like Molly Bloom."

"If I have ten minutes off, I go chasing up to see the horses or the cattle," said Mr. Raferty. "I'm a fanatic for animals as well as being a part-time Jungian dream therapist and all my other duties with the hotel and all."

"Have your own animals, do you?"

"I do, yeah. I have a few. Myself and the little gaffer, he's as big as meself now, we'll run a horse on the track and we'll lead the track, too. So it's a bit of fun. I train 'em and he rides 'em. And he only cost two hundred quid. Up against horses a hundred times that."

"Just have the one? Horse, that is?"

"We only got the one just now, you know. We just mess around with him. But we had two or three horses, but only ever just one on the track."

"Sounds like a lot of fun."

"We do have a lot of fun with him, and he doesn't cost too much to run because we've got the land to put him out on and we got the hay to feed him with. So it's a nice bit of a hobby."

"Every man needs a hobby," I declared.

"And yours would be what?" said he.

"She'll be down in a minute." He flinched enviously. "Bit of photography as well."

"Ach, and y'know it's nice when the young lads are able to do it, to run these horses around the track. And I do it myself. I was third myself at the races about six years ago. Even at my age. So it's a bit of an interest and it gets you away from the job for an hour or two. But then you meet somebody on the street and he says, 'God, you have a bloody great time of a soft life, you ride horses during the day, do you ever work?' Hah heh heh heh. And then you have to rise at four o'clock in the morning to sort some people out like last night for instance. Hah heh heh."

"Now, all that fine action last night, are you sure that wasn't all a Jungian dream? I'm normally a terribly light sleeper. A mild sigh from a hotel six blocks away can wake me up. Or a wineglass breaking in the next township."

"Well, it certainly wouldn't have last night. I think maybe that young girlfriend of yours is too much for you, she had you all tuckered out if I may be so bold as to give my opinion on a subject of such sensitivity to be sure."

"You underestimate me, Mr. Raferty, direct descendant as you claim to be of the famous wandering poet and blind Irish holy man."

"Could be. But I think she'd have me all tuckered out before you could say Oscar was an Englishman . . ."

"Oscar Wilde?"

"No, Oscar Tame."

When it came to the subject of bomb threats – as in, had he had any – he just shuddered and closed his eyes.

"I genuinely don't know anything about the IRA and I don't want to know anything about the IRA. And by the way, Raifteirí the poet wasn't totally blind, he could see fairly well out of one eye."

I mentioned that Ireland seemed to be very popular among the

Europeans, what with the drunk-but-very-quiet-and-polite German fishing parties and the *bon-appétit* French tourists eating the legs off the tables and the EEC-financed slum-clearance and highway-construction projects around the Dublin area —

"They just want to buy out Ireland, I presume," he said. "The Europeans that is. I can't see any future in that for quite a while."

He spoke of drunken senators getting in car wrecks and not getting charged, or getting sent to Canada for free liver transplants.

"Ach!" he said. "You want to get into our government? If your old man has been in there, or if you're a good footballer, you get in there 'cause the locals like you, you're a hero."

"You mean a guy who plays just for the local team? Doesn't have to play for the national team?"

"Not at all. The guys who play for the local team are better known than the players who play in the World Cup and all that. Or say your old man was in there, like in the government or whatever, and he died, so you get the sympathy vote. And we have the greatest shower of messers ever known running this country . . ."

"Messers?"

"Shower of messers. They don't know how to do anything. You could put a whole lot of them into a ready-mix concrete truck, turn it on, and you wouldn't get one brain out of it. Nobody should be let into the government until they have ten years in private enterprise. And proven themselves that they can make a go of it."

He told a joke or two about priests, then pointed upwards with a look of fake piety on his face.

"I'll never get up there," he said.

"You don't seem worried about it."

"I'll be with me pals."

Lourdes later mentioned that she'd been finding it difficult to get a straight yes or no answer out of the Irish. I told her I'd heard that was because there were no words in the Irish language for yes and no.

"But they all speak English, and there certainly are words for yes and no in English, aren't there?"

"This is true, there are last I checked. But even though the Irish by and large don't speak Irish and haven't for several generations, they still distrust the words yes and no in English."

"Instinct."

"Something like that. Yes and no are cheap words, mere hiccups, a little insulting perhaps, to the listener that is. For nothing is ever pure yes or no unless you're in a hurry and want to shake the supplicant off. Yes and no are absolutes in a relative universe, like black and white. They don't exist in the realm of true sincerity, of pure desire to be a friend and come clean. Such words cut conversation short and flat; they are pathetic little calls for closure; they are somehow unworthy of the genuine subtleties of intelligent discourse."

"Nothing is really yes or no, nothing is really black or white."

"That is so, actually, and probably has something to do with it."

"Let's see how long we can go without using them."

"You and me?"

"The two of us."

"Without saying yes or no?"

"That's what I mean."

"Good idea. Do you think it will have an effect on the genuine subtleties of our intercourse?"

"I can't wait to find out."

UNDER BEN BULBEN

There were no prehistoric monuments in H. V. Morton's *In Search of Ireland*. His mind filtered them out. Yet here we were, heading into Connemara, which he adored. We were following his route west from Spiddle along the north shore of Galway Bay, and there were megalithic tombs and little ring forts all over the place, practically in everybody's backyard.

Stone fences Morton does mention. He thinks they were so ubiquitous and enclosed such small patches of land, particularly in this area, because of the high population density. But it makes more sense to think that the enclosures were so tiny simply because there were so many stones in the fields. If the fields had been made larger, the fences would have had to be much higher, requiring much more work, and the stones would have had to be lugged further.

The fence builders weren't trying to keep people out or animals in or make fences per se. They were merely clearing the land for agricultural purposes. They had to do something with the rocks, so they piled them up in straight lines every twenty feet or so: the rockier the area, the closer together the fences, the smaller the enclosures.

And in almost every wall you'll see one boulder many times larger than the others. This would be an erratic – or sometimes, as at King Lear and the Three Daughters, a bonafide dolmen – and rather than try to move it, the builders would incorporate it into the fence, which would explain why the fields are so irregular in size and shape. Any stone that seemed too difficult to move would be incorporated into a fence. In agricultural matters, function traditionally follows form.

Protection from wild animals doesn't seem to have been a factor, because the fences aren't high enough to offer such protection. It doesn't appear that the land was being cleared to provide grazing for animals, for the animals were perfectly capable of grazing among the rocks. Those fields were cleared to provide garden land, pure and simple.

The old stone fences were everywhere along the sea coast here. There were houses sitting every which way, fairly dense population for such a remote part of the country, swarms of children coming home from school. All the little Irish cottages that would have been here in Morton's day had disappeared, leaving only modern little redbrick houses, with aluminum front doors, among the strangely patterned networks of ancient walls, Gulf Stream pink limestone beaches with turquoise water, stubby little palm trees, stubby herds of cattle.

Morton was a brilliant and indefatigable crowd-pleaser as far as the describing of landscapes was concerned. But he needed to be; he was writing for a popular audience that didn't travel much, bourgeois travel being too expensive and time-consuming, and he was writing for a pre-television audience that had not become sated with colour images and documentaries from all ends of the earth. Every technological change seems to alter our psychology profoundly (though certain futurists maintain technological changes take our psychology where it wants to go anyway). Morton was writing for a different crowd. "The talk rattled on as Irish talk does," he writes, "leaping and jumping about like a leprechaun on a hill."

It rained when Morton came charging through these parts, but today in Connemara it was a beautiful sunny day in early spring. We stopped to gaze at the ruins of a fairy-tale castle on an island in the middle of a lake. The lake was a field of diamonds, picking up light from the sky and reflecting it in all directions at a higher intensity for anyone who cared to observe it. The castle was almost as big as the island, and its ramparts were covered with thick green ivy, just as the lake was surrounded by thick green forest. As the sun moved lower in the sky, the diamonds caught fire with a bright gold flame.

We discovered our first North American-style motel in Ireland. It was called the Connemara Inn and it was falling apart and had been closed for fifteen years.

A rumpled Brendan Behan in early middle age was stumbling along the main street of the remote town of Clifden at the western end of the Connemara Peninsula. He had a rumpled newspaper in his pocket, with a number of articles he wanted to read again or show a friend to prove a point. He was wearing a long, rumpled black over-coat, flecked with cat hairs and cigarette ash, had long, rumpled black hair, and he was an awful mess. His coat collar was turned up, yet he had a sweet, innocent look on his face, like Dylan Thomas, and his eyes met mine with an expression that said, simply, I wouldn't mind becoming your best friend, that is if you happen to be in need of such a thing, and really when you think of it who isn't?

He turned into the chemist's shop and I followed him. He was chat-ting with the young, handsome, well-groomed chemist, who never-theless had a terrible case of the shakes. These two seemed to be great drinking buddies. They were talking about some concert coming up, some group from Dublin. Brendan smoothed his newspaper out on the counter.

The chemist fixed my glasses, which had fallen apart on my face as we drove into Clifden. I handed him the tiny screw. He got out a razor blade to use as a screwdriver. I was afraid he'd cut himself, his hands were shaking so badly, which was a terrible thing to see in a man so young. The blade broke into pieces, but he kept at it with a little sliver of the original blade and finally got the screw in without bloodshed. He handed me the glasses and said, "You'll be needing these for all the scenery." He laughed when I asked how much that would be, and he wouldn't take a cent.

Lourdes missed all this, having remained in the purple Satori, parked diagonally on the broad main street of Clifden. She was sitting in the passenger seat, leaning up towards the rear-view mirror and grimacing as she plucked the occasional wayward curly hair out of her bushy eyebrows. She was so intent she didn't notice me coming from the left, nor the small group of kids and adults on the sidewalk to the right, watching her with looks of wonder on their faces, standing back a suitable distance so she wouldn't notice them staring.

In just about every Irish hotel there's a sign saying "Residents Only," though its meaning is far from clear, for nobody ever gets kicked out of the bar simply because they don't have a room – at least in my experience. Perhaps the sign is used as an excuse to get rid of any Tinkers who might come in. But at the Alcock Brown Hotel in Clifden there was a sign saying "Non-Residents Welcome." On the wall over the bar was a framed front page from a 1938 paper, with stories about Hitler, Czechoslovakia's impregnable defences, and a little story about Ireland's pavilion at the World's Fair in Glasgow, with its display of Irish butter, eggs, and bacon.

Excitement was mounting about Ireland's chances in the World Cup. The young bartender was wearing a World Cup T-shirt depicting a large green shamrock and a lot of little acronyms in green too. He explained the complicated procedure and listed the teams the Irish would have to beat before getting into the final.

"How did they qualify for the first round?"

"It was because they played in Europe, they played against four European teams."

"I bet you know the names of every player, right?"

"Oh, you gotta."

"And their age and where they're from and their height and weight and all their individual stats."

"Pretty well for sure."

"On the Irish team, that is."

"Oh, I don't know all that many on the other teams."

When H. V. Morton was in Clifden, he heard a lovely story about an Irishman, who had been in the United States for thirty years, coming back to Ireland to look up his younger brother, with whom he had not been in touch all that time. He got off the ship at Cork and hired a limousine and chauffeur to take him up to County Mayo to pay a surprise visit to his brother, who had supposedly been running the family farm all this time. Now the older brother was a "terrible teetotaller entirely," and severely chastised the chauffeur when he caught him "with his face in a pint of porter." But when he arrived at the farm, he discovered that his brother had sold it long ago and had bought a pub with the proceeds. They proceeded to the pub and found the brother sitting there behind the counter sound asleep and dead drunk. He tried to awaken him, but the fellow just snored all the louder, so finally the older brother commanded the chauffeur to drive him back to Cork, and he caught the next boat to the United States.

Also while in Clifden, Morton failed to impress the locals with his genially ostentatious display of wealth:

In the post office I waited while a young Connemara girl, fresh as a peach, painfully addressed a letter to New York; and then I drew twenty pounds in much-travelled one-pound notes – money that had been wired to me – and not one person in the post office showed any surprise, although this sum must have seemed to them real wealth.

Lourdes was stooping at the shore, cleaning her muddy boots in the clear waters of Lough Gill, a mile or two south and east of Sligo. From the shore could be seen William Butler Yeats's Lake Isle of Innisfree. My grade-10 teacher is whacking his desk with his yardstick, splinters of wood flying in all directions, and screaming that this is the greatest line in all of English poetry. "I thought it was Irish, sir." "Pipe down and listen, McFadden. Just listen to the *l*'s." He beats time by whacking the yardstick on his desk and intones mournfully, in the Dylan Thomas mode: "I hear lake water lapping with low sounds by the shore." I can't remember the teacher's name now. His wife taught gym at the same school. He had a bad back and a Ph.D., his thesis having been a brief-but-scintillating (so he told us) treatise on the works of Alfred North Whitehead, and he was always muttering, when things were going badly, as they always were, that he could triple his salary in advertising.

"Well, why don't you, sir?"

"How could I abandon you kids? My devotion and sense of responsibility to you is too great."

"We wouldn't mind, sir."

"Achh!"

He takes another yardstick and smashes it against his desk.

Lourdes was photographing me standing reverently by Yeats's limestone (he had insisted on limestone) grave marker – Yeats who, in spite of his chilling political ambiguities, had given our hearts so much mysterious pleasure. I had to arrive on this spot to understand his famous inscription, which Hugh Kenner wrongly finds arrogant:

Cast a cold Eye
On Life, on Death.
Horseman, pass by!

In A.D. 575 Saint Columba founded a monastery on the site where Yeats is now buried. And high above, like a cold eye in the clear air, sits the axe-faced Ben Bulben, on the slopes of which Diarmuid, much to Gráinne's dismay, was killed by the wild boar. Earlier in the day, in the shadow of the sacred Croagh Patrick, a perfect volcano-shaped mountain beloved of penitent holy pilgrims painfully trudging their rocky barefoot way to the top, stands an impressive statue of Saint Patrick. It was life-size and of recent vintage, but it looked down from the top of a much-older hundred-foot nineteenth-century imperious neoclassical pillar. The original statue had been taken down and replaced with Patrick, and the original engravings on the side panels of the base, no doubt offensive to true Irish sensibilities, had been chiselled out and new panels placed in: "I am Patrick, a sinner, most unlearned, the least of all the faithful, and utterly despised by man."

Then there was the volcanic Mount Nephra, in the heart of County Mayo, looming to the west of Lough Conn. Its bald head was flecked with dandruff-like snow, at least on one side, and on the other the snow patches were striated in long narrow parallel lines, like lines of cocaine, or like cornrows on the head of an aged Jamaican woman.

From the ruins of the thirteenth-century Errew Abbey, sitting on a tongue-shaped peninsula of deep pathless mud jutting out into Lough Conn, a little puff of grey cloud could be seen floating over Mount Nephra in the darkening blue sky. And through the field glasses from our side, a couple of hundred yards downside from the peak, could be seen the offset puckered shadowy volcanic crater, like a crater on the moon. The red fireball of the sun was setting over the early Victorian hunting lodge we'd passed two miles west of here. It was derelict but with all windows curiously intact, and dusty old curtains still hung in the upper windows.

Purple mountains surrounding us were lying low on the horizon – except for Mount Nephra, looming snowy and craggy in the immediate distance – and surrounding us on three sides were herds of cattle and broad stretches of silvery pink and golden water.

The grim grey cloud above Mount Nephra looked like a puff of smoke coming out of the crater, the crater resembling an old man's puckered navel. It was a kidney-shaped and kidney-coloured mountain, and its name means kidney.

For Lourdes's intellectual pleasure, though not to be taken seriously, I gave her my latest theory: The stones used in building wedge graves were taken from as close as possible to the spot where the dead person had been born and put down at the spot where he died.

Legends indicated that, at least in some cases, such graves were built at the spot where the person therein interred actually did die. Near Cahir, for instance, at the top of a mountain, there was a cairn grave in which lay the body of a poet who had been caught and murdered by enemies of the king. In order to confuse the invaders, the poet had agreed to flee the court in disguise, dressed in the king's gear, but he was caught and killed. The actual king, deeply moved by the poet's sacrifice, built the cairn grave, visible for ten miles in all directions, in a show of sorrow, gratitude, and respect for the great courage of the poet who died rather than admit he was not really the king. This was told to me by Mr. Looney.

"It's a wonderful story," said Lourdes. "I'd like to meet that man."

"I know you would, and you probably will."

"Ignorance is bliss, I believe that," she added.

"You do?"

"I do. For instance, this is a better trip for us than it would be if we knew a lot about archaeology. Archaeologists always look so miserable. They spend their whole lives working on one small problem."

The improvement in her English was taking my breath away.

Cherry blossoms, old abbeys, Fujiyama-style extinct volcanoes, sunsets, glorious lakes, mountains all around us, a great gibbous moon, and Lourdes Brasil had written her first poem in English:

Pale moon flying in the sky
How do you stay up there so high?
I've never seen you look so grand
Flying above old Ireland.

FARMER TROLLOPE

We were staying a few days later at a guest house run by Mr. and Mrs. Trollope on a dairy farm near Belfast. We had been referred to this charming spot by the Royal Ulster Constabulary.

"I won't shake hands, I've been milking the cows," said Farmer Trollope.

"They must be nice and clean then," said Lourdes, meaning the hands.

Farmer Trollope was a sober, quiet man, the sort you want to tell stories to, ask naïve questions of, and hope for his approval. He was the proud possessor of a hundred dairy cows. He was in the process of getting rid of the last of the beef cattle. He invited us to wander around the farm.

"We were over in Donegal Town and Letterkenny late yesterday afternoon, in County Donegal," I told him. We had spent hours fooling around in the casino, playing the little slot machines, and wandering around town. People-watching is particularly pleasant in the part

of the world where your ancestral family springs from, and I kept passing folks who looked like members of the McFadden family, long-dead
aunts and uncles, younger versions of aging cousins, a dead ringer for
my brother dressed in blue coveralls.

"That fellow would be a farmer," said Farmer Trollope.

It had occurred to us to venture east across the border to Derry,
then south to visit Boa Island and White Island, a good step south of
Derry, because we were interested in the archaeological sites there. It
was an interesting border crossing, with plenty of mean-looking characters with machine-guns. Always very conscious of the direction in
which he was travelling, Morton rhapsodizes about going *south* from
Donegal, part of the Republic, into Northern Ireland. "An English
reader who has not studied the map will wonder how I performed such
an unnatural feat. It is simple" – as simple as going north from Canada
into the United States, as one can do at several points here and there.

As in Morton's experience at customs, every second car was having
a complete inspection, even inside the hub caps. But tourists were
having an easy time of it. We sailed through. Derry was a glorious
sight from the highway but the countryside was so drenched in hyp-
notic moonlight, and the roads were so good and free of traffic, we
simply couldn't enter the city, we felt compelled to continue driving
through the night without stopping. Our hair was blowing in the
wind, and the wind was blowing through our hearts. Derry, a walled
city, was even more beautiful than York and Chester, according to
Morton, who said the city is called "Londonderry" only by tourists
and on maps. I recalled my days as a boy soprano having to sing
"Londonderry Air" on occasion at meetings of the Gaelic Society.

And we ended up in Belfast.

"And you went to the police?" said Farmer Trollope.

"Well, we didn't *intend* to go to the police. But we thought maybe
there'd be a place to stay out near the airport. It was late, we couldn't
find anything in Belfast; there must have been hotels, but for security
reasons I suppose the hotels had no signs out front."

"That would be right."

"We kept running into police roadblocks and cul-de-sacs and being told at gunpoint to turn around and head back the way we came. Then we got stopped at a police roadblock on a very dark road on the way to the airport. The policeman said, 'Would you be going to the airport to catch a plane, sir? Or are you going to pick somebody up?'"

"That would be the constabulary all right."

"You can tell by what he said?"

"Only the constabulary talk like that."

"And so I later realized these must have been trick questions, that is if we had answered yes to either we would have been in jeopardy, because there are no night flights in or out of Belfast."

"Of course."

"So I told him actually we were just looking for a place to spend the night, which of course was true."

"Of course it was true. They would have known that."

"And they said, 'Would a guest house be all right, sir?' All very polite. I said, 'That would be perfect.' They said, 'Just drive in here.' And a nice old fellow, armed to the teeth mind you, got on the phone and started calling around. He phoned one lady, Mrs. McGraw. All filled up."

"That would be the wife's sister."

"Of course. So then he said, 'Well, I'll call Mrs. McGraw's sister, Mrs. Trollope.' I felt like a right bloody fool, and I told him so. He said, 'Oh, don't worry at all. This happens all the time. The Common Market is going to build a large hotel right next to the airport, but right now there is nothing.'"

"Indeed," said the farmer, "it does happen all the time. People has phoned up maybe half three, four o'clock in the morning. Lots of times."

Today I remember Farmer Trollope fondly, with even more fondness than I felt towards him during our brief time together. As far as the

Troubles were concerned, he was at ground zero, but he was as moderate as anyone in the Republic, a passionately obsessed moderate, however. Like all of us, he probably had blind spots and ugly aspects to his personality, but I didn't see any of it. He seemed kind, not highly educated, but very kind and serious – serious about his country and the life he was living in it. I liked him immensely, but I had to leave before I realized that Farmer Trollope was a good man, thoughtful and straight down the middle, and one could feel the pain of his being an Ulsterman lying just under the surface, and the pain of trying to be a moderate in an immoderate country.

A cute little red-haired boy in blue coveralls with little rubber boots, a miniature version of the Irish farmer's uniform, North or South, approached us with a shy look on his face. You could imagine the father sometimes wondering if he were raising the child only to have him gunned down or blown up by the bad guys on the other side.

"He's on holidays," said the farmer. "He's a full-time farmer this week. Aren't you, Leonard?"

The little boy glanced at me to see if this had registered and if I was suitably impressed.

Four British soldiers had been killed and several injured. Their military vehicle was blown up. It happened about seven-thirty that morning just outside Downpatrick. It was on the radio. The bomb had been placed in a pothole and wired to a detonator up on a hill overlooking the road. The caravan of military vehicles went by at the same time every morning. The guys on the hill let off the blast just as the first truck came over the pothole, and the truck blew up, killing everyone in it, and the culprits got away.

The blast produced four more inconsolable mothers and another round of curses for Ireland. Their sons were supposed to be there in a peacekeeping capacity, like Canadians in Somalia.

But Farmer Trollope hadn't heard the news, and wasn't that

interested in discussing it. He politely suggested, for the first time of many, that we might like to go to the Ballyclare cattle auction. Beef cattle, heifers, dairy stock.

"Where would Downpatrick be from here?"

"'Twould be thirty mile. Not too bad a distance."

"Bit of trouble there this morning?"

"In Downpatrick?" He looked surprised.

My face and tone had given it all away. He pure and simple didn't want to know about it.

"Did you hear about that?"

"No, we never listen to the news at all."

"I don't blame you."

"If you travel this country," said Farmer Trollope, "you'll find about six hard areas where there's high unemployment and lots of people with nothing to do. Nothing better to do, I mean."

"Nothing much worse to do either," said Lourdes, who had been having a good cry in the background.

"We've got a lot of publicity about bombings and shootings, but when you look at America it's ten times worse. We have an American friend, he carries his own gun. It's not done here. Unless you're on the security force or need personal protection, it's not legal here."

"I don't know how he got it through the security checks."

"Oh, the American man didn't bring it. He couldn't bring his gun here."

"Oh, I thought you meant he was carrying it around here."

"No, in America he had to carry it. He said he had to, I don't know. And he said he'd used it, too."

"That's all they do over there. More guns than people to shoot. It's not like that in Canada yet. We've got a bit of catching up to do."

We were strolling back to the barn and were almost up to our ankles in mud. Not cows in general, but "my cows," said Farmer Trollope, as if he'd sent them to bovine music-appreciation classes.

"My cows like music. We can get five gallons of milk per day more playing the radio than we can if we don't play it."

"What kind of music do they like?"

He was waiting for that. He flicked a switch and the barn filled with the bouncy, bovine sounds of a string orchestra softly playing a slow version of "Please Don't Talk About Me When I'm Gone."

"They like soft music," he said.

"None of this heavy-metal stuff."

"Not too much. The general idea of music is, if I come in with buckets and make a noise or bang the gate or a door bangs – well then they jump, they're scared. But with the continuous music, even if it's noisy rock and roll, then the cows don't scare to a sudden noise. So they relax and they give more milk."

While listening to Mozart it often occurred to me that if I were a cow I'd give more milk with this glorious music being piped into the barn. Further, a recent study at the University of California at Irvine found that listening to Mozart for ten minutes could boost your IQ ten points, temporarily, that is, of course. This Mozart was something else. I visualized a whole herd of cattle, each with an IQ of ten.

"Have you ever tried Mozart on them?"

"Tried what?"

"Mozart."

"What's that?"

"Like, Mozart."

Blank look.

I don't know what was the matter with me. Maybe I was still trying to figure out if he meant five gallons extra a cow or five gallons extra *in toto*. I should have just said classical music.

Farmer Trollope may not have known beans about classical music, but I didn't know beans about cattle. He spoke about TV monitors for pregnant cows so when he's in the house and he sees some action starting up on the monitor he goes running out to the barn with a huge pincer mechanism to assist in the delivery. And he spoke about foxes from the surrounding woods stealing into the barn and dragging the afterbirths across the fields and into their den.

"I live in a big city. What exactly is a heifer? I used to know but I bloody well forgot."

"A heifer's a heifer until it gets into calf; a bull calf's a bull calf until it gets into stud."

"Right. And they just stand here like this all day long, do they?"

Oh my God, we sophisticated urbanites!

"Yes."

"Dull life."

"They seem to like it. We feed them nuts."

"What kind of nuts? Peanuts? Brazil nuts?" Señorita Brasil, who was playing hide and seek with Leonard, looked up, and our eyes connected for a moment.

"No, well, it's a special kind of nut to develop the cow from the day it is born."

I reached down and put my arms around three small black calves. "What are these little guys?"

"These here are what we call bull calves. These were born between December and the end of January."

I had a naïve curiosity about how dairy farmers had kept the multitudinous strains of cattle separate down through the millennia, since the cattle culture in Ireland went back five thousand years and the old sagas and legends are full of cattle raids.

"Surely all cows and all bulls can mate," I offered.

"Yes. Pretty well."

"It's amazing you can still keep the strains separate after all these centuries."

"It sounds complicated. It's not complicated."

Lourdes came back out of breath from playing with Leonard.

"We been so busy playing I missed a lot of your talk, except for the bit about Brazil nuts."

"It's pretty complicated, this cattle business," I said.

"Well," said Farmer Trollope, "the Good Lord gave me two ears and one mouth, so I try to listen twice as much as I talk."

I wanted to pop into Belfast, see it by day, but Farmer Trollope wouldn't hear of it. He suggested once again, patiently and politely, that I might be better off going to the Ballyclare market to see the cattle being sold off. He thought it would be great entertainment for a tourist. He gave directions, then said, if you see a car with a trailer, follow it. I wasn't too fussy on the idea, because all the tourist brochures had photos of cattle-market scenes, and it seemed to me the Ballyclare market would be a lot more organized and less fun than the fairs Morton was always visiting or stumbling upon fortuitously on his tour so long ago. We'd leave that for the tourists.

"We like people to come here and have a good impression. Because this country has got such a hard bad name. We like people to go into the towns and look around, but if you go into Belfast and have a bad day, you go home with a bad impression."

"I see."

"About three weeks ago there was a party come from England, what you might call a scooter club. Little wee scooters, about five hundred of them. They came for a meeting, and everybody brought their scooters. And they came off the boat at Belfast, the boat over from Liverpool, and they would drive their scooters to a bar called Buck Lodge, just over here. It's a hotel."

"We saw that last night, but we were already coming to your place."

"And they all congregated there. And about forty of them drove through part of Belfast which was a particularly bad area, and the people who lived there, they stoned the people on the scooters, and they were made very much unwelcome." A Biblical tone was affecting the rhythm of his narrative. "And they come in here that night to stay, four or five of them, and they said in the morning, 'We'll never be back in our life. This place is a complete lunatic asylum. And we're going back home today.'"

"What part of Belfast was that?"

"What we call West Belfast."

"Notorious. The Falls Road area. It's a poor Catholic area."

"Well, we're Protestant. But there's as bad Protestant areas as Catholic. And there's no doubt about that. Now, Falls Road is a Roman Catholic area and Shankill Road is a Protestant area. And there's no truck between them, no truck at all, believe you me. But we prefer to try not to call them Roman Catholic or Protestant, because that would be a negative thing. This whole thing is a political thing, you know. But you do have a Republican Protestant, people who are Protestant but who side with the Republic of Ireland, and we have some Catholics who would side very much with the North of Ireland, the Catholic Loyalists. And I don't suppose you hear very much about that in the papers."

"No, sir."

"So you don't know really, but it's very much a political thing."

My impression that he was optimistic of a settlement turned out to be false.

"I cannot see a settlement, owing to the fact that it's been going for eight hundred years. We've had a particularly bad time lately, and it's mainly due to politics and unemployment. I maintain that if everybody had a job and worked from eight o'clock in the morning to five or six o'clock at night they'd just want to go home and sit down and behave themselves."

"If everyone was working, everyone would be cooperating," said Lourdes.

"That is what I believe. I have employees who are Roman Catholic and I have employees who are Protestant, and we work together one hundred per cent, it's never mentioned. The papers, they always say that a Roman Catholic man was shot or a Protestant man was shot. And they always call Roman Catholics Republicans, even when they live up here. This is a slight embarrassment which causes problems with Catholic people and Protestant people working in the same place."

"I imagine it would."

"I'll be going to the Ballyclare market today and there will be as many Roman Catholics there as Protestants there, and there'll not be one gun there and there won't be one explosion there and I'll sell my cattle to whoever has the best money and I'll buy my cattle from whoever has cattle I like best – the cattle I like best, not the person. It's just these hard areas, you know, the fine young ones will turn up and they'll get it going again and somebody'll get his head blown off."

"But you don't pay any attention to the news."

"Well, the newspapers and the radio and the television, they get me fed up. I say it's very wrong to say a Roman Catholic man was shot or a Protestant man was shot because it encourages people to, like, keep score, and to do what they call these, uh —"

"Tit-for-tat killings?"

"That's the term. So I think if they cut off newspapers and radio and television, that should help a lot."

✦ ✦ ✦

An Irish neighbour sticks her head in and says she heard I'd been to Ireland, and had I been in the North as well? She says she's from Portaferry, near Belfast. Her parents brought her to Canada when she was six, and they settled in a small town in Southern Ontario, her dad a minister. A few years later, the parents not finding Canada to their taste, they returned to Ireland. But the kids hated the cold and pleaded to go back to Canada, because they'd by this time been spoiled by central heating. And so the family came back to Canada, and this time they stayed.

She says she remembers riots, rubber bullets, being caught up in all of that, burning effigies of the Pope, watching off in the distance as the Catholics burned effigies of the Queen.

"Bad-mannered people with low IQs."

"It's utter insanity," she says.

"You were right involved in all of that?"

"Yes, I was."

"Like burning effigies of the Pope?"

"Yes."

She says her parents just loved Ian Paisley and still do, *in absentia*. She remembers going to his church in the early eighties and seeing armed soldiers on the roof as she entered. She too has heard that Paisley had a place in Canada – in Ontario, she says it was, but she doesn't know where.

She says her parents and most northern Protestants really detest the Catholics, they think they are subhuman in every way, and even after all these years in Canada her father hasn't changed. He hates everything to do with Quebec, for instance, and France. In fact he almost died when his daughter went to live in Paris for a year and then to Montreal for five years.

She says her parents would rather she married a person of a different race, an African for instance, or an Asian, than an Irish Catholic. She has an uncle who married a Catholic, and they won't have anything to do with him.

She read some of what I've written about Farmer Trollope. Yes, she says, he's a good one all right, really good.

In a conversation in Belfast close to seventy years ago, Morton told someone he felt it was only a matter of time before union between the North and the South occurred. "How could we be ruled by a lot of Catholics?" replied the man.

MANY A SONG WAS
SUNG AT TARA

Downpatrick was not only the site of that morning's massacre, it was the place where Saint Patrick launched his campaign to introduce Christianity to the Irish in the fifth century. And his bones were said to be lying in the churchyard of Downpatrick Cathedral.

In spite of the horror of this morning's events, there was a peculiar sense of enchantment, as the road south from Belfast straightened out and, at the end of it, far in the distance, appeared the cathedral sitting high on its hill, which commanded a view to the flat horizon in all directions. It was as if we were entering another world, more ethereal, with spirits flying thick in the air and passing through each other like clouds, but with faces, and looking down at the earth with amusement. The cathedral was sitting in splendour high on the Hill of Down, a site of great mythical and strategic importance long before the time of Patrick.

The huge black granite stone, lying on its back in the churchyard, had Patrick's name engraved on it with such simplicity and beauty as would tend to lessen the likelihood of its authenticity being questioned. It's true the stone had been placed there only recently, in 1900, but it was sitting on the exact spot cited by ancient tradition as Patrick's grave. Trouble is, there are so many traditions. For instance, William of Malesbury, writing in the early twelfth century, states that on either side of the altar in a little wattle church at Glastonbury, Somerset, were the tombs of Saint Patrick and Saint Indract.

Heading out of Downpatrick to the seaside town of Saul, where Patrick was said to have landed in 432 (though he was also said to have landed at Dundrum further south), we were stopped at a checkpoint and had a machine gun stuck in our faces. But as soon as I opened my mouth and asked, with an exaggerated Boston accent, if the machine gunner knew where we could get a hot dog and a Coke and the latest baseball scores, we were allowed to drive on. Lucky he didn't know that baseball season hadn't started yet.

We drove down the coast through Ardglass and Newcastle. When we stopped to buy a paper somewhere between Maggy's Leap and Annalong, the shopkeeper refused to sell me one because all I had was Irish money, that is from the Republic, even though it was perfectly legal tender and the bed-and-breakfast last night had no problem with it. His attitude wasn't particularly nasty, just unpleasantly stubborn and sullen, as if he wanted to punish tourists for going to the South, and I didn't feel like arguing, as I seldom do. I had not come to Ireland to argue, but only to watch and listen.

Soon we were driving along where the Mountains of Mourne sweep down to the sea, as the old song by the immortal Percy French has it:

> So I'll wait for the wild rose that's waiting for me
> Where the Mountains of Mourne sweep down to the sea.

It took hours for us to get across the border back into the Republic, not because we were being questioned, but because everyone else seemed to be. A traffic jam ensued, as bad as anything I'd seen anywhere.

We drove down to Drogheda at the mouth of the Boyne. Drogheda was founded by the Vikings in the tenth century but is the site of an ancient burial mound said to contain the bones of the warrior-poet Amergin, who arrived from Spain a few centuries before Christ. Amergin was the son of Míl, who gave his name to the Milesians, the Celtic race that invaded Ireland about that time, although, as Jack Roberts maintains, perhaps invasion is too strong a word. Or, if Mr. Looney is to be believed, it's too weak a word.

Drogheda was captured by Cromwell in 1649. Two thousand defenders were killed, with many survivors being sent to the West Indies. We decided against zipping in to Saint Peter's Church to catch a look at the severed head of Oliver Plunkett, the Irish saint who was executed for treason in London in 1681. His head was snatched from the fire, but it couldn't be brought back to Ireland until 1721. I'd already seen dozens of saints' heads in Italy, and even Galileo's forearm, and Lourdes was no stranger to this melancholy brand of morally uplifting pathology.

And as promised we revisited Newgrange. The weather was fine this time, and we even managed to penetrate the long passage tunnel into the central cruciform chamber, the holy of holies. But we were with a guided tour, and the guide was rather remote and bored, and had a voice like a parrot. We were left with a feeling of having violated something unimaginably sacred, sophisticated, mysterious. There could be no faulting the modern restoration, it was a brilliant and inspired piece of work. But the ancient pre-Celtic gods of Ireland, the Tuatha Dé Danann, who had descended from the sky and inhabited the land for millennia, were definitely not in attendance.

The Hill of Tara afforded a spectacular panoramic view of the surrounding plain. Other than that there wasn't much to see, just a powerful sense of atmosphere, no doubt in part because the two of us had the whole place to ourselves. There was no one else in sight, and we could see for miles in all directions (except, unfortunately, down). The feelings were seeping up through the ground, like Keats's unheard music, silent moans, groans, sighs, screams, shouts, laughter, and harps and flutes, and the unmistakable sound of hearts breaking.

Tara was the home of the high kings of Ireland from before the sacking of Troy up to the tenth century A.D., almost to the time of the first Norman invasions. And before the Celtic kings took over, there were the Tuatha Dé Danann kings, characters such as Nuada of the Silver Hand and Lughaidh Lámhfhada.

In those ancient days one can imagine stonecutting teams resting at Tara on the last stop on the way to Newgrange with massive chunks of brilliant white quartzite quarried in the Wicklow Mountains south of Dublin.

Many a song was sung at Tara, many a tale told, many a harp plucked, many a heart broken. Many of the impossible legends of Ireland had their birth on this hill. And when a king died, he became a god.

Tara, *Teamhair* in Irish, was said to have been named after a Milesian princess named Tea, or Thea, who took up residence on the hill and had a wall, or *mhair*, built like one she had seen and admired in Spain. So Tea's Wall became Tara, which became the heart of ancient Celtic Ireland.

The five ancient provinces – Connaght, Munster, Ulster, Leinster, and Meath – surrounded Tara like petals around the eye of a daisy in a way reminiscent of what is known of the imperial geography of the ancient Mayan civilization. Five roads radiated out from Tara, one for each of the five provinces. From here bands of soldiers set out to do battle with the Romans in Britain and France. The surrounding countryside was much different then. Or was it? On a good map, one sees that there still are five roads radiating out from the vicinity of the Hill of Tara. Morton believed they disappeared eons ago, but they're still there. They are minor roads by today's standards, but each in its winding way can be seen to make its way into each of the five ancient provinces.

It might be mentioned in passing that, in addition to the political geography being similar, the Mayans had a feathered serpent-god called Kulkulcan, while the Irish Celts had a heroic demi-god called Cúchulainn. Cúchulainn was probably a Tuatha dé Danann name.

Horrible battles were fought at Tara. It was the site, for instance, of a famous massacre staged by King Dúnlaing of Leinster in which thirty royal princesses were killed along with three thousand people altogether, in A.D. 222. With the coming of Christianity, the battles apparently became larger and more frequent, although there were also frequent (but short) periods of harmony and stability.

There's nothing to fight over now. Just a silent treeless hill, impregnated with a sense of sadness even under a blue afternoon sky. The hill is a gently sloping three hundred feet high, covered with green grass and decorated here and there with ancient earthworks, mounds, modern bronze plaques, a modern (and much-disliked) statue of Saint Patrick, and a well-loved legendary standing stone called the *Lia Fáil*, the Stone of Destiny. Kings were inaugurated at the site of this stone, and if the stone approved of the crowning it would roar three times. The stone is also said to have been Jacob's pillow, brought to Ireland by the Milesians. It's popularly known as *Bod Fhearghuis*, Fergus's Penis.

The hill sits behind and above a small old country church and graveyard. The effect is one of silence, like the Zen gardens of sand and rock in Kyoto. If I were a real Irishman, living in Ireland, and concerned about the spiritual well-being of my country, I would oppose any further plans to excavate or recreate the Mound of the Hostages, or the old *Teach Míodhchuarta*, which was a banquet hall 750 feet long, perhaps the largest banquet hall in human history, or the Royal Enclosure, or the Royal Seat, or Cormac's House. That Tara is in silence today is good for the soul of the country, in my view. If it were filled with the sounds of excavation and construction once again, and thence with the shouts of ignorant tourists, the entire country would have lost something. The silence and sadness of the Hill of Tara today is doing more to keep the spirit of Tara alive than a billion dollars worth of excavation and restoration.

Mr. Looney would agree to a point. More money should be spent on the little-known and completely unexcavated sites, like Motte Knockgraffon. No more should be spent on the famous spots, he might say. But then again, it would be great to see what is under the soil at Tara, for, as Mr. Looney said, we need to understand who we were in order to figure out who we are.

"I came to the Hill of Tara as a man should, at sunset, and alone, to say good-bye to Ireland," says Morton at the end of his book.

And in Yeats's words:

> At the grey round of the hill
> Music of a lost kingdom
> Runs, runs and is suddenly still.

At Thurles that evening we stayed in the same beautiful old hotel in which I'd stayed solo a few weeks earlier. Now we were creeping silently along the carpeted maze of corridors as we gigglingly studied the old framed prints showing Irish life as it was, photos of Thurles from a hundred years ago, old political cartoons of Irish political heroes outsmarting the English variety, and of course the obligatory foxhunting scenes. Then we went out and discovered a Chinese restaurant. Our waitress made me feel homesick, because she was the first Asian face I'd seen in a month. Our fortune cookies were ominous. Lourdes's said: "You will soon meet your true love." Mine said: "You will only ever love yourself."

The next day we appeared at Mr. Looney's door in Cahir. He glanced at me, then gave Lourdes a long, admiring look. Twice. And a third time when he heard her name, for he was a great lover of the holy wells that are found everywhere in County Tipperary, and these wells, where people go for prayer and healing, are often referred to as Lourdes grottoes. Also he had a natural admiration for hot babes. And he wasn't one of those elderly hypocrites who manages to hide his still-sputtering libido from public scrutiny, as if it were some sick animal that should have been put to sleep decades ago. Lourdes repaid his glances with interest.

We simply wanted to ask if Mr. Looney would care to be treated to lunch in a nice restaurant we'd heard about in Cahir, but he insisted first on stopping off here and there to show us some of the beauty spots, rather than the historical sites, no doubt with Lourdes in mind. He was behaving in a most courtly manner towards her.

He took Lourdes, with me trailing along and feeling terribly left out, to swan-filled lakes and streams tucked away in surprisingly secret valleys among the hills, nature trails running through ancient oak forests, beautiful old Georgian mansions with commanding views out over great natural parks filled with deer and fountains and beautiful walled gardens. All this was for Lourdes. She was squealing with delight and throwing her arms around Mr. Looney. The old boy knew how to give a girl a good time, and he had Lourdes's undivided attention as I hobbled and limped along behind them.

It was a fine old restaurant, divided into a maze of small dining rooms, each with its own fireplace blazing away and each with its own busy bar. We had the salmon special, me with Guinness, Lourdes and Mr. Looney with tea. He was a strict, lifelong teetotaller and referred contemptuously to "boozers."

I had taken extensive notes on everything I remembered from our earlier conversations, but there was much I had missed, much I hadn't absorbed, and much I hadn't understood. I pulled out a little list of questions and a tape recorder and asked him to forgive me in advance if he caught me asking things he had already answered. And he kindly agreed to do so.

"First off, which historical sight, if you had to pick one out, is the most neglected in this area?"

"Moorstown Castle."

"And what period does that castle date from?"

"About the fourteenth century. It was the stronghold of the Keating clan. The Keatings originally came from Wales. They were gallowglasses. Castle Ballymacadam was another Keating stronghold from the early twelfth century, but people don't realize that, because that was before surnames were introduced into Ireland. And Adam was actually the surname of an early Keating from Wales."

"So Castle Ballymacadam is the castle of the town of the son of Adam?"

"That is correct."

"What do you think of the policies of the historical board in general? For instance when they select one site, almost as if at random, spending a lot of money on it, and neglecting all the others."

"With the Board of Works it's a matter of money. But they have an unhappy knack of taking over sites and preserving them, and it finishes them off."

"What exactly do you mean by that, Mr. Looney?"

"For example, in 1961 I reported a site here in the district going back to 4000 B.C. And four days after I reported it, they took it over as a national monument, both the site and the surrounding twenty acres. Now all of this was worthy of research, but up to now they haven't come back to do anything."

"And where exactly was this?"

"I'd rather not disclose the location."

"Why would that be?"

"At the present day there's a lot of vandalism and destruction of ancient monuments. And there's a lot of pilfering of important artifacts. That's why. But I did take you there during your first visit."

"Oh, there we go. You took me so many places."

"Well, I figured that. It can be confusing at first."

Actually I did remember the spot, but it would have been impossible for me to find it again unaided.

"So what do you think of metal detectors in general, people who go around the countryside with them?"

"I have no time whatsoever for metal detectors. I travel the countryside and I do it field by field and I find great pleasure in that type of work. But I have never used a metal detector."

"And you manage quite well without them."

"Quite well, because I'm solely an amateur enthusiast, and to find one unrecorded stone or artifact gives me more pleasure than anything I could find with a detector."

"I've heard people complain about road construction, construction crews in general, with many unrecorded antiquities disappearing under the blade of a bulldozer. Is this a big problem? And if so do you think there's anything that could be done about it?"

"Well, you cannot stop progress. And although it's true the bulldozer has done a lot of damage, it has done a lot of good as well. I think a lot depends upon the drivers of these bulldozers. If they don't report finds, it's possibly because they don't realize they're making a find. That can happen, too, because anything that has spent three or four thousand years in the soil is very delicate and a bulldozer can destroy it without anyone seeing it."

I asked Mr. Looney about the work he did in tracing family histories, particularly for North Americans and so on. Did some people find out more than they want to know?

"Well, if the average person wants to go back over his family history and be reasonably exact about it, there is a possibility I suppose that we'd find out something we'd rather we didn't know. There's an old saying that you'll find a skeleton in every cupboard. And I think it's a fairly true statement. But you must accept that you're going back into history, and what happens maybe a hundred or two hundred years ago it's not going to affect anyone at the present day, and it should be taken in that spirit, that it is history."

I told him that in high school I was an indifferent student and was unable to understand why we had to study history. Was there anything that could be done to motivate such a student today?

"I would say to a student like that, that if you want to go forward, you must know what's behind you. In other words, if you really want to know who you are or where you came from you have to check back on your roots. That's necessary, otherwise you'll be in ignorance of your past. You'll always know that there's something missing, that you're groping for something out there that you know is there, but you just can't quite find it. So it's very necessary to go back in the past in order to understand the future."

The subject of politics came up. Mr. Looney's voice dropped, and he said he could never talk about such things generally because "some of the fellows aren't very well informed and they get all heated up about it."

Mr. Looney was a true Irish patriot for whom Northern Ireland represented his heart's deepest wound. He said that Michael Collins and the others shouldn't have settled for partition, that they should have accepted defeat, they should have perhaps surrendered, then they could have regrouped and started over again. He pointed out that these were very young men – Michael Collins was only thirty-three, for instance – and they were dealing with career parliamentarians, they didn't have any experience, and they just made a fundamental and understandable political error. Then later, de Valera became president at thirty-nine, and he had a direct line of communication with Westminster.

"There are the things that are never brought out," he said. "De Valera was very close to the British intelligence."

When I asked about the extradition treaty that would allow the United Kingdom to bring suspected Irish terrorists back to Britain for trial, he simply shook his head sadly and said such a treaty would have been unthinkable twenty years ago.

I didn't ask Mr. Looney if he supported the IRA, or the Sinn Féin. But I think he would be a supporter, one of a mere 4 per cent in the twenty-six counties of the Republic. It's a greater challenge to see the romantic and idealistic side of the IRA today than it was when Mr. Looney was a young man, which was when his unwavering sentiments were formed.

MOTTE KNOCKGRAFFON

We visited the local Church of Ireland church and Lourdes took a picture of Mr. Looney and me standing at the front door with a bust of Henry VIII on my side and Martin Luther on Mr. Looney's side.

"The people of the church don't have a clue who these people are, not even the pastor," said Mr. Looney, "but to the best of my reckoning it's Henry VIII and Martin Luther."

As for the newspaper stories about the Tinkers, Mr. Looney said the people who were doing all the complaining had not spoken to the Tinkers at all. "They've not sat down and talked to them, that's what that's all about."

As for antiquities, wouldn't it be nice if, in order to attract more tourism, the government clearly marked and delineated all the Stone Age trackways all over Ireland, just to encourage tourists to come to Ireland and walk along them?

"They'd never do it," said Mr. Looney, "because the government doesn't know anything about the trackways, all they know is to count how many tourists order breakfast and how many people go here to lunch or there to lunch, that's all they know about. They don't want to admit they don't know anything, so they just say oh certainly not, we couldn't do that."

Further on metal detectors, the following day the London Observer ran a story headed "Pay Day for Mr. Pay." A printer named Keith Pay was under sedation for "nervous excitement" after making a big find in a cow pasture in Cheshire. He had been demonstrating his new metal detector to a friend, when it started emitting an ear-splitting noise. He dug down a few inches and found a horde of four lead-sealed pots full of coins dated between 1547 and 1685, covering the reigns of Edward VI, Elizabeth I, James I, and Charles I and II.

There were almost four thousand coins, all in mint condition.

I was limping along the back streets of Cashel at dusk after spending another cold couple of hours on the rock. Lourdes and Mr. Looney had become so enchanted with each other, I had discreetly taken off. We were to meet at Chez Hans later. I knew Lourdes was getting tired of me, which was not surprising. Only a day or two before I'd been musing aloud how I felt as if I were Morton, except for being a little deficient in the Messiah-complex department.

"I wouldn't say that," said Lourdes.

"What do you mean?"

"You are very pompous sometimes, and I think you have a bit of a megalomania problem."

"What? Me? A pompous megalomaniac? This is a joke, right?"

"No, it's not a joke."

"I'm known as the man with no ego."

"Now that's a joke."

As I passed the Cashel Folk Museum, famed for its tackiness, a glance through the open door revealed an unexpected sight: a splendid high cross, standing in the foyer, to one side of the cash register. A woman behind the ticket table explained that the cross had been standing in the main street of Cashel for a hundred years after having been brought in from the countryside, where it had been standing for a thousand years. But one day a truck hit it, and it fell down and smashed into several pieces. The people from the National Museum came down and carted the pieces away to Dublin.

"My husband wrote to the museum and asked them if they weren't doing anything with the pieces could he have them, and so they shipped them back to him. He put them back together and built his museum around it."

"He's done an impeccable job of putting it back together again."

In Ireland you see a lot of high crosses that were obviously in pieces and put together again, but the seams on this one were so clean you had to feel with your fingers to figure out where it was broken.

"He'll be pleased to hear that, I'm sure. In fact here he is now!"

The museum operator himself, Martin O'Dwyer, smelling fresh blood, appeared in the foyer and escorted me out back.

The museum turned out to be a little Walt Disney street of thatched-roof nineteenth-century shops: a typical butcher shop, typical kitchen, typical village pub, village smithy, and a little one-room house devoted to the Easter Rising, with framed news clippings and photos, rusty old sidearms, and someone's spectacles, removed just before execution.

This museum seemed to be aimed at the Irish tourists rather than the foreign ones. Perhaps that's why the guidebooks called it tacky. And Mr. O'Dwyer had built his very own chapel, complete with a good long row of carved-stone faces, just like at the more-famous Cormac's Chapel on the rock. I told him it looked just like the twelfth century. He gave me a delighted look, reminiscent of the looks old Mr. Looney had been giving Lourdes, not that I needed any reminders. And then he laughed.

"The archaeologists from Dublin," he said, "they came down and said those carvings were twelfth-century for sure." He might have been pulling my leg or maybe the archaeologists had been pulling his. "But I actually did carve them myself."

"Did you carve them a long time ago, or did you carve them intending to make them look old?"

"I carved them back in the twelfth century, I did."

"Seriously though, Mr. O'Dwyer, it's good to see the old arts aren't completely dead."

"There's still a little spark in the old arts yet."

"And those fellows who found the chalice, they got a lot of money out of that, didn't they? The Lukeswell Chalice." It turned out Mr. O'Dwyer knew the gentlemen and was definitely on their side.

"Oh they got big money, yeah. They got twenty-five thousand pounds each. One got fifty thousand plus expenses."

"I've heard some awful stories about them."

"Like what?"

"Well, about the one who actually found the chalice. I heard that it's common knowledge that he made several secret trips to the United States before it became public that he'd found the chalice. And it's thought that he found a lot of other things that he took over to the States and sold there."

"Quite probable, but I think contact was made with the National Museum prior to the trips. He was looking for a buyer, and that's why he was treated so badly by the National Museum."

"You mean because they didn't like him using a metal detector?"

"Well, no. You see, that was only a cover. Of course now, they want to discourage people wandering around with metal detectors, but what they didn't like was the idea that he might have tried to sell it, like the chalice, elsewhere."

"Like in the United States."

"Maybe."

"It must have been exciting to find it though. How deep was it?"

"It was only about that deep, and that big a hole." He indicated a hole about two feet deep and three feet around. "I have a piece of the corrosion that was around it even, you know. A big copper dish was over the chalice, and you know the way that copper gets corroded from being in the earth all that time. And I have a piece of that, the corrosion. But it was a very exciting find at the time, that was."

"Strange story."

"It is that, it is. They won't dig it up themselves. But they don't like it if you dig it up yourself."

"They want it to stay in the ground."

"They do."

"Well, Timmy Looney down there at Cahir, he claims he's found a burial mound twice as big as the one at Newgrange."

"Ooh, my God."

"And he's phoned the Board of Works, and they're not interested."

"They wouldn't be, it's true."

"He can't get them to come down and have a look at it."

"No help at all."

"He won't tell anybody where it is, though. He's afraid unauthorized people will start digging it up."

"He's right. I imagine it could be the Motte Knockgraffon he's talking about. You probably know it was built by the Normans, you know what I mean. But there's legends about Knockgraffon going back before the Normans ever came here, you know. And there's an underground in it, and I've always said there's an underground, and the motte was probably built on top of an already-built mound."

"That's pretty near here, isn't it?"

"It is. It's between Cahir and Cashel. Legend has it that the kings of Cashel lived down there at the Motte Knockgraffon before they came to the Rock of Cashel."

"Mr. Looney told me that, indeed. He called them the Kings of Munster."

"He would be right as well. It's true."

"And this would be long before the Normans came and built a castle on top of it. It looks like a mound with a lot of trees growing out of the top."

"It is that. It's a big, big mound. I'd say it was that one he was talking about."

"A burial mound for the burial of dead kings."

"That it is."

"Is it about that size, about twice as big as Newgrange? He says he's paced all around it."

"He's probably measured it, I'm not sure. You know, I wouldn't have paced it myself. But it is big."

"Have you been to Newgrange?"

"I have, and I've been out to that place, too. And I'd imagine Newgrange is as big as it. But the legends are there all about it."

"Where do you read about these legends?"

"Well, we heard about them. They're handed down, yeah."

"They must be written down though."

"I suppose they are, but I never seen them written up like that anywhere. But there's the one I like about the fellow with the hump. You know what I mean, and he went along to get a fairy, because the fairies were of course magnificent people in our childhood you know, we grew up with the fairies. And we called them leprechauns in those days. We grew up with all the folklore about the fairies and that. But this fellow was coming home one night, and the fairies were inside and they were all singing. And they were all singing in Irish of course: *Dé Luain, Dé Máirt, Dé Céadaoin, Déardaoin, Dé hAoine, Dé Sathairn, Dé Domhnaigh* . . ."

"I see. So the fairies were singing the days of the week."

"They were, and so as he came along they sang *Dé Luain, Dé Máirt, Dé Céadaoin* . . . That was Monday, Tuesday, Wednesday, you see? And they couldn't get the next day. And so they'd go back and they'd sing: *Dé Luain, Dé Máirt, Dé Céadaoin* . . . *Dé Luain, Dé Máirt, Dé Céadaoin* . . ."

"They just kept singing Monday, Tuesday, Wednesday, because they couldn't remember the word for Thursday."

"You've got it. And the man shouted out *Déardaoin*, which was —"

"The name for Thursday!"

"Right, and that was the one day they wanted, you know what I mean?"

"Yes. They couldn't finish the week till they remembered the day for Thursday. Something important was missing, and they couldn't proceed."

"That is so, and so they were very happy with his help and so they asked him what would he want for this thing, for helping them like that. And of course the one thing he wanted was to have the hump taken off his back. Which they duly done, you see. So he arrived back anyway, and he told everybody."

"He had no choice. They would notice his hump had gone and they would naturally want to know what had happened to it."

"That's right."

"They suspected maybe some supernatural goings-on. Humps don't just disappear like that."

"That's right. And so this other guy had this bad hump too, you see. And so he decided to go out and do the same thing. So he went out the same way, and he heard the fairies singing: *Dé Luain, Dé Máirt, Dé Céadaoin* . . . And the man jumped in and said *Déardaoin*. But they had known that one, you see."

"They knew it this time. The man jumped in too soon."

"He did."

"He was too eager. He wanted it too badly. He should have waited, because nobody likes to have his story interrupted when he's right in the middle of it. I hope my numerous interruptions aren't bothering you at all."

"No, in your case it's the sign of a good listener."

"Thank you. I try."

"And so the man jumped in too soon. So what they done, they put the other man's hump on this man's back. So he had two humps instead of one."

"Oh! Cruel and unusual punishment."

"The leprechauns were experts at that sort of thing."

Mr. O'Dwyer let out a big fat sigh.

"And there's loads of them about that, you know. And there's ones about the Rock too. They go away way back. And it's imagination and everything. Good story-telling."

"And morality."

"Right."

"And how to behave ethically."

"Right."

"And the virtue of honesty."

"Right."

"How the world has evil forces to punish people who are selfish and stupid and think only of themselves and their humps."

"Right."

"Did you grow up hearing the fairies were the people who lived here before the Celts came?"

"I did. I most certainly did."

"And pretty well everybody believed that, right?"

"That they did."

"And they were magic people; they could appear and disappear any time and all that."

"They were that, that's right."

"And they could control the weather?"

"I suppose they could, they were right clever. And there's a good story told about a fellow going out one morning and he meets a fairy. You know, the fairy was trapped. So he caught the fairy and he wouldn't let him go unless he told him where the crock of gold was."

"The famous crock of gold."

"It was. And so the fairy takes him over to the Dublin Road, and he says down there is the crock of gold. So the man says, 'How will I know it?' The fairy says there's a *buachalán*" – pronounced "booka-long" – "as we call it, a big yellow flower you see in the summer time, a big weed, that'll be growin' out of it. So the man went down the Dublin Road, and he saw the *buachalán* growing there. And he said,

I'll come back in the morning with me spade and I'll dig it up. Of course he arrived back the next morning and the whole place was full of *buachaláns.*"

I let out a big sneeze.

"God bless you. Allergic to the *buachalán,* are you?"

I laughed. "Not usually," I said.

Buachalán is the Irish word for ragweed.

"Ach, you could be on about legends and stories at this point forever, and you wouldn't have to repeat yourself."

The stories seemed to be the litter of a once-great religion.

"How old were you when you stopped believing?"

"In fairies? Hmm . . . You see, electrification first came here in the fifties or so, well no, a little bit before. I remember the first radio being here, you know what I mean, just one radio. That was magic of course. And we couldn't believe how this guy got inside this bloody thing. But it was all fairies before that, and *everybody* visited *everybody* you know. And you came in at night, and we all gathered around the fire, and of course the crack started as we called it; you sang, I gave a recitation, and you'd tell a story, and someone else would tell a story, and there were the wakes, too."

"The wild and wonderful wakes."

"It was at a real old-fashioned wake, in my time, I was only very little, but the snuff was there, and the clay pipes were there, and the drink was there. It was an outing, really, and processions."

"And then there's the song 'Finnegan's Wake,' where Finnegan's widow punches out his girlfriend for weeping and wailing too much."

"That's a good song, and I think Ireland is the only country in the world where you will have crack, where you get good sport and laughter, you know what I mean? I think we still know how to laugh in this country, you know. We haven't been spoiled. There's so many countries been spoiled. And I think commercialization done it all, you know. We're not as rich, I suppose, or as well off as other countries, you know, we haven't been spoiled. Television has ruined the world. In that way now, I mean it's a marvellous medium, don't get me wrong, but it's ruined it for people visiting each other together in each other's houses and talking. The art of conversation is nearly finished. You know what I mean?"

"I'm with you, but at least the art is still valued here. In many countries, Canada for instance, even the concept of the art of conversation is utterly foreign."

"I'm sorry to hear that. It's television. The television, even if you turn it down when somebody comes in, then your eyes go back to it. No, I love television, you know, the video and everything like that. But I be very selective in what I be watching. I love anything to do with history. It doesn't matter where it is in the world."

The story comes to an end with Timmy Looney and Lourdes Brasil sitting across from me at a table for four at Chez Hans at the foot of the Rock of Cashel. Chez Hans was in a nineteenth-century "Methodist edifice" (phrase stolen from John Updike), a handsome and spacious church. But never a service was held in it. The minister, just after he finished building the church, abandoned it and returned to his mother church, the Church of Ireland, having sorted out his difficulties with them.

"It must have cost money at the time, I'd say," said the waiter. He added that the church was built in 1850, and the renegade clergyman's name was, coincidentally, Morton – the Reverend James Morton. The church stayed under Morton's ownership, and when he died it passed on to his wife. It was used as a public hall for a century, and then in 1968 the current owner, "the boss," bought it off the local pawnbroker, into whose hands it had fallen.

"The boss, who does all the cooking," said the waiter.

Lourdes and Mr. Looney took no interest in my conversation with the waiter. They seemed radiantly unaware of me. They chatted away for an hour or two, with me occasionally contributing some banality. They luxuriated in their occasional silences, while I couldn't help wishing to be several counties away, or even an ocean away. The subject of food came up, as it tends to do in restaurants, and I mentioned one country, New Zealand, where cold asparagus sandwiches are considered a great delicacy.

"How were they flavoured?" Lourdes queried, politely.

"Flavoured with margarine." I could hear myself sounding like a fool. "Just cold, soggy, greasy, overcooked, mushy asparagus, wrapped in white bread with globs of margarine, and people line up for them."

Lourdes and Mr. Looney appeared to be secretly holding hands under the table.

"When you're in love," said Lourdes, "everything tastes – *delicioso.*" She gave me a weak little smile.

So did Mr. Looney.

Then Lourdes and Mr. Looney turned and gave great broad smiles to each other.

✦ ✦ ✦

The next twenty-four hours were gloomy, awkward, and cold. Mr. Looney and Lourdes said goodbye to me at the airport. An hour later, when my plane took off, I looked out the window with my field glasses. I can't say for sure it was them, but it looked like them, walking hand in hand through a boggy field towards a standing stone. Soon I was out over the Atlantic.

With numerous interruptions it took me well over a year to complete the first draft of this book. At that point I felt a desire to phone Mr. Looney, to see how he was doing, and to clarify some of his points.

Lourdes answered the phone.

Mr. Looney, she said, had needed someone to help him organize his material, to help with the cleaning, cooking, laundry, and so on, and generally to be a good companion for him in his declining years. I told her those were exactly my needs too. A silence ensued, then she burst into her high-pitched laughter I hadn't realized was so pleasant to listen to, even when it was at my expense.

Lourdes said she'd never been happier. In fact she'd been writing the best poetry of her life, reams of it. She had published a book and it had been shortlisted for the prestigious annual Lorca Prize.

I offered her my hearty congratulations.

She wanted to know if I had ever won any awards for my poetry.

"Oh, a few," I said, but I hadn't. So I bit my tongue, and my vague feeling of self-pity inched up another notch.

Coincidentally, the day I called was Lourdes's birthday. But not only that, it was Mr. Looney's birthday as well. They had both been born on October 11, almost sixty years apart.

"We're both Librans," said Lourdes. "Maybe that is why we are such good friends."

She wanted to know if I remembered the fat, red-faced, elderly man who had sold me the tip for my cane, and who had called me an old reprobate. He too had recently taken a very strong interest in the antiquities. The three of them had been on many field trips together, in far-flung parts of the Republic of Ireland, south of a line running between Galway and Dublin.

I asked if they had discovered anything interesting.

"It's all been very interesting for us, you know."

"You're getting to sound Irish."

"I know."

"And you've come to like the Irish."

"That happened during our trip together."

"Thanks for coming along."

"Thanks for inviting me."

"I didn't actually invite you."

"I remember."

"I don't know what to say."

"You never did."

"I suppose not."

"Did you wish to speak to Timmy?"

"Timmy?" I croaked and stuttered. "Let me call back tomorrow."

"He's right here."

"I have to go now, but I'll call back real soon."

I still haven't called back.

Every sixty-five years or so, it seems, a travel writer from another country arrives in Cahir, County Tipperary, and unintentionally effects a dramatic change in the life of Mr. Looney.

INDEX

Antrim (County), 226
Aran Islands, 9, 154-155, 184
Athassel Abbey, 110-112

Ballaghbeama Gap, 192
Ballinskelligs Bay, 196
Ballycarberry (Castle), 206
Ballyclare, 278, 281, 283
Ballydehob, 229
Ballymacadam (Castle), 292
Baltimore, 240-242
Bantry, 214
Béara Peninsula, 212-228
Beckett, Samuel, 244
Bede, Venerable, 48
Behan, Brendan, 13, 266
Belfast, 5, 17, 19, 27, 134,
  160, 173, 274-275, 281
Ben Bulben, 271-272
Blackwater Valley, 99
Blasket Islands, 185, 199
Boyne Valley, 146, 148, 199
Browne's Hill Dolmen, 65-69,
  74, 110
Burren, the, 168, 171, 176
Butlers, the, 88
Byrne, Gay, 5, 33, 41, 61, 93,
  128

Cahirciveen, 64, 192,
  206-207
Cahir, 73, 91, 96, 105-125,
  160, 255, 273, 290-291
Cappagh Cross, 160
Carlow, 64
Cashel (Folk Museum),
  297-305
Cashel (Rock), 45, 74, 93-96,
  106, 113, 117, 118, 202,
  296
Castlemaine Harbour, 178
Castletown Bearhaven, 213
Catholic University Church,
  29-30
Charters, Lady Margaret, 119
Chesterton, G. K., 101, 224
Chez Hans, 297, 305-306
Christ Church Cathedral, 86
Church Island, 197
Churchtown, 75
Claddagh, the, 155-167, 173
Clare (County), 168, 170,
  259

Clifden, 268-270
Cliffs of Moher, 45, 169
Clogheen, 112, 160
Colclough, William, 75
Collins, Michael, 294
Connemara (County), 134,
  254, 266, 268-270
Connolly, James, 18
Corc, King, 94
Cork (City), 31, 35, 65,
  125-136, 154, 164, 245, 253
Cork (County), 212-244
  passim
Cormac the Magnificent,
  King, 96, 208
Cormac's Chapel, 94-96,
  298
Craggaunowen Project, 176
Croagh Patrick, 272
Cromwell, Oliver, 64, 87,
  103, 113, 116, 171, 287
Cúchulainn, 289
Currane (Lough), 197

Derry (Londonderry), 138,
  249, 275
Derrynasaggart Mountains,
  245
De Valera, Eamonn, 294
Diarmuid and Gráinne,
  208-211, 271-272
Dingle Peninsula, 176-190,
  201, 250
Donegal (County), 142, 187,
  245, 274
Donnelly, Dan, 56-59
Downpatrick, 277-278, 285
Dowth, 151-152, 223
Drogheda, 147, 287
Dublin Zoo, 16-25, 129
Duleek Abbey, 148
Dún Aonghusa, 223
Dunbeg Fort, 185
Dunbrody Abbey, 71-75
Dunlaing of Leinster, King,
  289
Dunnamaggan, 81

Emmet, Robert, 32, 138
Ennis, 170, 176, 178
Enniskerry, 42
Errew Abbey, 272
Eyeries, 218-219, 224

Famine, the Great, 175-190
  passim
Farrell, Mariead, 172-174
Fir Bolg, 223
Fomonians, the, 223
French, Percy, 10, 286

Gaeltacht, the, 98, 184, 197
Gallarus Oratory, 186
Galway, 4, 109, 135, 152-168,
  173, 266
Gerald of Wales, 47-48
Gill (Lough), 271
Glendalough, 39, 45-50, 52
Golden, 112
Golden Vale, the, 123, 137
Gregory, Lady, 208
Gur (Lough), 143-145

Hag of Béara, 213
Harbison, Peter, 218
Haughey, Charles, 160-163
Healy Pass, 214
Heuston, John J., 18
Holy Cross Abbey, 74, 91-94

Inchiquin, Earl of (Murrough
  of the Burnings), 95-97
Inchiquin (Lough), 220, 224,
  235
Inch Peninsula, 178
Irish Republican Army, 31,
  36, 39, 43, 90, 163,
  172-174, 248-249, 263,
  295
Irish Country Women's
  Association, 149
Iveragh Peninsula, 189, 199,
  208-209

Joyce, James, 1, 29, 43, 131,
  249, 262

Kealkil, 226
Keane, John B., 10-12
Keane, Molly, 41
Keatings, the, 122, 292
Kells Priory, 79-85 passim
Kenmare, 192, 225, 249
Kerry (County), 8, 14, 64,
  134, 142, 169, 194, 202
Kilcullen, 51-59
Kildare, 52, 55, 62

Kilkee, 169
Kilkenny, 51, 79, 80, 81, 85-89, 261
Killarney, 111, 189, 191, 206, 225, 250
Kilmalkedar, 186
Kinsale, 125, 127
Kinsella, Thomas, 213
Kinsellas, the, 72-74, 91
Knightstown, 199
Knockanouganish (Mountain), 212
Knockatee (Mountain), 212
Knockmealdown Mountains, 99, 106
Knowth, 151-152, 223

Lámhfhada, Lughaidh, 288
Leacanabualie (Fort), 206
Leap, 219
Ledwidge, Francis, 48
Letterkenny, 274
Lia Fail, 289
Limerick, 65, 95, 136, 142, 177, 203-205, 259
Lios, the, 144
Lismore, 99, 125
Listowel, 8-9
Looney, Tim, 98, 103, 105-124, 160, 168-169, 207, 219, 273, 287, 290-308

Macgillicuddy's Reeks, 189, 192
McKenna, Siobhan, 178
MacMahon, Brian, 127
Macroom, 225, 245-249
Mayo (County), 4, 129, 171, 270, 272
Middleton, Doctor, 64
Míl, 287
Milesians, the, 287
Milesius, King, 110
Moorstown (Castle), 292
Morton, H. V., 2-308 passim
Motte Knockgraffon, 290
Mount Melleray, 98-104, 106, 166
Mourne (County), 386

Naas, 142
Nephra (Mountain), 272
Newgrange, 45, 74, 106, 148-152, 215, 223, 287

Newman, John Henry Cardinal, 29-30
Nuada of the Silver Hand, 288

O'Brien, Brian, 112
O'Brien, Edna, 4
O'Brien, King Dónal Mór, 91, 94
O'Casey, Sean, 9, 12
O Crohan, Tomás, 185
O'Duffy, General Eoin, 65
Offaly (County), 31
O'Riordan, Liz, and Patricia Connery, 188, 202

Paisley, Ian, 160-163, 283
Pembroke, Earl of, 74
Phoenix Park, 16-25
Plunkett, Oliver, 150, 287
Pollen, John Hungerford, 29, 86
Portmagee, 197, 199
Price, Archbishop, 95

Quais, the, 159

Raifteirí the Poet, 261-263
Rath Luirc, 136-145
Ring of Hook, 75
Ring of Kerry, 189
Roberts, Jack, 219-220, 234-239, 287
Roy, James Charles, 179
Royal Ulster Constabulary, 274

Saint Bechaum, 114-115, 121
Saint Brendan, 176, 186
Saint Brigid, 62
Saint Canice's Cathedral, 93
Saint Catherine's Church, 30
Saint Columba, 271
Saint Edmond's Priory, 113
Saint Finan, 197
Saint Indract, 286
Saint Kevin (Caoimhín), 45-48
Saint Mary's Cathedral, 95
Saint Patrick, 95, 115, 191, 272, 285-286, 289
Saint Patrick's Cathedral, 94-95, 113
Saint Peter's Church, 287
Saint Stephen's Green, 28-29

Sally Gap, 42
Scott, Sir Walter, 94
Severin, Tim, 176
Sherkin Island, 242-244, 257
Sinn Féin, 248-249, 295
Skellig Michael, 195
Skibbereen, 137, 164, 219, 234
Skull, 230, 233
Slane, 146
Slieve Miskish Mountains, 214
Sligo (County), 223, 271
Sneem, 193
Spiddle, 266
Staigue (Fort), 194, 207, 210
Strongbow, 72, 85-86
Synge, John Millington, 9, 155, 184

Tara, 45, 287-290
Tarbert Race, 169
Thea (Tea), 288
Thurles, 90-91, 290
Tinkers, 51, 53, 55, 113-114, 155-167, 251-253, 296
Tintern Abbey, 72-75
Tipperary (County), 72, 92, 105, 106, 291
Tone, Wolfe, 138
Tralee, 144, 182, 250
Trappist Monks, 100-104, 166
Trinity College, 58, 118
Tuatha Dé Danann, 116, 222-223, 227, 287-288
Tuosist, 212, 216

Uragh, 219-228, 249

Valentia Island, 199, 204
Vere, Aubrey de, 93

Waterford, 51, 71, 73, 79, 81, 91
Waterville, 195
Watkins, Alfred, 236-237
Wellington Monument, 16
Wexford (County), 179
Wicklow (County), 39, 41, 288
William of Malesbury, 286

Yeats, William Butler, 1, 9-11, 70, 90, 169, 224, 271, 290